THE ENGLISHMAN ABROAD

The Great Briton on the Rhine

THE ENGLISHMAN ABROAD

HUGH AND PAULINE MASSINGHAM

ALAN SUTTON
1984

Alan Sutton Publishing Limited
Brunswick Road · Gloucester

Copyright © Compilation and Introduction,
Hugh and Pauline Massingham, 1962

First published 1962
This edition published 1984

British Library Cataloguing in Publication Data

Massingham, Hugh
    The Englishman abroad.
    1. Travellers—England
    I. Title   II. Massingham, Pauline
    910'.8921 G242

    ISBN 0-86299-143-9

Printed and bound in Great Britain

CONTENTS

Part III: The Middle Distance

PART IV: WIDER HORIZONS

ILLUSTRATIONS

*The frontispiece and, except where otherwise stated, the illustrations
in text, are from 'The Foreign Tour of Messrs Brown, Jones and
Robinson', by Richard Doyle, 1855.*

INTRODUCTION

THESE PAGES can be seen as a painless armchair journey. No bother about tickets. No guilty moments with the customs. Or they can be read, especially on a winter's night, to jog the memory and remind one of the sunny pleasures of other times. There will float through the cancerous fog the shining cheeks of oranges, the grin of lemons, the saucy blue of opulent grapes. But we like to think that an anthology has this advantage over the ordinary travel book. A writer who goes out to explore a remote or a familiar country is always consistent. He may be clever or he may be stupid; he may feel that he is on sacred ground or he may be an unbeliever and turn even the innermost mysteries into irony and laughter. Whatever he is, he will, whether supping with the natives, or inspecting Rome, or merely idling on the beach, put forward a point of view that inevitably reduces the vast complexities of society into a simple and recognizable pattern. Life, as we all know, is not like that, and the point of an anthology is that it mixes everything up. Present Shelley and Byron with exactly the same scene and few of us would realize that they were talking about the same subject. Rome inspired the devout: prickly Protestants saw it as a City of the Plains where corrupt and mendicant friars padded through the streets, growing fat on a backward and superstitious people. Elizabeth Barrett Browning cries out in ecstasy when she is living in Florence; others find Italy dirty, fly-bound, hopelessly sordid. In our own day Mr William Sansom can find the meaning of a place in a detail that the glazed eye does not notice—a white slab of fish, a lonely but potent shell on the seashore. All these views are equally true and equally false. The French are the majestic St Joans of de Gaulle's imagination, but to some people they are also ridiculous frogs—mean, croaking, theatrical, and speaking a language that no true Englishman would use. The shell on the seashore can be kicked idly away or it can be seen as explaining the mystery of the world.

The merit of an anthology is that, by letting these contradictory views quarrel with one another, it can sharpen the traveller's eye. Having shown him the ludicrous prejudices of others, it can help him to fight against his own. It can make him humble and restore to him the crowing delight of the child. The ideal traveller, in fact, is not a man who goes out to teach, but a man who goes out to learn. He is a person who, in his most censorious moments, even as he wickedly observes the Italians juggling with spaghetti or listens to the tiresome

yodelling of the Swiss, can look at himself and realize that he is
equally funny—that his favourite dish is fish and chips, that his grey
trousers and sports coat can make him seem inexpressibly comic to a
Spaniard or an Arab.

But what emerges from this anthology is not a map of Europe but a
careful portrait of the Englishman in all his improbability. The myth is
that the English love travel. Mr Cyril Connolly was the first to start the
new snobbery: we are now in a time when no civilized person can hold
up his head unless he admires Sartre and knows of a little restaurant
on the Left Bank where one can dine superbly for a few shillings.
Even the masses have rushed in: the Channel boats are so over-
loaded that they can scarcely waddle, and a lonely traveller finds that
he cannot walk along the more frequented roads without taking the
risk of being run down by motorists who think that he has no right to
exist. What most people do not realize is that this enthusiasm is a
comparatively modern development. In the past we had a much
more lordly attitude. To judge from the advice given to our fathers
before setting out from their comfortable mansions and castles, their
destinations might have been the alligator swamps of Africa or the
frozen wastes of Lapland. Dr Chambers warns his readers in 1875
against those messy dishes on the Continent which not only lead to
'rancid indigestion' but to 'flatulence or diarrhoea'. The traveller
should even avoid eating on a train journey and should take with him
a few cold but nourishing snacks—'bread, eggs, chickens, game,
sandwiches, Cornish pasties, almonds, oranges, captain's biscuits,
water, and sound red wine, or cold tea. . . .' The Englishman abroad
would also be well advised to learn a little elementary cooking before
he leaves civilization. To drive the lesson home, Dr Chambers tells the
sad story of a friend of his who 'was once considerably non-plussed
in Norway, after he had bargained for some lamb, by having the
animal handed over to him bleating, with a request that he would
return the skin in the evening. The task', he adds, 'was accomplished
under difficulties, but the details are unpleasant'.

The Rev. E. J. Hardy pointed out in 1887 other inconveniences and
perils. In calculating the chances of finding 'health and pleasure' from
a tour abroad, we must take into account the uncouth social habits of
the foreigner—the 'nervous irritation', for instance, 'involved in
waiting hours past our usual meal-times'. Nor is this all. The traveller
can never be sure of a good night's sleep because 'just as we have dined
off fellow creatures smaller fellow-creatures may sup off us'. These
ravening companions are a constant source of complaint. The English,
Cardinal Newman says, 'have no idea of what a Sicilian flea is'. Robert
Southey is even more forthright. At midnight, he says, he 'was at

supper, not where I eat, but where I was eaten. The ingenious gentleman', he goes on, 'who communicated his discovery to the public, in the Encyclopaedia, that ninety millions of mites' eggs amount exactly to the size of one pigeon's egg, may, if he please, calculate what quantity of blood was extracted from my body, in the course of seven hours; the bed being six feet two and a half, by four feet five, and as populous as possible in that given space.'

Of course, our fathers, and especially our grandfathers and great-grandfathers, had more to complain about than we have. The roads were flinty, the beds more spartan, the meals uncertain. On the other hand our great-grandfathers had one or two advantages. These were the days of our opulence; like the lords of creation, we could pay, not with doubtful paper but with ringing, spinning, irresistible guineas—a magpie's dream. The rich and the serious went on what was known as the Grand Tour and many of them travelled as if they were emperors. The Grand Tour, despite its high-sounding title, was hardly more than a donkey trot: it meant, if one were to complete one's education, travelling through France and Italy, seeing Vienna, looking at the Rhine, and admiring the Alps. And one did this in a luxury that nowadays seems almost as fabulous as the Thousand and One Nights. When Byron set off he had a circus of seven servants and five carriages. He even took along some livestock in case he should find that he might be faced by starvation on the way.

The truth is that, far from ardently loving foreign travel, the English have a curious hate-love towards it. The born traveller—the man who is without prejudices, who sets out wanting to learn rather than to criticize, who is stimulated by oddity, who recognizes that every man is his brother, however strange and ludicrous he may be in dress and appearance—has always been comparatively rare. 'The object of travelling', says Hazlitt, 'is to see and learn; but such is our impatience of ignorance, or the jealousy of our self-love, that we generally set up a certain preconception . . . and are surprised at a quarrel with all that does not conform to it.' Exactly. We admire what we recognize and guffaw like a donkey at anything that would not happen in the cosy familiar whirl of Deal and Bournemouth and Blackpool. Because we drink beer, we mock at the Frenchman for his addiction to wine. And because we like a cut off the roast and two veg., we despise an Italian's love for what we regard as contemptible pap.

Of course, there are exceptions—Byron, for instance. Being such an eccentric himself, the wildest extravaganza only made him feel that he was among friends. He blossoms absurdly in Lisbon 'because I love oranges, and talk bad Latin to the monks, who understand it, as it is like their own, and I goes into society (with my pocket pistols), and I swims the Tagus all across it once, and I rides on an ass or a mule, and swears Portuguese, and have got the diarrhoea. . . .' There you have the perfect traveller who sees how comic he is in a vastly comic world. Walpole is also of this convivial company: he can hardly wait to dress up and flit from one ball to the next. Then there is Gibbon, who placidly settles down in Lausanne and reflects how fortunate he is not to be still breathing the sour air of the House of Commons. Boswell, perhaps, is the most engaging of them all. Like the rest of us, whether we are at home or abroad, he is full of good resolution. 'Yesterday', he tells himself, 'you did very well. You read an immensity of Greek.' This was on a Sunday and the next day he had even greater cause for congratulation. 'Yesterday', he says, 'you did delightfully. You did not commit one fault in any respect the whole day. . . . You admired *La Comtesse* in church, but not imprudently. . . . This is a fine tale to tell.' But alas! the flesh is weak and he can never keep up his high standards for long. 'You eat too much wild duck', he chides himself, and 'so was a little gloomy.' Soon there was also much worse to confess. At seven o'clock one morning, his 'blood took a fine flow'; . . . there came a woman with a basket of chocolate to sell. 'I toyed with her and found she was with child. Oho! a safe piece . . . ' and at the end of it all, he asks in amazement, 'Bless me, have I now committed adultery?'

But for the most part the English traveller passed through France and Italy with a critical rather than an appreciative eye. What dirt! What darkness! What a distressing lack of refinement! Swinburne gets in such a rage that he can hardly contain himself. 'Of *all the beasts* of countries', he writes from Mentone, 'I reckon this about caps them. . . . A calcined, scalped, rasped, scraped, flayed, broiled, . . . mangy, grimy, parboiled country *without* trees, water, grass, fields—*with* blank, beastly senseless olives. . . .' Carlyle, swearing at large as usual, finds Paris a perpetual nightmare. The Bois de Boulogne is a 'dirty scratchy place . . . with paltry bits of trees on each hand'. He finds the noise insupportable and fails to get as much as a blink of sleep the whole night through. Southey travels through Spain, Portugal, and the Netherlands and cannot find a good word to say about them. Brussels is 'too much Frenchified'. The Lisbon streets are 'very agreeable: if you walk under the houses you are drenched by the water-spouts; if you attempt the middle, there is a torrent; would you go between the two, there is the dunghill'. As for Madrid he can only quote two lines of doggerel in farewell—

He who likes thee does not know thee,
He who knows thee does not like thee.

For all his good advice, his warnings against prejudice, his pleas for understanding, Hazlitt cannot sometimes restrain an insolent guffaw; there is no Englishman, he reflects smugly while observing French manners at the dinner table, 'who spouts Shakespeare one moment, the next picks his teeth with his fork, and then sticks it into a potatoe to help you to it'. Shelley is perhaps the biggest prig of the lot. 'What do you think?' he asks in disgust, writing from Italy. 'Young women of rank actually eat—you will never guess what—*garlick*!' Poor Byron— 'he is quite corrupted by living among these people'.

Added to these natural prejudices, at least in Victorian times, was the hatred of Roman Catholicism. Southey cannot even put up with the noise of church bells. They were, he says when he is staying in Liège, 'very loud, frequent, and troublesome—this annoyance alone would have told us we were in a Catholic country'. Ruskin is not much better. He admits that the outside and west façade of St Peter's is 'very fine'; on the other hand 'the inside would make a nice ball-room but is good for nothing else'. Even Newman, in his Anglican days, talks of Naples as if it were little better than a later Sodom and Gomorrah. 'Religion', he complains, 'is turned into a mere occasion of worldly gaiety—as in the history of the Israelites—and the sooner we are out of so bad a place the better.'

What is so curious is that when the Victorian gets away from the safer and familiar tracks; when he really has something to complain about, he shows a stoicism and sympathy that are wholly admirable. It may be that anybody who has gone through the rigours of an English public school finds the primitive conditions of Arab society almost a home from home. To die from a thousand and one cuts on some arid patch in the Middle East recalls the unspeakable tortures of the dorm, the memories of the twisted arm, the kick in the groin. It is certain that the off-hand cruelty of the Arabs aroused all the secret and repellent sadism of T. E. Lawrence. And it is not only the men who travel dry-eyed along these remote and flinty by-ways. Lady Hester Stanhope walls herself up in Mount Lebanon and grows dottier and dottier as the years go by. And yet there is surely something more to all this than an apprenticeship at Eton and Harrow, Cheltenham and Rugby. The Victorian who forsook the cosy reassurance of the vicarage and the manse and set out to explore the distant corners of the earth, was compelled to do so by an insatiable curiosity. He—or she— had the authentic spirit of the explorer—of the person who wants to find out, who is not only prepared for the unusual but welcomes it. He does not complain about the fleas; he would be surprised if these companionable and democratic little creatures did not fall upon him during his travels. He does not expect an inn, a bed, obsequious service, a meal at every stop: he knows that he has left what passes for civilization far behind him. Small mercies become precious ones, and having freed himself from prejudice and convention he can be entranced by the mystery of his fellow creatures. Doughty fades into the Arab landscape and Gertrude Bell walks unselfconsciously with a Bedouin 'finger in finger'. Even Emily Eden, in the breathless intervals between the last ball and the next, gets a disturbing intimation of what the British may be storing up for themselves in India. 'In short', she writes in a melancholy moment, 'Delhi is a very suggestive and moralizing place—and somehow I feel that we horrid English have just "gone and done it", merchandised it, revenued it, and spoilt it all.'

But Gertrude Bell should have the last word on these pioneers. 'I want to tell you, just you', she writes, 'who knows and understands everything, that I'm acutely conscious of how much life has given me. I've got back now to the wild feeling of joy in existence. . . .' And there, though not quite in the same words, speak Elizabeth Barrett Browning, Doughty, Boswell—all the happy travellers, in fact.

One or two words of explanation should be added. There are no explorers in these pages, because explorers are to the ordinary traveller what the Saint is to the average church congregation. Then most of these quotations are taken from letters and travel books, and we have reluctantly excluded poetry on the ground that the poet is more revealing about himself, at least as a traveller, when he writes in prose. Finally, we have cheated a little over the Grand Tour by including the whole of Germany and not just the Rhineland.

Part I

OPENING STEPS

THE FIRST WHIFF

... I REMEMBER being much amused last year, when landing at Calais, at the answer made by an old traveller to a novice who was making his first voyage.

'What a dreadful smell!' said the uninitiated stranger, enveloping his nose in his pocket handkerchief.

'It is the smell of the continent, sir,' replied the man of experience. And so it was.—Mrs Frances Trollope, *Paris and the Parisians in 1835.*

BRIGHTON TO DIEPPE

Paris, August 21, 1843. DEAREST HANNAH,—What people travel for is a mystery. I have never during the last forty-eight hours had any wish so strong as to be at home again. . . . I could very well add a chapter to the 'Miseries of Human Life'. For example:—

Groan 1. The Brighton railway; in a slow train; a carriage crowded as full as it would hold; a sick lady smelling of aëther; a healthy gentleman smelling of brandy; the thermometer at 102° in the shade, and I not in the shade, but expos'd to the full glare of the sun from noon till half after two, the effect of which is that my white trowsers have been scorched into a pair of very serviceable nankeens.

Groan 2. And for this Fanny is answerable, who made me believe that the New Steyne Hotel at Brighton was a good one. A coffee-room ingeniously contrived on the principle of an oven, the windows not made to open; a dinner on yesterday's pease-soup, and the day before yesterday's cutlets; not an ounce of ice; and all beverages, wine, water, and beer,—in exactly the state of the Church of Laodicea.

Groan 3. My passage to Dieppe. We had not got out of sight of the Beachy Head lights, when it began to rain hard. I was therefore driven into the cabin, and compelled to endure the spectacle, and to hear the unutterable groans and gasps, of fifty sea-sick people. I went out when the rain ceased; but everything on deck was soaked. It was impossible to sit; so that I walked up and down the vessel all night. . . .

Groan 4. The custom-house. I never had a dispute with custom-house officers before, having found that honesty answered in England, France, and Belgium, and corruption in Italy. But the officer at Dieppe, finding among my baggage some cotton stockings which had not been yet worn, threatened to confiscate them, and exacted more than they were worth—between thirteen and fourteen francs—by way of duty.

I had just bought these unlucky stockings to do honour to our country in the eyes of foreigners; being unwilling that the washerwomen of Paris and Orleans should see an English Member of Parliament's stockings either in holes or darned. See what the fruits of patriotism are! Groan 5. Mine inn at Dieppe. I need not describe it, for it was the very same at which we stopped for a night in 1840. . . . I did not discover where I was till too late. I had a cup of coffee worse than I thought any French cook could make for a wager. In the bedroom, where I dressed, there was a sort of soap which I had half a mind to bring away, that men of science might analyse it. . . . I shaved with it, and the consequence is that I look as if I had that complaint which our mother held in such horror. If I used such cosmetics often, I should be forced to beg Queen Victoria to touch me.—Lord Macaulay, *Letters*.

THE WRONG APPROACH

The first thing an Englishman does on going abroad is to find fault with what is French, because it is not English. If he is determined to confine all excellence to his own country, he had better stay at home.— William Hazlitt, *Notes of a Journey Through France and Italy*, 1826.

HOW TO KNOW A PLACE

October 3, 1753. It is certain that no man can be much pleased himself, or please others much, in any place where he is only a bird of passage for eight or ten days; neither party thinking it worth while to make an acquaintance, still less to form any connection, for so short a time; but when months are the case, a man may domesticate himself pretty well; and very soon not be looked upon as a stranger. This is the real utility of travelling, when, by contracting a familiarity at any place, you get into the inside of it, and see it in its undress. This is the only way of knowing the customs, the manners, and all the little characteristical peculiarities that distinguish one place from another; but then this familiarity is not to be brought about by cold, formal visits of half an hour; no, you must show a willingness, a desire, an impatience, of forming connections, *il faut s'y prêter, et y mettre du liant, du désir de plaire*.—Lord Chesterfield, *Letters*.

THE ENGLISH SERVANT

Athens, January 14, 1811. I believe I have mentioned to you more than once that I swam (in imitation of Leander, though without his lady) across the Hellespont, from Sestos and Abydos. Of this, and all other particulars, F., whom I have sent home with papers, &c., will apprise you. I cannot find that he is any loss; being tolerably master of the Italian and modern Greek languages, which last I am also studying with a master, I can order and discourse more than enough for a reasonable man. Besides, the perpetual lamentations after beef and beer, the stupid, bigoted contempt for every thing foreign, and insurmountable incapacity for acquiring even a few words of any language, rendered him, like all other English servants, an incumbrance. I do assure you, the plague of speaking for him, the comforts he required (more than myself by far), the pilaws (a Turkish dish of rice and meat), which he could not eat, the wines which he could not drink, the beds where he could not sleep, and the long list of calamities, such as stumbling horses, want of *tea*!!! &c., which assailed him, would have made a lasting source of laughter to a spectator, and inconvenience to a master. After all, the man is honest enough, and in Christendom, capable enough; but in Turkey, Lord forgive me! my Albanian soldiers, my Tartars and Janissary, worked for him and us too, as my friend Hobhouse can testify.—Lord Byron, *Letters*.

TEALESS LANDS

ENGLISH SERVANTS, whom no wise person would take on the Continent, are nowhere more useless, or greater encumbrances, than in this hungry, thirsty, tealess, beerless, beefless land: they give more trouble, require more food and attention, and are ten times more discontented than their masters, who have poetry in their souls; an aesthetic love of travel, for its own sake, more than counterbalances with them the want of material gross comforts, about which their pudding-headed four-full-meals-a-day attendants are only thinking.—Richard Ford, *Gatherings From Spain*, 1846.

SIMPLE TRAVELLERS

Calais. YOUR IDLE people that leave their native country, and go abroad for some reason or reasons which may be derived from one of these general causes:—

> *Infirmity of body,*
> *Imbecility of mind, or*
> *Inevitable necessity.*

The two first include all those who travel by land or by water, labouring with pride, curiosity, vanity, or spleen, subdivided and combined *in infinitum*.

The third class includes the whole army of peregrine martyrs; more especially those travellers who set out upon their travels with the benefit of the clergy, either as delinquents, travelling under the direction of governors recommended by the magistrate;—or young gentlemen, transported by the cruelty of parents and guardians, and travelling under the direction of governors recommended by Oxford, Aberdeen, and Glasgow.

There is a fourth class; but their number is so small, that they would not deserve a distinction, were it not necessary, in a work of this nature, to observe the greatest precision and nicety, to avoid a confusion of character: and these men I speak of, are such as cross the seas, and sojourn in a land of strangers, with a view of saving money for various reasons and upon various pretences; but as they might also save themselves and others a great deal of unnecessary trouble by saving their money at home,—and, as their reasons for travelling are the least complex of any other species of emigrants, I shall distinguish these gentlemen by the name of

Simple Travellers.

Laurence Sterne, *A Sentimental Journey Through France and Italy*, 1768.

ENGLISH INSOLENCE

Ghent (1840). How THEY hate us, these foreigners, in Belgium as much as in France! What lies they tell of us; how gladly they would see us humiliated! Honest folks at home over their port-wine say, 'Ay, ay, and very good reason they have too. National vanity, sir, wounded— we have beaten them so often'. My dear sir, there is not a greater error in the world than this. They hate you because you are stupid, hard to please, and intolerably insolent and air-giving. I walked with an Englishman yesterday, who asked the way to a street of which he pronounced the name very badly to a little Flemish boy: the Flemish boy did not answer; and there was my Englishman quite in a rage, shrieking in the child's ear as if he must answer. He seemed to think that it was the duty of 'the snob', as he called him, to obey the gentleman. This is why we are hated—for pride. In our free country a trades-man, a lacquey, or a waiter will submit to almost any given insult from a gentleman; in these benighted lands one man is as good as another; and pray God it may soon be so with us! Of all European people, which is the nation that has the most haughtiness, the strongest preju-dices, the greatest reserve, the greatest dulness? I say an Englishman of the genteel classes. An honest groom jokes and hobs-and-nobs and makes his way with the kitchen-maids, for there is good social nature in the man; his master dare not unbend. Look at him, how he scowls at you on your entering an inn-room; think how you scowl yourself to meet this scowl. To-day, as we were walking and staring about the place, a worthy old gentleman in a carriage, seeing a pair of strangers, took off his hat and bowed very gravely with his old powdered head out of the window: I am sorry to say that our first impulse was to burst out laughing—it seemed so supremely ridiculous that a stranger should notice and welcome another.—W. M. Thackeray, *Contributions to 'Punch'*.

TRAVAIL

WHEN CALCULATING . . . our chances of obtaining health and pleasure from a tour abroad, we must think of the nervous irritation involved in waiting hours past our usual meal-times, of never being sure of sleep at night—suspecting, as we must, that just as we have dined off fellow-creatures, smaller fellow-creatures may sup off us!—of having frequently to go through a heated argumentation, or else submit our plans to those of our companions in travel, or *travail*.—Rev. E. J. Hardy, *Manners Makyth Man*, 1887.

A SAFE WAY WITH WATER

WHEN THE water of a place is bad, it is safest to drink none that has not been filtered through either the berry of a grape, or else a tub of malt. These are the most reliable filters yet invented.—Samuel Butler, *Note Books*, 1912.

THE TRIALS OF LEARNING FRENCH

31 October 1763. IT IS certain that I have the greatest desire to learn French, but I fear that I am not learning it quickly. Perhaps my keen desire makes me think myself worse in acquiring the language than I am. I certainly take a great deal of pains to improve. I write two pages of a theme every morning. I read for two hours in the works of Voltaire every evening. When I do not understand words perfectly, I look them up in the dictionary, and I write them down with their meanings. Every Wednesday I have the pleasure of passing the evening in a literary society where it is not permitted to speak a word of anything but French; and I dine at Mr. Brown's, where there are two ladies who do not speak English, and where for that reason it is always necessary to speak French. Yet I cannot observe that I am making rapid progress. In writing, I am slow and clumsy, and in speaking I

have great difficulty in expressing myself and often make terrible blunders. Instead of saying, 'Would you like to play at shuttlecock?' (*volant*), I said, 'Would you like to play at robber?' (*voleur*); and instead of, 'Mademoiselle, I am entirely at your service' (*tout ce qu'il vous plaira*), I said, 'Mademoiselle, I am something (*quelque chose*) that will please you.' Such blunders make a man very ridiculous.—Boswell, *Boswell in Holland.*

How they saw Belgium

THE TRUE TRAVELLER

IF [this book] appeals to anyone, it will appeal to a class of men who take to travel in a different spirit altogether, and who frankly admit that what they seek under other skies is neither profitable, nor useful, nor edifying information of any kind, but merely this—the stimulant of a new mental experience. No doubt their taste in this respect is for nothing but a more refined form of dram-drinking; and that perhaps may be thought sufficiently immoral and frivolous. And yet such men after all are the only true travellers, for it is they alone who really love change for the sake of change, taking it into their system as a smoker inhales smoke, and finding it exhilarate them like a kind of spiritual haschish. All other travellers are travellers merely by accident. They go to distant places for some definite object, which it so happens is to be had at a distance only—a picture gallery, a gaming-table, or a good climate in January—but they would like it as well or better if they could find it nearer home, whilst as for the excursionist, who in the course of a single holiday is 'personally conducted' through India, Japan, and America, it can hardly be said that he has ever left home at all. He has virtually sat still and looked at a moving peep-show. The globe has gone round before him, he has not gone round the globe.—W. H. Mallock, *In an Enchanted Island*, 1889.

ENCUMBRANCES

NO LADY who values her peace on the journey, or desires any freedom of mind or movement, will take a maid. What can a poor English girl do who must dispense with home-comforts, and endure hardships that she never dreamed of, without the intellectual enjoyments which to her mistress compensate (if they do compensate) for the inconveniences of Eastern travel? If her mistress has any foresight, or any compassion, she will leave her at home. If not, she must make up her mind to ill-humour or tears, to the spectacle of wrath or despondency, all the way.— If she will have her maid, let her, at all events, have the girl taught to ride,—and to ride well: or she may have much to answer for. To begin to ride at her years is bad enough, even at home, where there may be a choice of horses, and the rides are only moderate in length. What is a poor creature to do who is put upon a chance horse, ass, or camel, day by day, for rides of eight hours' long, for weeks together? The fatigue and distress so caused are terrible to witness, as I can testify,—though we were happily warned in time, and went unencumbered by English servants altogether. Of course, the lady herself is sure of her ability to ride to this extent; or she will put herself into training before she leaves home.—Harriet Martineau, *Eastern Life, Present and Past*, 1846.

COOKING APPRENTICESHIP

A KNOWLEDGE of simple methods of preparing food is often a great comfort to a traveller. A friend of mine was once considerably non-plussed in Norway, after he had bargained for some lamb, by having the animal handed over to him bleating, with a request that he would return the skin in the evening. The task was accomplished under difficulties, but the details are unpleasant. This is an extreme contingency, which need not be provided against by all vacation barristers acquiring the art of butchering; but still it is worth while to learn in your own kitchen how to prepare an omelet, fry fish, eggs and ham, cut and grill a steak off a joint, boil and fry potatoes, scrabble eggs, mull wine (if it happens to be sour), boil coffee, make 'Liebig' into good soup, &c. These accomplishments may be brought into play without wandering very far from home; and it is astonishing how popular they render those sometimes troublesome fellow-travellers, the ladies of the party—Thomas King Chambers, *A Manual of Diet in Health and Disease*, 1875.

SENSUALITY OF A SWINE

London, May 10, O.S., 1748. THE END which I propose by your education, and which (if you please) I shall certainly attain, is, to unite in you all the knowledge of a scholar, with the manners of a courtier; and to join, what is seldom joined in any of my countrymen, books and the world. They are commonly twenty years old before they have spoken to anybody above their schoolmaster, and the Fellows of their college. If they happen to have learning, it is only Greek and Latin; but not one word of modern history, or modern languages. Thus prepared, they go abroad, as they call it; but, in truth, they stay at home all that while; for being very awkward, confoundedly ashamed, and not speaking the languages, they go into no foreign company, at least none good; but dine and sup with one another only, at the tavern. Such examples, I am sure, you will not imitate, but even carefully avoid. You will always take care to keep the best company in the place where you are, which is the only use of travelling: and (by the way) the pleasures of a gentleman are only to be found in the best company; for that riot, which low company most falsely and impudently call pleasure, is only the sensuality of a swine.—Lord Chesterfield, *Letters*.

A POET'S EYE

Calais. I PITY the man who can travel from Dan to Beersheba, and cry, 'Tis all barren;—and so it is: and so is all the world to him who will not cultivate the fruits it offers. I declare, said I, clapping my hands cheerily together, that was I in a desert, I would find out wherewith in it to call forth my affections:—if I could not do better, I would fasten them upon some sweet myrtle, or seek some melancholy cypress to connect myself to;—I would court their shade, and greet them kindly for their protection;—I would cut my name upon them, and swear they were the loveliest trees throughout the desert: if their leaves wither'd, I would teach myself to mourn;—and when they rejoiced, I would rejoice along with them.—Laurence Sterne, *A Sentimental Journey Through France and Italy*, 1768.

BIRTH OF A MASTERPIECE

1764–65. THE USE of foreign travel has been often debated as a general question; but the conclusion must be finally applied to the character and circumstances of each individual. With the education of boys, *where* or *how* they may pass over some juvenile years with the least mischief to themselves or others, I have no concern. But after supposing the previous and indispensable requisites of age, judgment, a competent knowledge of men and books, and a freedom from domestic prejudices, I will briefly describe the qualifications which I deem most essential to a traveller. He should be endowed with an active, indefatigable vigour of mind and body, which can seize every mode of conveyance, and support, with a careless smile, every hardship of the road, the weather, or the inn. The benefits of foreign travel will correspond with the degrees of these qualifications; but, in this sketch, those to whom I am known will not accuse me of framing my own panegyric. It was at Rome, on the 15th of October, 1764, as I sat musing amidst the ruins of the Capitol, while the bare-footed fryars were singing vespers in the Temple of Jupiter, that the idea of writing the decline and fall of the city first started to my mind. But my original plan was circumscribed to the decay of the city rather than of the empire, and though my reading and reflections began to point towards the subject, some years elapsed, and several avocations intervened, before I was seriously engaged in the execution of that laborious work.—Edward Gibbon, *Memoirs*.

HUNGRY WORK

BUT THOUGH every one travels in these days, just as every one reads, there are as few good travellers as there are good readers. The people who ask at lending libraries for the very newest book only to have to say 'they saw it, and liked it', are precisely those who rush to and fro all over the earth, and return as empty as they set out. Travelling is either useful or not according to the motive with which it is undertaken. Some there are whose sole object is to get over a number of countries just to have to say they were in them. Such globe-trotters neither improve themselves nor increase their happiness. They never do anything they themselves care for, but follow conventionalism as the best tourist's guide. They admire by means of their *Baedekers* and *Murrays*, and are 'charmed' with the things with which they ought to be charmed. In picture galleries they do not look at the pictures, but

They 'do' Cologne Cathedral

read before them out of a guide-book, for the sake of future conversation, a short notice of the birth and death of 'this eminent artist'. It has been said that 'life would be tolerable but for its pleasures', and in their heart of hearts many would like going on the Continent, only for its art-galleries, museums, cathedrals, and objects of interest generally. 'Hungry work it is doing pictures. I have always to eat two steaks after each collection; besides, it tires the neck so!'—this is the honest confession once heard by the writer on coming out of a celebrated gallery.—Rev. E. J. Hardy, *Manners Makyth Man*, 1887.

C

JOHNSON'S VIEWS

I MENTIONED a friend of mine who had resided long in Spain, and was unwilling to return to Britain. JOHNSON. 'Sir, he is attached to some woman.' BOSWELL. 'I rather believe, Sir, it is the fine climate which keeps him there.' JOHNSON. 'Nay, Sir, how can you talk so? What is *climate* to happiness? Place me in the heart of Asia, should I not be exiled? What proportion does climate bear to the complex system of human life? You may advise me to go to live at Bologna to eat sausages. The sausages there are the best in the world; they lose much by being carried.'—Boswell's *Life of Johnson*, 1791.

KEEPING FIT

WHEN ACTUALLY on a carriage or railway journey it is unwise to make large meals. They are sure to be swallowed in a hurried manner, and in a state of heat and excitement very unfavourable to digestion. The best way is to make no meal at all till the journey is over, but to carry a supply of cold provisions, bread, eggs, chickens, game, sandwiches, Cornish pasties, almonds, oranges, captain's biscuits, water, and sound red wine, or cold tea, sufficient to stay the appetites of the party, and let a small quantity be taken every two or three hours.

If this plan be adopted, not only is activity of mind and body preserved, but that heat and swelling of the legs which so often concludes a long day's journey is avoided. Attention to the matter is particularly necessary when the journey continues all night, and for several days in succession, since varicose veins and permanent thickening of the ankles have sometimes resulted from this exertion being combined with too long fasts and hurried repletion at protracted intervals.—Thomas King Chambers, *A Manual of Diet in Health and Disease*, 1875.

ATLANTIC CROSSING

1842. ABOUT MIDNIGHT we shipped a sea, which forced its way through the skylights, burst open the doors above, and came raging and roaring down into the ladies' cabin, to the unspeakable consternation of my wife and a little Scotch lady—who, by the way, had previously sent a message to the captain by the stewardess, requesting him, with her compliments, to have a steel conductor immediately attached to the top of every mast, and to the chimney, in order that the ship might not be struck by lightning. They and the handmaid before-mentioned, being in such ecstasies of fear that I scarcely knew what to do with them, I naturally bethought myself of some restorative or comfortable cordial; and nothing better occurring to me, at the moment, than hot brandy-and-water, I procured a tumbler-full without delay. It being impossible to stand or sit without holding on, they were all heaped together in one corner of a long sofa—a fixture extending entirely across the cabin—where they clung to each other in momentary expectation of being drowned. When I approached this place with my specific, and was about to administer it with many consolatory expressions to the nearest sufferer, what was my dismay to see them all roll slowly down to the other end! And when I staggered to that end, and held out the glass once more, how immensely baffled were my good intentions by the ship giving another lurch, and their all rolling back again! I suppose I dodged them up and down this sofa for at least a quarter of an hour, without reaching them once; and by the time I did catch them, the brandy-and-water was diminished, by constant spilling, to a tea-spoonful. To complete the group, it is necessary to recognise in this disconcerted dodger, an individual very pale from sea-sickness, who had shaved his beard and brushed his hair, last, at Liverpool: and whose only article of dress (linen not included) were a pair of dreadnought trousers; a blue jacket, formerly admired upon the Thames at Richmond; no stockings; and one slipper.—Charles Dickens, *American Notes*.

FIRST INTRODUCTION

1753. IN MY childhood I had once studied the French grammar, and I could imperfectly understand the easy prose of a familiar subject. But when I was thus suddenly cast on a foreign land I found myself deprived of the use of speech and of hearing; and, during some weeks, incapable not only of enjoying the pleasures of conversation, but even of asking or answering a question in the common intercourse of life. To a home-bred Englishman every object, every custom was offensive; but the native of any country might have been disgusted with the general aspect of his lodging and entertainment. I had now exchanged my elegant apartment in Magdalen College for a narrow, gloomy street, the most unfrequented of an unhandsome town, for an old inconvenient house, and for a small chamber ill-contrived and ill-furnished, which, on the approach of winter, instead of a companionable fire, must be warmed by the dull invisible heat of a stove. From a man I was again degraded to the dependence of a schoolboy . . . I received a small monthly allowance for my pocket-money; and helpless and awkward as I have ever been, I no longer enjoyed the indispensable comfort of a servant. My condition seemed as destitute of hope as it was devoid of pleasure: I was separated for an indefinite, which appeared an infinite term from my native country. . . . Such was my first introduction to Lausanne; a place where I spent nearly five years with pleasure and profit, which I afterwards revisited without compulsion, and which I have finally selected as the most grateful retreat for the decline of my life.—Edward Gibbon, *Memoirs.*

WILD MEN

Paris. AFTER a young man has employed his time to advantage at a public school, and has continued his application to various branches of science till the age of twenty, you ask, what are the advantages he is likely to reap from a tour abroad . . . ?

However persuaded he may be of the advantages enjoyed by the people of England, he will see the harshness and impropriety of insulting the natives of other countries with an ostentatious enumeration of those advantages; he will perceive how odious those travellers make themselves, who laugh at the religion, ridicule the customs, and insult the police of the countries through which they pass, and who never fail to insinuate to the inhabitants that they are all slaves and bigots. Such bold Britons we have sometimes met with, *fighting* their way through Europe, who, by their continual broils and disputes, would lead one to imagine, that the angel of the Lord had pronounced on each of them the same denunciation which he did on Ishmael the son of Abraham, by his handmaid Hagar: 'And he will be a wild man, and his hand will be against every man, and every man's hand against him.' If the same unsocial disposition should creep into our politics, it might arm all the powers in Europe against Great Britain, before she gets clear of her unhappy contest with America.—John Moore, *A View of Society and Manners in Italy,* 1795.

AN ABSURD PRACTICE

1775. IN ENGLAND, it becomes every day more and more the custom to send young people to travel in foreign countries immediately upon their leaving school, and without sending them to any university. Our young people, it is said, generally return home much improved by their travels. A young man who goes abroad at seventeen or eighteen, and returns home at one and twenty, returns three or four years older than he was when he went abroad; and at that age it is very difficult not to improve a good deal in three or four years. In the course of his travels, he generally acquires some knowledge of one or two foreign languages;

a knowledge, however, which is seldom sufficient to enable him either to speak or write them with propriety. In other respects, he commonly returns home more conceited, more unprincipled, more dissipated, and more incapable of any serious application either to study or to business, than he could well have become in so short a time, had he lived at home. By travelling so very young, by spending in the most frivolous dissipation the most precious years of his life, at a distance from the inspection and controul of his parents and relations, every useful habit, which the earlier parts of his education might have had some tendency to form in him, instead of being rivetted and confirmed, is almost necessarily either weakened or effaced. Nothing but the discredit into which the universities are allowing themselves to fall, could ever have brought into repute so very absurd a practice as that of travelling at this early period of life. By sending his son abroad, a father delivers himself, at least for some time, from so disagreeable an object as that of a son unemployed, neglected, and going to ruin before his eyes.—Adam Smith, *The Wealth of Nations.*

GARLIC

IN ALMOST all country places out of England it is impossible to avoid the greasy dishes which are apparently preferred by all except our own countrymen; and a frequent consequence is rancid indigestion, with nauseous taste in the mouth, and flatulence or diarrhoea. A few drops of vinegar or lemon-juice and a little cayenne pepper in the plate are the readiest correctives.

Another article of cuisine that offends the bowels of unused Britons is garlic. Not uncommonly in southern climes an egg with the shell on is the only procurable animal food without garlic in it. Flatulence and looseness are the frequent results. Bouilli, with its accompaniments of mustard sauce and water melon, is the safest resource, and not an unpleasant one, after a little education.—Thomas King Chambers, *A Manual of Diet in Health and Disease*, 1875.

MORES

London, April 30, O.S., 1750. . . . You know what you are sent abroad for. It is of much more consequence to know the *Mores multorum hominum* than the *Urbes.* Pray continue this judicious conduct wherever you go, especially at Paris, where, instead of thirty, you will find above three hundred English herding together, and conversing with no one French body.

The life of *les Milords Anglais* is regularly, or if you will, irregularly, this. As soon as they rise, which is very late, they breakfast together, to the utter loss of two good morning hours. Then they go by coach-fuls to the Palais, the Invalides, and Notre-Dame; from thence to the English coffee-house, where they make up their tavern party for dinner. From dinner, where they drink quick, they adjourn in clusters to the play, where they crowd up the stage, drest up in very fine clothes, very ill made by a Scotch or Irish tailor. From the play to the tavern again, where they get very drunk, and where they either quarrel among themselves, or sally forth, commit some riot in the streets, and are taken up by the watch. Those who do not speak French before they go, are sure to learn none there. Their tender vows are addressed to their Irish laundress, unless by chance some itinerant English-woman, eloped from her husband, or her creditors, defrauds her of them. Thus, they return home, more petulant, but not more informed, than when they left it; and show, as they think, their improvement, by affectedly both speaking and dressing in broken French.—Lord Chesterfield, *Letters*.

JOHN BULL

1824. THERE IS a wonderful *keeping* in our prejudices; we reason as consistently as absurdly upon the confined notions we have taken up. We put the good, wholesome, hearty, respectable qualities into one heap and call it English, and the bad, unwholesome, frivolous, and contemptible ones into another heap, and call it French; and whatever does not answer to this pretended sample, we reject as spurious and partial evidence. Our coxcomb conceit stands over the different races of mankind, like a smart serjeant of a regiment, and drills them into a pitiful uniformity, we ourselves being picked out as the *élite du corps*, and the rest of the world forming the forlorn hope of humanity. One would suppose, to judge from the conversation of the two nations, that all Frenchmen were alike, and that all Englishmen were personified by a particular individual, nicknamed John Bull. The French have no idea that there is any thing in England but roast-beef and plum-pudding, and a number of round, red faces, growing fat and stupid upon such kind of fare; while our traditional notion of the French is that of *soup-maigre* and wooden shoes, and a set of scare-crow figures corre-sponding to them. All classes of society and differences of character are by this unfair process consolidated into a sturdy, surly English yeoman on the one side of the Channel, or are boiled down and evaporate into a shivering, chattering valet-de-chambre, or miserable half-starved peasant on the other.—William Hazlitt, *Notes of a Journey Through France and Italy*.

HOME AGAIN

FOR ARGUMENT'S sake, let us take the return to England in a likely month, October. Aboard the Channel steamer, if it is English, mixed portents show. There is the pleasure and reassurance of bacon and eggs served among silverish coffee pots on white damask tablecloths of good area at about three shillings and sixpence, after you have become used to paying eight or ten shillings for something similar served on paper. So far so good. But later, in the bar, the first shadow falls—a first contact is made with the great English puritan undertow. Something about the bar-man. Something different from the volatile ease to which you have become accustomed. He is so solid, so near to being grim, a man of stern self-possessed movement who as he takes your money looks pointedly away—as though money or drink should not be mentioned. It may be a seaman's trick, like looking away when he talks to you. But it is suggestive too of justice dispensed, as though he had provided some permitted ration of vice which he is powerless to withhold. Of course he is a nice fellow and will have a chat if you invite him. And perhaps he is simply acting the impassivity of the best English service—but to me it is the Puritan shadow.

Somewhere about three-quarter's way across the Channel the sky becomes clouded and finally Dover appears colourless in what almost seems to be grey mist, but is not, is no more than lightlessness. I am biassed about the weather? A bit: but it is surprising how many times this is so, how often a dismal sky provides a pall of what next is to come, the Customs.

Now I must confess to a personal inability to pass through the Customs without being knocked cock-eyed by guilt. I am a rotten smuggler, and so I never smuggle. But even so I feel thoroughly in the wrong. Something, I feel, however explicable, will be held against me. The Customs Officers are usually most polite. I imagine they are also wise, and magically perceptive: I have always felt that if I had charge of the education of a young man I would try to smuggle him for a period into a Custom Officers' School, if there is such a thing—there I feel he would learn better than anywhere else how to size up the intentions of his fellow men. However . . . passed clean by those careful-eyed gentlemen, I would tread more or less relieved onto the railway platform: but the sense of guilt is never compensated for; I am without doubt upset.

The bookstall for a paper or two, your seat—and the first result of nostalgia's assuagement, nausea. Headlines just the same as when you left, still the same kind of old grumble, new murder. Advertisements

brighter and hollower than ever. However . . . patience, don't take it
too hard, you'll be allowed a drink as soon as a hundred teas have been
served, and in any case you'll soon be THERE. You'll soon be kissing
loved ones, shaking liked ones, pacing the hearth and opening the
post. (It is about here that I ought to say I am no anglophobe. I like
England and I always want to get home; I am not forever grumbling
for the Latin sun, I cannot be wrapped up in that old parcel.) Meanwhile, isn't it strange to sit in a varnished electric-canoe of a train after
all those tall steel caravans the other side of the water?—William
Sansom, *Blue Skies, Brown Studies,* 1961.

THE OLD-FASHIONED CARRIAGE

THE POOR modern slaves and simpletons who let themselves be
dragged like cattle, or felled timber, through the countries they imagine
themselves visiting, can have no conception whatever of the complex
joys, and ingenious hopes, connected with the choice and arrangement
of the travelling carriage in old times. The mechanical questions first,
of strength—easy rolling—steady and safe poise of persons and
luggage; the general stateliness of effect to be obtained for the abashing
of plebian beholders; the cunning design and distribution of store-
cellars under the seats, secret drawers under front windows, invisible
pockets under padded lining, safe from dust, and accessible only by
insidious slits, or necromantic valves like Aladdin's trap-door; the
fitting of cushions where they would not slip, the rounding of corners
for more delicate repose; the prudent attachments and springs of
blinds; the perfect fitting of windows, on which one-half the comfort
of a travelling carriage really depends; and the adaptation of all these
concentrated luxuries to the probabilities of who would sit where, in
the little apartment which was to be virtually one's home for five or
six months;—all this was an imaginary journey in itself, with every
pleasure, and none of the discomfort, of practical travelling.—John
Ruskin, *Praeterita,* 1899.

IRON RATIONS

ON THE Continent the household bread is usually unwholesome and
nasty, and captain's biscuits are never to be obtained. It is prudent to
carry a store of them to use when the staff of life is found especially
abominable. This does not apply to Spain, where delicious, white, firm,
fine-grained bread can be procured in places where it is the only thing
eatable by a dainty person.—Thomas King Chambers, *A Manual of
Diet in Health and Disease,* 1875.

A mountain walk

RETURN OF THE MARTYRS

IT IS an amusing sight, when staying at Dover, in the end of September, to watch the boats coming from Calais. What an army of tourists! A rather sensational display of ice-hatchets and Alpen-stocks advertise the fact that their owners are lovers of scenery—unless, indeed, they have climbed the Swiss mountains merely for the sake of bringing home conversational material for the next 'season'. . . . But did not all these tourists 'go on the continent' for the sake of their health? and if so, why do they look so pale and worn? Why do they give one the impression that they are returning from war, rather than from a pleasure trip? Is it because they have slept in their clothes for a night or two, are covered with the begriming effects of steam-travelling, and are still suffering from sea-sickness? 'Some of you', I thought, as I once stood on the Admiralty Pier, in proud superiority to sea-sickness, watching its victims coming in pairs up the gangway steps, 'some of you seemed to have missed one of the chief objects of travelling—health. You will soon get over your sea-sickness, and be the better for it; but you have evidently worked too hard, and the effects of that will last much longer. Had you taken your tour more easily, you would have returned from it refreshed, instead of looking quite worn out, as you do now.'—Rev. E. J. Hardy, *Manners Makyth Man*, 1887.

GUIDE-BOOKS

FOR EVERY traveller who has any taste of his own, the only useful guide-book will be the one which he himself has written. All others are an exasperation. They mark with asterisks the works of art which he finds dull, and they pass over in silence those which he admires. They make him travel long miles to see a mound of rubbish; they go into ecstasies over mere antiquity. Their practical information is invariably out of date. They recommend bad hotels and qualify good ones as 'modest'. In a word, they are intolerable.

How often have I cursed Baron Baedeker for sending me through the dust to see some nauseating Sodoma or drearily respectable Andrea del Sarto! How angry I have been with him for starring what is old merely because it is old! And how I have hated him for his lack of discrimination! He has a way of lumping all old things of one class together and treating them as if, being made at the same period, their merit was exactly equal. . . . Imbecile!—Aldous Huxley, *Along the Road*, 1925.

Part II

THE GRAND TOUR

BYRON'S ESTABLISHMENT

Ravenna, August [probably 10th], 1821. LORD B.'s establishment consists, besides servants, of ten horses, eight enormous dogs, three monkies, five cats, an eagle, a crow, and a falcon; and all these, except the horses, walk about the house, which every now and then resounds with their unarbitrated quarrels, as if they were the masters of it. . . .

After I have sealed my letter, I find that my enumeration of the animals in this Circean Palace was defective, and that in a material point. I have just met on the grand staircase five peacocks, two guinea hens, and an Egyptian crane.—Shelley, *Letters*.

DISCOVERY OF VENICE

Venice (1909?). I CAME to Venice in August for a six weeks' holiday; and lived and worked and slept on my *barcheta* almost always. It seemed that, by staying on, I could most virtuously and most righteously cheat autumn and winter. Such was the effect of this kind of Venetian life on me, that I felt no more than twenty-five years old, in everything excepting valueless experience and valuable disillusion. The bounding joy of vigorous health, the physical capacity for cheerful (nay, gay) endurance, the careless, untroubled mental activity, the perfectly gorgeous appetite, the prompt, delicate dreamless nights of sleep, which betoken healthy youth—all this (with indescribable happiness) I had triumphantly snatched from solitude with the sun and the sea. I went swimming half a dozen times a day, beginning at white dawn, and ending after sunsets which set the whole lagoon ablaze with amethyst and topaz. Between friends, I will confess that I am not guiltless of often getting up in the night and popping silently over-board to swim for an hour in the clear of a great gold moon—*plenilunio* —or among the waving reflections of the stars. (O my goodness me, how heavenly a spot that is!) When I wanted change of scene and anchorage, I rowed with my two gondoglieri; and there is nothing known to physiculturalists (for giving you 'poise' and the organs and figure of a slim young Diadymenos) like rowing standing in the Mode Venetian. It is jolly hard work; but no other exercise bucks you up as does springing forward from your toe-tips and stretching forward to the full in pushing the oar, or produces such exquisite lassitude at night when your work is done. And I wrote quite easily for a good seven hours each day. Could anything be more felicitous?

And one day, I replenished my stock of provisions at Burano; and at sunset we rowed away to find a station for the night. Imagine a twilight world of cloudless sky and smoothest sea, all made of warm, liquid, limpid heliotrope and violet and lavender, with bands of burnished copper set with emeralds, melting, on the other hand, into the fathomless blue of the eyes of the prides of peacocks, where the moon rose, rosy as mother-of-pearl. Into such glory we three advanced the black *barcheta*, solemnly, silently, when the last echo of *Ave Maria* died.

Slowly we came out north of Burano into the open lagoon; and rowed eastward to meet the night, as far as the point marked by five *pali*, where the wide canal curves to the south. Slowly we went. There was something so holy—so majestically holy— in the evening silence, that I would not have it broken even by the quiet plash of oars. I was lord of time and place. No engagements cried to be kept. I could go when and where I pleased, fast or slow, far or near. And I chose the near and the slow. I did more. So unspeakably gorgeous was the peace on the lagoon just then, that it inspired me with a lust for doing nothing at all but sitting and absorbing impressions motionlessly. That way come thoughts, new, generally noble.

The wide canal, in which we drifted, is a highway. I have never seen it unspeckled by the *sandali* of Buranelli fishers. Steam-boats and tank-barges of fresh water for Burano, and the ordinary barks of carriage, disturb it, not always, but often. My wish was to find a smaller canal, away—away. We were (as I said) at the southern side, at the southward curve marked by five *pali*. Opposite, on the other bank, begins the long line of *pali* which shows the deep-water way right down to the Ricevitoria of Treporti; and there, at the beginning of the line, I spied the mouth of a canal which seemed likely to suit me. We rowed across to it, and entered. It tended north-eastward for two or three hundred metres, and then bended like an elbow north-westward. It looked quite a decent canal, perhaps forty metres in width, between sweet mud-banks clothed with sea-lavender about two-foot lengths above high-water mark in places. We pushed inshore, near to the inner bank at the elbow, stuck a couple of oars into the mud fore and aft, and moored there.

Baicolo and Caicio got out the draught board and cigarettes, and played below their breath on the *puppa*; while I sat still, bathing my soul in peace, till the night was dark and Selene high in the limpid sapphire-blue. Then they lighted the *fanali*, and put up the impermeable awning with wings and curtains to cover the whole *barcheta*; and made a parmentier soup to eat with our wine and *polenta*. And, when kapok-cushions had been arranged on the floor, and summer sleeping bags laid over them, we took our last dash overboard, said our prayers, and

Grand Canal

went to bed. Baicolo at *prova* with his feet towards mine amidships, and Caicio under the *puppa* with his feet well clear of my pillowed head. So, we slept.

Soon after sunrise I awakened: it was a sunrise of opal and fire: the boys were deep in slumber. I took down the awning, and unmoored quietly, and mounted the *puppa* to row about in the dewy freshness in search of a fit place for my morning plunge. I am very particular about this. Deep water I must have—as deep as possible—I being what the Venetians call 'appassionato per l'acqua'. Beside that, I have a vehement dyspathy against getting entangled in weeds or mud, to make my toe-nails dirtier than my finger-nails. And, being congenitally myopic, I see more clearly in deep water than in shallow, almost as clearly, in fact, as with a concave monocle on land. So I left the *barcheta* to drift with the current, while I took soundings with the long oar of the *puppa*, in several parts of the canal, near both banks as well as in the middle. Nowhere could I touch bottom; and this signified that my bathing place was more than four metres in depth. Needless to say that I gave a joyful morning yell, which dragged from sleep the luxury-loving Baicolo to make coffee, and the faithful dog Caicio to take my oar and keep the *barcheta* near me; and then I plunged overboard to revel in the limpid green water. Lord, how lovely is Thy smooth salt water flowing on flesh!—Frederick Rolfe, *Letters*.

LOW CUNNING

... To COMPLETE this tissue of charges against French manners, they are full of *tracasserie*, of trick and low cunning; they are a thorough 'nation of shopkeepers'. All their *bonhommie* and complaisance are at an end, as soon as their interest is concerned. They are rude or polite, just as they think they can make most by it. A French gentleman travelling in company with others, gets a cup of coffee at a little shop for three-halfpence, and laughs at you for paying two francs for a bad breakfast at the inn. They demand payment for board and lodging beforehand, which shows either a grasping disposition or a want of confidence. Besides, you cannot depend on them for a moment. A restless inconsequentiality runs through all they do. They seem naturally desirous of escaping from obligations of every kind. If they cut a throat, it is that of some relation from being *ennuyé* with a repetition of the same intercourse—*toujours perdrix*. If you make a bargain with them and someone else comes and offers them a *sou* more, they take it, and smile at your disappointment, or pretend not to have understood you. If they can impose on you for once, they think it a wonderful achievement, and consider the loss of your custom nothing.

This would be looking too far forward. Therefore, they can never be a commercial people; for commerce has a long memory and long hands.—William Hazlitt, *Essays.*

PARIS AFTERNOONS

PARIS AFTERNOONS: Book-stalls along the quais, with old prints that nobody wants, naughty novels corseted in cellophane; animal shops on the Quai de Gesvres; ferrets, squirming and clucking in the straw, with red eyes and little yawns which reveal their fine white teeth; marmosets chattering over their stump of rotten banana, moulting parrots; the mysterious ailing nocturnal creature that one is always tempted to buy—'c'est un binturong, monsieur'—and then the walk back over the bridge; poplar leaves eddying in the yellow river; misty black-and-grey streets of the Left Bank; discreet shops full of *bibelots*, bad modern paintings, Empire clocks.

Disorder of the hotel bedroom; books, paintings, clothes and red plush; shadows lengthening, the desirable afternoon sleep with its bewildering nightmare-starts and awakenings, its flash-backs to the past. Then the purple Neon lights shining in at the window and the concierge on the telephone: 'Il y a quelqu'un en bas qui vous demande.' 'Voulez-vous lui dire de monter.'—Palinurus, *The Unquiet Grave*, 1944.

A CHILD'S MEMORIES

IN THIS visit to Paris, I was extremely taken up with the soft red cushions of the arm-chairs, which it took one half an hour to subside into after sitting down,—with the exquisitely polished floor of the salon, and the good-natured French 'Boots' (more properly 'Brushes'), who skated over it in the morning till it became as reflective as a mahogany table,—with the pretty court full of flowers and shrubs in beds and tubs, between our rez-de-chaussée windows and the outer gate,—with a nice black servant belonging to another family, who used to catch the house-cat for me; and with an equally good-natured fille de chambre, who used to catch it back again, for fear I should teaze it, (her experience of English boy-children having made her dubious of my intentions);—all these things and people I remember,—and the Tuileries garden, and the 'Tivoli' gardens, where my father took me up and down a 'Russian mountain', and I saw fireworks of the finest. But I remember nothing of the Seine, nor of Notre Dame, nor of anything in or even out of the town, except the windmills on Mont Martre.—John Ruskin, *Praeterita*, 1899.

D

ENGLISH HABITS

THE FRENCH have a notion that, go where you may, to the top of a
pyramid or to the top of Mont Blanc, you are sure to meet an Englishman reading a newspaper.—Henry Labouchère, *Diary of the Besieged
Resident in Paris,* 1871.

THEATRES AT PARIS

Circa 1844. AFTER GOING to these theatres, seeing the houses all full,
and hearing the laughter ringing through every one of them, one is
puzzled to know what the people respect at all, or what principle they
do believe in. They laugh at religion, they laugh at chastity, they
laugh at royalty, they laugh at the Republic most pitilessly of all; when
France, in the piece called the 'Foire aux Idées', says she is dying under
nine hundred doctors, to each of whom she is paying a daily fee of
five-and-twenty francs, there was a cheer of derision through the
house. The Communists and their schemes were hooted with a still
more hearty indignation; there is a general smash and bankruptcy of
faith; and, what struck me perhaps most as an instance of the amazing
progress of the national atheism, is to find that the theatre audiences
have even got to laugh at military glory. They have a song in one of
the little plays which announces that France & Co. have closed that
branch of their business; that they wish to stay at home and be quiet,
and so forth; and strange to say, even the cry against perfidious
England has died out; and the only word of abuse I read against our
nation was in a volume of a novel by poor old Paul de Kock, who
saluted the Lion with a little kick of his harmless old heels. . . .

Sir, these funny pieces at the plays frightened me more than the most
bloodthirsty melodrama ever did, and inspired your humble servant
with a melancholy which is not to be elicited from the most profound
tragedies. There was something awful, infernal almost, I was going to
say, in the gaiety with which the personages of these satiric dramas
were dancing and shrieking about among the tumbled ruins of ever so
many ages and traditions. I hope we shall never have the air of 'God
save the King' set to ribald words amongst us—the mysteries of our
religion, or any man's religion, made the subject of laughter, or of a
worse sort of excitement. In the famous piece of 'La Propriété c'est
le Vol', we had the honour to see Adam and Eve dance a polka, and
sing a song quite appropriate to the costume in which they figured.
Everybody laughed and enjoyed it—neither Eve nor the audience ever
thought about being ashamed of themselves; and, for my part, I

looked with a vague anxiety up at the theatre roof, to see that it was not falling in, and shall not be surprised to hear that Paris goes the way of certain other cities some day.—W. M. Thackeray, *Contributions to 'Punch'*.

THE BEAUTY OF FLORENCE

Florence, June 6, 1854. I LOVE Florence, the place looks exquisitely beautiful in its garden-ground of vineyards and olive trees, sung round by the nightingales day and night, nay, sung *into* by the nightingales, for as you walk along the streets in the evening the song trickles down into them till you stop to listen. Such nights we have between starlight and firefly-light, and the nightingales singing . . . ! If you take one thing with another, there is no place in the world like Florence, I am persuaded, for a place to live in. Cheap, tranquil, cheerful, beautiful, within the limit of civilization yet out of the crush of it.—Elizabeth Barrett Browning, *Letters*.

FRENCH HOUSES

Paris, May 5, 1765. I ARRIVED here this day sevennight, my dear Netty, & am so taken up with everything I see, that I hardly know where I am. In the first place, the town is beautifull, & the people so genteel, that it's a real amusement to drive about the streets. . . . Ld and Ly Hertford are very civil to me, there was never anything so beautiful as their house is, it is quite a pallace, even here where the stile of houses in general are charming in my oppinion. 'Tis true they are inconvenient & dirty, but for one's own appartments they are delightful. In the first place, they are mostly upon the ground floor, & have every one a garden (where there are horse-chestnuts for shade); the rooms are large, the windows immense & all down to the ground, the furniture very fine (if new), for there are comodes even in our lodgings, & looking glasses in every part of the room & very large ones. The houses are dirty & cold, but yet I own I like the stile of them infinitely. —Lady Sarah Lennox, *Life and Letters*.

THE MUSICIANS OF CAPRI

Capri, March, 1854. IT IS as purple, as purple as the pelisse Miss Baxter used to wear this time last year—and there are 1, 2, 3 little ships dotting the sea line, and the blue ocean seems *swelling* over, gently dancing landward as if it would hop into my windows. Night & morning come musicians with song & roundelay. O my stars how sick I am of their noise! They have bawled it under my windows and spoiled my work. —W. M. Thackeray, *Letters.*

CARNIVAL

Florence, February 27, 1740. I HAVE done nothing but slip out of my domino into bed, and out of bed into my domino. The end of the Carnival is frantic, bacchanalian; all the morn one makes parties in masque to the shops and coffee-houses, and all the evening to the operas and balls. *Then I have danced, good gods! how I have danced!* The Italians are fond to a degree of our country dances: *Cold and raw* they only know by the tune; *Blowʒybella* is almost Italian, and *Buttered peas* is *Piʒelli al buro.* There are but three days more; but the two last are to have balls all the morning at the fine unfinished palace of the Strozzi; and the Tuesday night a masquerade after supper: they sup first, to eat *gras,* and not encroach upon Ash-Wednesday. What makes masquerading more agreeable here than in England, is the great deference that is showed to the disguised.—Horace Walpole, *Letters.*

VERDICT ON THE FRENCH

Paris, October 12th, 1763. . . . OF ALL the people I have ever known, I think the French are the least capable of feeling for the distresses of their fellow creatures.—Tobias Smollett, *Travels Through France and Italy.*

A HAPPY MIGRATION

Lausanne, September 5th, 1785. LAST SPRING (not to wear the metaphor to rags) I saw Lausanne in a new light, during my long fit of the Gout; and most boldly declare, that either in health or sickness I find it far more comfortable than your huge metropolis. In London my confinement was sad and solitary; the many forgot my existence when they saw me no longer at Brookes's; and the few, who sometimes cast a thought or an eye on their friend, were detained by business or pleasure, the distance of the way, or the hours of the house of commons. . . . Here the objects are nearer, and more distinct, and I myself am an object of much larger magnitude. People are not kinder, but they are more idle, and it must be confessed that, of all nations on the globe, the English are the least attentive to the old and infirm; I do not mean in acts of charity, but in the offices of civil life. During three months I have had round my chair a succession of agreeable men and women, who came with a smile, and vanished at a nod; and as soon as it was agreeable I had a constant party at cards, which was sometimes dismissed to their respective homes . . . without the least trouble or inconvenience to myself. In a word, my plan has most completely answered; and I solemnly protest, after two years' tryal, that I have never in a single moment repented of my transmigration.—Edward Gibbon, *Letters*.

DR ARNOLD'S THOUGHTS AT LAKE COMO

August 3, 1829. I FANCY how delightful it would be to bring one's family and live here; but then, happily, I think and feel how little such voluptuous enjoyment would repay for abandoning the line of usefulness and activity which I have in England, and how the feeling myself helpless and useless, living merely to look about me, and training up my children in the same way, would soon make all this beauty pall, and appear even wearisome. But to see it as we are now doing, in our moments of recreation, to strengthen us for work to come, and to gild with beautiful recollections our daily life of home duties;—this, indeed, is delightful, and is a pleasure which I think we may enjoy without restraint. England has other destinies than these countries—I use the word in no foolish or unchristian sense—but she has other destinies; her people have more required of them; with her full intelligence, her restless activity, her enormous means, and enormous difficulties; her pure religion and unchecked freedom; her form of society, with so much of evil, yet so much of good in it, and such immense power conferred by it;—her citizens, least of all men, should not think of their own rest or enjoyment, but should cherish every faculty and improve every opportunity to the uttermost, to do good to themselves and to the world. Therefore these lovely valleys, and this surpassing beauty of lake and mountain, and garden and wood, are least, of all men, for us to covet; and our country, so entirely subdued as it is to man's uses, with its gentle hills and valleys, its innumerable canals and coaches, is best suited as an instrument of usefulness.—Dean Stanley's *Life of Dr Arnold*.

FRENCH CONVERSATION

Paris, Sept 22, 1765. THE FRENCH affect philosophy, literature, and free-thinking: the first never did, and never will possess me; of the two others I have long been tired. Free-thinking is for one's self, surely not for society; besides one has settled one's way of thinking, or knows it cannot be settled, and for others I do not see why there is not as much bigotry in attempting conversions from any religion as to it. I dined to-day with a dozen *savans*, and though all the servants were waiting, the conversation was much more unrestrained, even on the Old Testament, than I would suffer at my own table in England, if a single footman was present. For literature, it is very amusing when one has nothing else to do. I think it rather pedantic in society; tiresome when displayed professedly; and, besides, in this country one is sure it is only the fashion of the day. Their taste in it is worst of all: could one believe that when they read our authors, Richardson and Mr Hume, should be their favourites . . . ?

In their dress and equipages they are grown very simple. We English are living upon their old gods and goddesses; I roll about in a chariot decorated with cupids, and look like the grandfather of Adonis.—Horace Walpole, *Letters*.

A TALK WITH ROUSSEAU

Saturday 15 December (1764). . . . ROUSSEAU. 'Good-bye. You are a fine fellow.' BOSWELL. 'You have shown me a great goodness. But I deserved it.' ROUSSEAU. 'Yes. You are malicious; but 'tis a pleasant malice, a malice I don't dislike. Write and tell me how you are.' BOSWELL. 'And you will write to me?' ROUSSEAU. 'I know not how to reach you.' BOSWELL. 'Yes, you shall write to me in Scotland.' ROUSSEAU. 'Certainly; and even at Paris.' BOSWELL. 'Bravo! If I live twenty years, you will write to me for twenty years?' ROUSSEAU. 'Yes.' BOSWELL. 'Good-bye. If you live for seven years, I shall return to Switzerland from Scotland to see you.' ROUSSEAU. 'Do so. We shall be old acquaintances.' BOSWELL. 'One word more. Can I feel sure that I am held to you by a thread, even if of the finest? By a hair?' (Seizing a hair of my head.) ROUSSEAU. 'Yes. Remember always that there are points at which our souls are bound.' BOSWELL. 'It is enough. I, with my melancholy, I, who often look on myself as a despicable being, as a good-for-nothing creature who should make his exit from life—I shall be upheld for ever by the thought that I am bound to Monsieur Rousseau. Good-bye. Bravo! I shall live to the end of my days.' ROUSSEAU. 'That is undoubtedly a thing one must do. Good-bye.'—Boswell, *Boswell on the Grand Tour*.

AN ENGLISH BISHOP AT MASS

AT SIENA last spring, prowling round outside the cathedral, we saw an English ecclesiastic in a stringed, sub-shovel hat. He had a young lady with him, presumably a daughter or niece. He eyed us with much the

Boswell in the dress of a Corsican chief

same incurious curiosity as that with which we eyed him. We passed them and went inside the duomo. How far less impressive is the interior (indeed I had almost said also the exterior) than that of San Domenico! Nothing palls so soon as over-ornamentation.

A few minutes afterwards my Lord and the young lady came in too. It was Sunday and mass was being celebrated. The pair passed us and, when they reached the fringe of the kneeling folk, the bishop knelt down too on the bare floor, kneeling bolt upright from the knees, a few feet in front of where we stood. We saw him and I am sure he knew we were looking at him. The lady seemed to hesitate but after a minute or so, she knuckled down by his side and we left them kneeling bolt upright from the knees on the hard floor.

I always cross myself and genuflect when I go into a Roman Catholic church, as a mark of respect, but Jones and Gogin say that any one can see I am not an old hand at it. How rudimentary is the action of an old priest! I saw one once at Venice in the dining-room of the Hotel la Luna who crossed himself by a rapid motion of his fork just before he began to eat, and Miss Bertha Thomas told me she saw an Italian lady at Varallo at the table-d'hôte cross herself with her fan. I do not cross myself before eating nor do I think it incumbent upon me to kneel down on the hard floor in church—perhaps because I am not an English bishop. We were sorry for this one and for his young lady, but it was their own doing.—Samuel Butler, *Note Books*, 1912.

THE WONDER OF THE WORLD

Cremona, 1844. I HAVE never in my life been so struck by any place as by Venice. It is *the* wonder of the world. Dreamy, beautiful, inconsistent, impossible, wicked, shadowy, d——able old place.—Charles Dickens, *Letters*.

SLEEPLESS NIGHT

Paris, Oct. 1851. EHEU! I have not had such a night these many years, hardly in my life before. My room had commodes, cheffoniers, easy-chairs, and a huge gilt *pendule* (half an hour wrong) was busy on the mantelpiece; but on the bed was not a rag of curtain, the pillow of it looked directly to the window, which had *battants* (*leaves*, not sashes), no shutters, nor with all its screens the possibility of keeping out the light. Noises from the street abounded, nor were wanting from within. Brief, I got no wink of sleep all night; rose many times to make readjustments of my wretched furniture, turned the pillow to the foot, &c.; stept out to the balcony four or five times, and in my dressing-gown and red night-cap *smoked* a short Irish pipe there (lately my poor mother's), and had thoughts enough, looking over the Tuileries garden there, and the gleam of Paris city during the night watches. I could have laughed at myself, but indeed was more disposed to cry. Very strange: I looked down on armed patrols stealthily scouring the streets, saw the gleam of their arms; saw sentries with their lanterns inside the garden; felt as if I could have leapt down among them— preferred turning in again to my disconsolate truckle bed. Towards two o'clock the street noises died away; but I was roused just at the point of sleep by some sharp noise in my own room, which set all my nerves astir;—I could not try sleep again till half-past four, when again a sharp noise smote me all asunder, which I discovered now to be my superfluous friend the heterodox *pendule* striking (all wrong, but on a sharp loud bell, doubly and trebly loud to my poor distracted nerves just on the act of closing into rest) the *half*-hour! This in waking time I had not noticed; this, and the *pendule, in toto,* I now stopt; but sleep was away; the outer and the inner noises were awake again; sleep was now none for me—perhaps some hour of half stupor between six and seven, at which latter hour I gave it up; and determined, first, to have a tub to wash myself in; secondly, not for any consideration to try again the feat of 'sleeping' in that apartment for one.—Thomas Carlyle, *Excursion (Futile Enough) to Paris.*

HUNTING

Greenwich, June 30, O.S., 1751. I SUPPOSE you have hunted at Compiègne. The King's hunting there, I am told, is a fine sight. The French manner of hunting is gentleman-like; ours is only for bumpkins and boobies.—Lord Chesterfield, *Letters.*

THE DUKE OF WELLINGTON'S SIMPLICITY

Cambray, 1818. WE GOT to Vitry about ten. The Duke [of Wellington] had driven much faster than us, so as to have time to answer his letters, and to have the return dispatches ready for Hope. The inn we found him in was the most miserable concern I have ever beheld—so small and so wretched that after we had entered the gate I could not believe that we were right, till the Duke, who had heard the carriage enter, came out of a little wretched parlour in the gateway, without his hat, and on seeing me said:—'Come in here, Creevey: dinner is quite ready.' Dinner accordingly was brought in by a couple of dirty maids, and it consisted of four dishes—2 partridges at the top, a fowl at the bottom, fricassee of chicken on one side and something equally substantial on the other. . . .

The Duke had left Paris at 5 in the morning, and had come 130 miles, and a cold fowl was all that had been eaten by his party in the coach during the day. Altho' the fare was so scanty, the champagne the commonest of stuff, and the house so bad, it seemed to make no impression on the Duke. He seemed quite as pleased and as well satisfied as if he had been in a palace. He and I had a very agreeable conversation for an hour or an hour and a half, principally about the improvements going on in France, which had been begun by Buona-parte—land, &c., &c.—and then we all went to bed.

In the morning we all breakfasted together at five o'clock punctually. Our fare was tea in a great coffee-pot about two feet high. We had cups to drink out of, it is true; but no saucers. The Duke, however, seemed quite as satisfied with everything as the night before; and when I observed, by way of a joke, that I thought the tea was not so very bad, considering it was made, I supposed, at Vitry:—'No', said he, with that curious simplicity of his, 'it is not: I brought it with me from Paris.'—*The Creevey Papers.*

HOTEL LIFE IN CALABRIA

IT IS customary here not to live *en pension* or to pay a fixed price for any meal, the smallest item, down to a piece of bread, being conscien-tiously marked against you. My system, elaborated after consider-able experimentation, is to call for this bill every morning and, for the first day or two after arrival, dispute in friendly fashion every item, remorsely cutting down some of them. Not that they overcharge; their honesty is notorious, and no difference is made in this respect between a foreigner and a native. It is a matter of principle. By this system, which must not be overdone, your position in the house gradually changes; from being a guest, you become a friend, a brother. For it is your duty to show, above all things, that you are not *scemo*—witless, soft-headed—the unforgivable sin in the south. You may be a forger or cut-throat—why not? It is a vocation like any other, a vocation for *men*. But whoever cannot take care of himself—i.e. of his money—is not to be trusted, in any walk of life; he is of no account; he is no man. I have become firm friends with some of these proprietors by the simple expedient of striking a few francs off their bills; and should I ever wish to marry one of their daughters, the surest way to predispose the whole family in my favour would be this method of amiable but unsmiling contestation.

Of course the inns are often dirty, and not only in their sleeping accommodation. The reason is that, like Turks or Jews, their owners do not see dirt (there is no word for dirt in the Hebrew language);

they think it odd when you draw their attention to it. I remember complaining, in one of my fastidious moments, of a napkin, plainly not my own, which had been laid at my seat. There was literally not a clean spot left on its surface, and I insisted on a new one. I got it; but not before hearing the proprietor mutter something about 'the caprices of pregnant women. . . .'—Norman Douglas, *Old Calabria*, 1915.

SOCIAL LIFE IN PARIS

Paris, February the 12th, 1763. SUPPERS, as yet I am pretty much a stranger to, and I fancy shall continue so: for Paris is divided into two Species who have but little communication with each other. The one who is chiefly connected with the men of letters dine very much at home, are glad to see their friends, and pass the evenings till about nine in agreeable and rational conversation. The others are the most fashionable, sup in numerous parties, and always play or rather game both before and after supper. You may easily guess which sort suits me best. Indeed, Madam, we may say what we please of the frivolity of the French, but I do assure you that in a fortnight passed at Paris I have heard more conversation worth remembering, and seen more men of letters among the people of fashion, than I had done in two or three winters in London.—Edward Gibbon, *Letters*.

POETS IN PINK SHIRTS

Rue de Lubeck, Paris, 1893. COMING HOME early this morning after a very noisy party in the Latin Quarter, I found your delightful letter. I have been drinking absinthe with poets and their loves. Bobbinette—isn't that a lovely name?—is a lovely creature, as delicate and innocent-looking and playful as if no such thing as the marriage-bond existed, and as if Latin Quarter manners set the code of morals for the world. I have been having a most amusing time with these queer people—all so gracious and friendly to me. I never really touched the life of Paris before.

To-day I have a breakfast-party at St. Germain. My guests will be arriving—poets in straw hats and pink shirts.—*The Life and Letters of Sir Edmund Gosse*.

LEMONS

IT IS only thirty miles to Messina, but the train takes two hours. It winds and hurries and stops beside the lavender grey morning sea. A flock of goats trails over the beach near the lapping wave's edge, dismally. Great wide deserts of stony river-beds run down to the sea, and men on asses are picking their way across, and women are kneeling by the small stream-channel washing clothes. The lemons hang pale and innumerable in the thick lemon groves. Lemon trees, like Italians, seem to be happiest when they are touching one another all round. Solid forests of not very tall lemon trees lie between the steep mountains and the sea, on the strip of plain. Women, vague in the orchard under-shadow, are picking the lemons, lurking as if in the undersea. There are heaps of pale yellow lemons under the trees. They look like pale, primrose-smouldering fires. Curious how like fires the heaps of lemons look, under the shadow of foliage, seeming to give off a pallid burning amid the suave, naked, greenish trunks. When there comes a cluster of orange trees, the oranges are red like coals among the darker leaves. But lemons, lemons, innumerable, speckled like innumerable tiny stars in the green firmament of leaves. So many lemons! Think of all the lemonade crystals they will be reduced to! Think of America drinking them up next summer.—D. H. Lawrence, *Sea and Sardinia*, 1923.

A HEAP OF LITTLENESS

Paris, February 2, 1839. THE SKY was clear, though it was very cold, and the snow covered everything. I resolved to go to Versailles. The palace is a huge heap of littleness. On the side towards Paris the contrast between the patches of red brick in the old part and the attempt at classical magnificence in the later part is simply revolting. Enormous as is the size of the Place des Armes, it looks paltry beyond description. The statues which used to stand at Paris on the bridge in front of the Chamber of Deputies are ranged round this court. Wretched strutting things they were; horses storming like captains of banditti blustering through a bad melodrama on a second-rate theatre. I had hoped never to have seen them again when I missed them on the bridge; and I fancied, more fool I, that the Government might have had the good taste to throw them into the Seine. In the middle of the court is an equestrian statue of Louis XIV. He showed his sense, at least, in putting himself where he could not see his own architectural performances. I was glad to walk through the Orangerie, and thence I went some little way into the gardens. The snow was several inches deep; but I saw enough to satisfy me that these famous grounds, in meanness and extravagance, surpassed my expectations; and my expectations were not moderate. The garden façade of the palace is certainly fine by contrast with the other front; but when the enormous means employed are compared with the effect, the disproportion is wonderful. This façade is about 2,000 feet in length and is elevated on a lofty terrace. It ought to be one of the most striking works of human power and art. I doubt whether there be anywhere any single architectural composition of equal extent. I do not believe that all the works of Pericles—nay, that even St. Peter's, colonnade and all—cost so much as was lavished on Versailles; and yet there are a dozen country houses of private individuals in England alone which have a greater air of majesty and splendour than this huge quarry. Castle Howard is immeasurably finer.—Lord Macaulay, *Letters*.

THE MONSIEURS OF PARIS

NOR SHALL we then need the monsieurs of Paris to take our hopeful youth into their slight and prodigal custodies, and send them over back again transformed into mimics, apes, and kickshows.—Milton, *Works*.

LAKE SCENE

Ratzeburg, 1799. THE WHOLE lake of Ratzeburg is one mass of thick transparent ice, a spotless mirror of nine miles in extent. The lowness of the hills, which rise from the shores of the lake, precludes the awful sublimity of Alpine landscape, yet compensates for the want of it by beauties, of which this very lowness is a necessary condition. Yester-morning I saw the lesser lake completely hidden by mist; but the moment the sun peeped over the hill, the mist broke in the middle, and in a few seconds stood divided, leaving a broad road all across the lake; and between these two walls of mist the sunlight burnt upon the ice, forming a road of golden fire, intolerably bright, and the mist-walls themselves partook of the blaze in a multitude of shining colours. This is our second frost. About a month ago, before the thaw came on, there was a storm of wind; and during the whole night, such were the thunders and howlings of the breaking ice, that they have left a conviction on my mind, that there are sounds more sublime than any sight can be, more absolutely suspending the power of comparison, and more utterly absorbing the mind's self-consciousness in its total attention to the object working upon it. Part of the ice which the vehemence of the wind had shattered, was driven shoreward and froze anew. On the evening of the next day, at sun-set, the shattered ice thus frozen, appeared of a deep blue, and in shape like an agitated sea; beyond this, the water, that ran up between the great islands of ice which had preserved their masses entire and smooth, shone of a yellow green; but all these scattered ice-islands, themselves, were of an intensely bright blood colour,—they seemed blood and light in union. On some of the largest of these islands, the fishermen stood pulling out their immense nets through the holes made in the ice for this purpose, and the men, their net-poles, and their huge nets, were a part of the glory; say rather, it appeared as if the rich crimson light had shaped itself into these forms, figures, and attitudes, to make a glorious vision in mockery of earthly things.—S. T. Coleridge, *The Friend.*

THE EVIL OF NOON DINNERS

Luchon (Garonne), June, 1787. IN THIS arrangement of the day, no circumstance is so objectionable as that of dining at noon, the consequence of eating no breakfast; for as the ceremony of dressing is kept up, you must be at home from any morning's excursion by twelve o'clock. This single circumstance, if adhered to, would be sufficient to destroy any pursuits, except the most frivolous. Dividing the day exactly in halves, destroys it for any expedition, enquiry, or business that demands seven or eight hours attention, uninterrupted by any calls to the table or the toilette: calls which, after fatigue or exertion, are obeyed with refreshment, and with pleasure. We dress for dinner in England with propriety, as the rest of the day is dedicated to ease, to converse, and relaxation; but by doing it at noon, too much time is lost. What is a man good for after his silk breeches and stockings are on, his hat under his arm, and his head *bien poudré?*—Can he botanize in a watered meadow?—Can he clamber the rocks to mineralize?—Can he farm with the peasant and the ploughman?—He is in order for the conversation of the ladies, which to be sure is in every country, but particularly in France, where the women are highly cultivated, an excellent employment; but it is an employment that never relishes better than after a day spent in active toil or animated pursuit; in something that has enlarged the sphere of our conceptions, or added to the stores of our knowledge.—I am induced to make this observation, because the noon dinners are customary all over France, except by persons of considerable fashion at Paris. They cannot be treated with too much ridicule or severity, for they are absolutely hostile to every view of science, to every spirited exertion, and to every useful pursuit in life.—Arthur Young, *Travels in France.*

ITALIAN GARDEN

1765. HE WHO loves the beauties of simple nature, and the charms of neatness, will seek for them in vain amidst the groves of Italy. In the garden of the Villa Pinciana, there is a plantation of four hundred pines, which the Italians view with rapture and admiration: there is likewise a long walk, of trees extending from the garden-gate to the palace; and plenty of shade, with alleys and hedges in different parts of the ground: but the groves are neglected; the walks are laid with nothing but common mould or sand, black and dusty; the hedges are tall, thin, and shabby; the trees stunted; the open ground, brown and parched, has scarce any appearance of verdure. The flat, regular alleys of evergreens are cut into fantastic figures; the flower gardens embellished with thin cyphers and flourished figures in box, while the flowers grow in rows of earthen-pots, and the ground appears as dusky as if it was covered with the cinders of a blacksmith's forge. The water, of which there is great plenty, instead of being collected in large pieces, or conveyed in little rivulets and streams to refresh the thirsty soil, or managed so as to form agreeable cascades, is squirted from fountains in different parts of the garden, through tubes little bigger than common clyster-pipes. It must be owned indeed that the fountains have their merit in the way of sculpture and architecture; and that here is a great number of statues which merit attention: but they serve only to encumber the ground, and destroy that effect of rural simplicity, which our gardens are designed to produce. In a word, here we see a variety of walks and groves and fountains, a wood of four hundred pines, a paddock with a few meagre deer, a flower-garden, an aviary, a grotto, and a fish-pond; and in spite of all these particulars, it is, in my opinion, a very contemptible garden, when compared to that of Stowe in Buckinghamshire, or even to those of Kensington and Richmond.—Tobias Smollett, *Travels Through France and Italy*.

AGREEABLE SURPRISE

Calais, 1802. WE WERE all three too much awake by the new scene to try for any repose, and the hotel windows sufficed for our amusement till dinner; and imagine, my dearest sir, how my repast was seasoned, when I tell you that, as soon as it began, a band of music came to the window and struck up '*God save the King*'. I can never tell you what a pleased emotion was excited in my breast by this sound on a shore so lately hostile, and on which I have so many, so heartfelt motives for wishing peace and amity perpetual. . . !

Beggars we saw not—no, not one, all the time we stayed or sauntered; and for civility and gentleness, the poorest and most ordinary persons we met or passed might be compared with the best dressed and best looking walkers in the streets of our metropolis, and still to the disadvantage of the latter. I cannot say how much this surprised me, as I had conceived an horrific idea of the populace of this country, imagining them all transformed into bloody monsters.

Another astonishment I experienced equally pleasing, though not equally important to my ease; I saw innumerable pretty women and lovely children, almost all of them extremely fair. I had been taught to expect nothing but mahogany complexions and hideous features instantly on crossing the strait of Dover. When this, however, was mentioned in our party afterwards, the Highlander exclaimed, 'But Calais was in the hands of the English so many years, that the English race there is not yet extinct.'—Fanny Burney, *Diary and Letters of Madame D'Arblay.*

GARDEN SOLITUDE

Brescia (July 10, 1748). MY GARDEN was a plain vineyard when it came into my hands not two years ago, and it is, with a small expense, turned into a garden that (apart from the advantage of the climate) I like better than that of Kensington. The Italian vineyards are not planted like those in France, but in clumps, fastened to trees planted in equal ranks (commonly fruit-trees), and continued in festoons from one to another, which I have turned into covered galleries of shade, that I can walk in the heat without being incommoded by it. I have made a dining-room of verdure, capable of holding a table of twenty covers; the whole ground is three hundred and seventeen feet in length, and two hundred in breadth. You see it is far from large; but so prettily disposed (though I say it), that I never saw a more agreeable rustic garden, abounding with all sort of fruit, and produces a variety of wines. I would send you a piece if I did not fear the customs would make you pay too dear for it. I believe my description gives you but an imperfect idea of my garden. Perhaps I shall succeed better in describing my manner of life, which is as regular as that of any monastery. I generally rise at six, and as soon as I have breakfasted, put myself at the head of my weeder women and work with them till nine. I then inspect my dairy, and take a turn among my poultry, which is a very large inquiry. I have, at present, two hundred chickens, besides turkeys, geese, ducks, and peacocks. All things have hitherto prospered under my care; my bees and silkworms are doubled, and I am told that, without accidents, my capital will be so in two years' time. At eleven o'clock I retire to my books: I dare not indulge myself in that pleasure above an hour. At twelve I constantly dine, and sleep after dinner till about three. I then send for some of my old priests, and either play at piquet or whist, till 'tis cool enough to go out. One evening I walk in my wood, where I often sup, take the air on horseback the next, and go on the water the third. The fishery of this part of the river belongs to me; and my fisherman's little boat (where I have a green lutestring awning) serves me for a barge. He and his son are my rowers without any expense, he being very well paid by the profit of the fish, which I give him on condition of having every day one dish for my table. Here is plenty of every sort of fresh-water fish (excepting salmon); but we have a large trout so like it, that I, that have almost forgot the taste, do not distinguish it.

We are both placed properly in regard to our different times of life: you amidst the fair, the gallant, and the gay; I in a retreat, where I enjoy every amusement that solitude can afford. I confess I sometimes wish for a little conversation; but I reflect that the commerce of the world gives more uneasiness than pleasure, and quiet is all the hope that can reasonably be indulged at my age.—Lady Mary Wortley Montagu, *Letters.*

NELSON IN FRANCE

November, 1783. WE SLEPT at Dover, and next morning at seven o'clock put to sea with a fine north-west wind, and at half-past ten we were safe at breakfast in Monsieur Grandsire's house at Calais. . . . Sterne's 'Sentimental Journey' is the best description I can give of our tour. Mac advised me to go first to St. Omer, as he had experienced the difficulty of attempting to fix in any place where there are no English; after dinner we set off, intended for Montreuil, sixty miles from Calais: they told us we travelled *en poste*, but I am sure we did not get on more than four miles an hour. I was highly diverted with looking what a curious figure the postilions in their jack boots, and their rats of horses, made together. Their chaises have no springs, and the roads generally paved like London streets; therefore you will naturally suppose we were pretty well shook together by the time we had travelled two posts and a half, which is fifteen miles, to Marquise. Here we [were] shown into an inn—they called it—I should have called it a pigstye: we were shown into a room with two straw beds, and, with great difficulty, they mustered up clean sheets; and gave us two pigeons for supper, upon a dirty cloth, and wooden-handled knives—O what a transition from happy England!—Horatio, Viscount Nelson, *Letters.*

STAID MANNERS

1770. IN THE court of Milan, as in several others in Italy, there are many who fall in with the dress and carriage of the French. One may, how-ever, observe a kind of awkwardness in the Italians, which easily discovers the airs they give themselves not to be natural. It is indeed very strange there should be such a diversity of manners, where there is so small a difference in the air and climate. The French are always

E

open, familiar, and talkative: the Italians, on the contrary, are stiff, ceremonious, and reserved. In France every one aims at a gaiety and sprightliness of behaviour, and thinks it an accomplishment to be brisk and lively: the Italians, notwithstanding their natural fieriness of temper, affect always to appear sober and sedate; insomuch that one sometimes meets young men walking the streets with spectacles on their noses, that they may be thought to have impaired their sight by much study, and seem more grave and judicious than their neighbours. —Joseph Addison, *Remarks on Italy*.

LORD CURZON IN LAUSANNE

Beau Rivage Hotel, Lausanne. TEN MINUTES later the glass doors again gyrated and Lord Curzon, magnificent and smiling, stood upon the threshold. Slowly and benignly he bowed to the managers: to the journalists he made a friendly gesture at once welcoming and dismissive: he proceeded to the lift. Seizing the green foot-rest from Sir William Tyrrell, I hurried through the crowd towards the staircase: 'Tiens', exclaimed a French journalist, indicating the foot-rest, 'le trône de Bagdad.' I pushed past him and arrived on the first floor just as Lord Curzon was leaving the lift. He paused at the doorway of his apartment and surveyed it. 'How ghăstly!' he sighed. He walked towards the window, pulled aside the yellow cretonne curtain, and gazed across to the lights of Evian. 'How positively ghăstly,' he repeated.—Harold Nicolson, *Some People*, 1927.

THE FRENCH GRIN

1718. I HAVE been running about Paris at a strange rate with my sister, and strange sights have we seen. They are, at least, strange sights to me, for after having been accustomed to the gravity of the Turks, I can scarcely look with an easy and familiar aspect at the levity and agility of the airy phantoms that are dancing about me here, and I often think that I am at a puppet-shew amidst the representations of real life. I stare prodigiously, but nobody remarks it, for every body stares here; staring is à la mode—there is a stare of attention and *intérêt*, a stare of curiosity, a stare of expectation, a stare of surprise, and it would greatly amuse you to see what trifling objects excite all this staring. This staring would have rather a solemn kind of air, were it not alleviated by grinning, for at the end of a stare there comes always a grin, and very commonly the entrance of a gentleman or a lady into a room is accompanied with a grin, which is designed to express complacence and social pleasure, but really shews nothing more than a certain contortion of muscles that must make a stranger laugh really, as they laugh artificially. The French grin is equally remote from the cheerful serenity of a smile, and the cordial mirth of an honest English horse-laugh. . . . Does not King David say somewhere, that *Man walketh in a vain shew?* I think he does, and I am sure this is peculiarly true of the Frenchman—but he walks merrily and seems to enjoy the vision, and may he not therefore be esteemed more happy than many of our solid thinkers, whose brows are furrowed by deep reflection, and whose wisdom is so often clothed with a mistly mantle of spleen and vapours?—Lady Mary Wortley Montagu, *Letters*.

A MISERABLE RACE

Milan, April 20, 1818. THE PEOPLE here, though inoffensive enough, seem both in body and soul a miserable race. The men are hardly men; they look like a tribe of stupid and shrivelled slaves, and I do not think that I have seen a gleam of intelligence in the countenance of man since I passed the Alps. The women in enslaved countries are always better than the men; but they have tight-laced figures, and figures and mien which express (O how unlike the French!) a mixture of the coquette and prude, which reminds me of the worst characteristics of the English.—Shelley, *Letters*.

A CITY IN THE COUNTRY

Paris: July 7 (1851). WELL, now we are in Paris and have to forget the 'belle chiese'; we have beautiful shops instead, false teeth grinning at the corners of the streets, and disreputable prints, and fascinating hats and caps, and brilliant restaurants, and M. le Président in a cocked hat and with a train of cavalry, passing like a rocket along the boulevards to an occasional yell from the Red. Oh yes, and don't mistake me! for I like it all extremely, it's a splendid city—a city in the country, as Venice is a city in the sea.—Elizabeth Barrett Browning, *Letters*.

NEWMAN IN ROME

Rome: March 5, 1833. WE ARRIVED at this wonderful place only Saturday last (March 2) from Naples. . . . Of course, I have seen very little of it; but the effect of every part is so vast and overpowering— there is such an air of greatness and repose cast over the whole, and, independent of what one knows from history, there are such traces of long sorrow and humiliation, suffering, punishment and decay, that one has a mixture of feelings, partly such as those with which one would approach a corpse, and partly those which would be excited by the sight of the spirit which had left it. . . . Oxford, of course, must ever be a sacred city to an Oxonian, and is to me. It would be a strange want of right pride to think of disloyalty to it, even if our creed were not purer than the Roman; yet the lines of Virgil keenly and affectionately describe what I feel about this wonderful city. Repeat them in your memory every word, and dwell on each. '*Urbem, quam dicunt Romam, Meliboee, putavi, stultus ego!*' &c.—John Henry Newman, *Letters.*

A BOARDING-HOUSE

AN ACQUAINTANCE of mine is settled in a French boarding-house. What scenes we have (fit to make us die with laughter) in going over the messes and manners of the place! How we exult in the *soup-maigre!* How we triumph in the *bouillé*, as hard as a bullet! If a single thing were good, it would ruin us for the evening. Then the knives will not cut—and what a thing to set down a single fowl before six people, who seem all ready to fall upon it and tear it in pieces! What meanness and wretched economy! Why don't they get a good substantial joint of meat, in which there would be *cut and come again?* If they had common sense they would. And then the lamentable want of decency and propriety is another never-failing and delightful topic. The child is unswaddled before company, and the dirty clothes for the next week's wash are left stewing in the window all dinner-time. The master is such a Goth too, a true Frenchman! When carving he flourishes his knife about in such a manner as to endanger those who sit near him, and stops in the middle with the wing of a duck suspended on the point of his fork, to spout a speech out of some play. Dinner is no sooner over than he watches his opportunity, collects all the bottles and glasses on the table, beer, wine, porter, empties them into his own, heaps his plate with the remnants of fricassees, gravy, vegetables, mustard, melted butter, and sops them all up with a large piece of bread, wipes his plate clear as if a dog had licked it, dips his bread in some other dish that in his hurry had escaped him, and finishes off by picking his teeth with a sharp-pointed knife. He then, having satisfied his most urgent wants, amuses himself during the dessert by putting salt into the governess's fruit, and giving a pinch of snuff to a cat which is seated in his lap with a string of beads round its neck. What exquisite refinement! Surely, the English are a century behind the French in civilisation and politeness! Is it not worth while to run the gauntlet of a French boarding-house, to pay a hundred and sixty francs a month, and be starved, poisoned, talked, stung to death, to arrive at so consoling a reflection? It may be said that this is a vulgar Frenchman in a

low rank of life: I answer that there is no such character in any rank of life in London—who spouts Shakespear one moment, the next picks his teeth with his fork, and then sticks it in a potatoe to help you to it.
—William Hazlitt, *Essays.*

THE RUINS OF POMPEII

Naples, July 15, 1840. WE HAVE just left Pompeii, after having spent two hours in walking over the ruins. Now what has struck me most in this extraordinary scene, speaking historically? That is, what knowledge does one gain from seeing an ancient town destroyed in the first century of the christian era, thus laid open before us? I do not think that there is much. I observed the streets crossing one another at right angles: I observed the walls of the town just keeping the crown of the hill, and the suburbs and the tombs falling away directly from the gates: I observed the shops in front of the houses,—the streets narrow, the rooms in the houses very small; the dining-room in one of the best was twenty feet by eighteen nearly. The Forum was large for the size of the town; and the temples and public buildings occupied a space proportionably greater than with us. I observed the Impluvium, forming a small space in the midst of the Atrium. And I think, farther, that Pompeii is just a thing for pictures to represent adequately; I could understand it from Gell's book, but no book can give me the impressions or the knowledge which I gain from every look at the natural landscape. Then, poetically, Pompeii is to me, as I always thought it would be, no more than Pompeii; that is, it is a place utterly unpoetical. An Osco-Roman town, with some touches of Greek corruption—a town of the eighth century of Rome, marked by no single noble recollection, nor having—like the polygonal walls of Cicolano—the marks of a remote antiquity and a pure state of society. There is only the same sort of interest with which one would see the ruins of Sodom and Gomorrah, but indeed there is less. One is not authorised to ascribe so solemn a character to the destruction of Pompeii; it is not a peculiar monument of God's judgments, it is the mummy of a man of no worth or dignity,—solemn, no doubt, as everything is which brings life and death into such close connexion, but with no proper and peculiar solemnity, like places rich in their own proper interest, or sharing in the general interest of a remote antiquity, or an uncorrupted state of society. The towns of the Cicolano are like the tomb of a child,—Pompeii is like that of Lord Chesterfield.
—Dean Stanley's *Life of Dr Arnold.*

GLIMPSE OF HELL

Maison Laurenti, Mentone, January 19th, 1861. MANY THANKS for
your letter, which a comfortable letter it was, but creates violent
wishes to get back to England. For of *all the beasts* of countries I ever
see, I reckon this about caps them. I also strongly notion that there
ain't a hole in St. Giles's which isn't a paradise to this. How any pro-
fessing Christian as has been in France and England can look at it,
passes me. It is more like the landscape in Browning's *Childe Roland*
than anything I ever heard tell on. A calcined, scalped, rasped, scraped,
flayed, broiled, powdered, leprous, blotched, mangy, grimy, parboiled,
country *without* trees, water, grass, fields—*with* blank, beastly, senseless olives and orange-trees like a mad cabbage gone indigestible; it is
infinitely liker hell than earth, and one looks for tails among the
people. And such females with hunched bodies and crooked necks
carrying tons on their heads, and looking like Death taken seasick.
Ar-r-r-r-r! Gr-r-r-rn!—Algernon Charles Swinburne, *Letters*.

ON THE WAY TO FLORENCE

1765. HAVING SATISFIED my curiosity at Rome, I prepared for my
departure, and as the road between Radicofani and Montefiascone is
very stony and disagreeable, I asked the banker Barazzi, if there was
not a better way of returning to Florence, expressing a desire at the
same time to see the cascade of Terni. He assured me that the road by
Terni was forty miles shorter than the other, much more safe and easy,
and accommodated with exceeding good *auberges*. Had I taken the
trouble to cast my eyes upon the map, I must have seen, that the road
by Terni, instead of being forty miles shorter, was much longer than
the other: but this was not the only mistake of Signiore Barazzi. Great
part of this way lies over steep mountains, or along the side of preci-
pices, which render travelling in a carriage exceeding tedious, dreadful,
and dangerous; and as for the public houses, they are in all respects the
most execrable that ever I entered. I will venture to say that a common
prisoner in the Marshalsea or King's-Bench is more cleanly and
commodiously lodged than we were in many places on this road. The
houses are abominably nasty, and generally destitute of provision:
when eatables were found, we were almost poisoned by their cookery:
their beds were without curtains or bedstead, and their windows
without glass; and for this sort of entertainment we payed as much as
if we had been genteely lodged, and sumptuously treated. I repeat it
again, of all the people I ever knew, the Italians are the most villainously
rapacious.—Tobias Smollett, *Travels Through France and Italy*.

An Italian view

MACAULAY AND THE OLIVES

November 2, 1838. As I approached Florence, the day became brighter;
and the country looked, not indeed strikingly beautiful, but very
pleasing. The sight of the olive-trees interested me much. I had,
indeed, seen what I was told were olive-trees, as I was whirled down
the Rhone from Lyons to Avignon; but they might, for anything I
saw, have been willows or ash-trees. Now they stood, covered with
berries, along the road for miles. I looked at them with the same sort of
feeling with which Washington Irving says that he heard the nightingale for the first time when he came to England, after having read
descriptions of her in poets from his childhood. I thought of the
Hebrews, and their numerous images drawn from the olive; of the
veneration in which the tree was held by the Athenians; of Lysias's
speech; of the fine ode in the Oedipus at Colonos; of Virgil and

Lorenzo de' Medici. Surely it is better to travel in mature years, with all these things in one's head, than to rush over the Continent while still a boy!—Lord Macaulay, *Letters*.

THE TWO ITALIES

Naples, December 22, 1818. THERE ARE *two* Italies. . . . The one is the most sublime and lovely contemplation that can be conceived by the imagination of man; the other is the most degraded, disgusting, and odious. What do you think? Young women of rank actually eat—you will never guess what—*garlick*! Our poor friend Lord Byron is quite corrupted by living among these people. . . .—Shelley, *Letters*.

A DREAM OF ST PETER'S

Rome, October 30th, 1780. IMMEDIATELY after breakfast I repaired again to St. Peter's, which even exceeded the height of my expectations. I could hardly quit it. I wish his Holiness would allow me to erect a little tabernacle within this glorious temple. I should desire no other prospect during the winter; no other sky than the vast arches glowing with golden ornaments, so lofty as to lose all glitter or gaudiness. But I cannot say I should be perfectly contented, unless I could obtain another tabernacle for you. Thus established, we would take our evening walks on the field of marble; for is not the pavement vast enough for the extravagance of the appellation? Sometimes, instead of climbing a mountain, we should ascend the cupola, and look down on our little encampment below. At night I should wish for a constellation of lamps dispersed about in clusters, and so contrived as to diffuse a mild and equal light. Music should not be wanting: at one time to breathe in the subterraneous chapels, at another to echo through the dome.

The doors should be closed, and not a mortal admitted. No priests, no cardinals: God forbid! We would have all the space to ourselves, and to beings of our own visionary persuasion.—William Beckford, *Italy, Spain, and Portugal*.

BAD MARKSMEN

Calais. *C'est bien comique*, 'tis very droll, said the lady smiling, from the reflection that this was the second time we had been left together by a parcel of nonsensical contingencies,—*c'est bien comique*, said she.

—There wants nothing, said I, to make it so, but the comic use which the gallantry of a Frenchman would put it to,—to make love the first moment,—and an offer of his person the second.

—'Tis their *fort*, replied the lady.

—It is supposed so at least;—and how it has come to pass, continued I, I know not; but they have certainly got the credit of understanding more of love, and making it better than any other nation upon earth: but for my own part, I think them arrant bunglers; and, in truth, the worst set of marksmen that ever tried Cupid's patience.— Laurence Sterne, *A Sentimental Journey Through France and Italy*, 1768.

INSOLENT OFFICIAL

January 1, 1839. I SHALL not soon forget the three days which I passed between Rome and Naples. . . . At the frontier the custom-house officer begged me to give him a place in my carriage to Mola. I refused, civilly, but firmly. I gave him three crowns not to plague me by searching my baggage, which indeed was protected by a *lascia passare*. He pocketed the three crowns, but looked very dark and sullen at my refusal to accept his company. Precious fellow; to think that a public functionary to whom a little silver is a bribe is fit society for an English gentleman!—Lord Macaulay, *Letters*.

CLIMBING

Switzerland, 1868. WE TOOK a guide up the Wylerhorn but the top being clouded dismissed him and stayed up the mountain, lunching by a waterfall. Presently after long climbing—for there was a good chance of a clearance—we nearly reached the top, when a cloud coming on thick frightened me back: had we gone on we should have had the view, for it cleared quite. Still we saw the neighbouring mountains well. The snow is often cross-harrowed and lies too in the straightest paths as though artificial, which again comes from the planing. In the sheet it glistens yellow to the sun. How fond of and warped to the mountains it would be easy to become! For every cliff and limb and edge and jutty has its own nobility.—Two boys came down the mountain yodelling. —We saw the snow in the hollows for the first time. In one the surface was crisped across the direction of the cleft and the other way, that is across the broader crisping and down the stream, combed: the stream ran below and smoke came from the hollow; the edge of the snow hewn in curves as if by moulding-planes.—Crowd of mountain flowers—gentians; gentianellas; blood-red lucerne; a deep blue glossy spiked flower like plantain, flowering gradually up the spike, so that at the top it looks like clover or honeysuckle; rich big harebells glistening black like the cases of our veins when dry and heated from without; and others. All the herbage enthronged with every fingered or fretted leaf.—Firs very tall, with the swell of the branching on the outer side of the slope so that the peaks seem to point inwards to the mountain peak, like the lines of the Parthenon, and the outline melodious and moving on many focuses.—I wore my pagharee and turned it with harebells below and gentians in two rows above like double pan-pipes. In coming down we lost our way and each had a dangerous slide down the long wet grass of a steep slope.—*The Journals and Papers of Gerard Manley Hopkins.*

LAZINESS

Florence, Oct. 2, 1740. YOU WOULD be as much amazed at us as at anything you saw: instead of being deep in the liberal arts, and being in the Gallery every morning, as I thought of course to be sure I would be, we are in all the idleness and amusements of the town. For me, I am grown so lazy, and so tired of seeing sights, that, though I have been at Florence six months, I have not seen Leghorn, Pisa, Lucca, or Pistoia; nay, not so much as one of the Great Duke's villas. I have contracted so great an aversion to inns and post-chaises, and have so absolutely lost all curiosity, that, except the towns in the straight road to Great Britain, I shall scarce see a jot more of a foreign land.—Horace Walpole, *Letters.*

PIETY

July, 1738. AT FOUR we took boat, when I could not but observe the decency of the Papists above us who are called Reformed. As soon as ever we were seated (and so every morning after), they all pulled off their hats, and each used by himself a short prayer for our prosperous journey. And this justice I must do to the very boatmen (who upon the Rhine are generally wicked even to a proverb), I never heard one of them take the name of God in vain, or saw any one laugh when anything of religion was mentioned. So that I believe the glory of sporting with sacred things is peculiar to the English nation!—John Wesley, *Journal.*

OLIVES

Golfo della Spezia, Italia, 18 Dec., 1913. AT THIS time of the year all the women are out in the olive woods—you have no idea how beautiful olives are, so grey, so delicately sad, reminding one constantly of the New Testament. I am always expecting when I got to Tellaro for the

letters, to meet Jesus gossiping with his disciples as he goes along
above the sea, under the grey, light trees. Now the hills are full of
voices, the peasant women and children all day long and day after day,
in the faint shadow of olives, picking the fallen fruit off the ground,
pannier after pannier full.—D. H. Lawrence, *Letters*.

QUEEN VICTORIA IN PARIS

St Cloud, 23rd August, 1855. I DO NOT intend to attempt any description, for I have no time for anything of the sort; besides I have no
doubt you will read the papers, and I know good Van de Weyer has
written *au long* to you about it all. I will therefore only give in a few
words my impressions.

I am *delighted, enchanted, amused,* and *interested,* and think I never
saw anything more *beautiful* and gay than Paris—or more splendid
than all the Palaces. Our reception is *most* gratifying—for it is enthusiastic and really kind in the highest degree; and Maréchal Magnan
(whom you know well) says that such a reception as I have received
every day here is much greater and much more enthusiastic even than
Napoleon on his return from his victories had received! Our entrance
into Paris . . . was quite *overpowering*—splendidly decorated—
illuminated—immensely crowded—and 60,000 troops out—from the
Gare de Strasbourg to St Cloud, of which 20,000 Gardes Nationales,
who had come great distances to see me.

The Emperor has done wonders for Paris, and for the Bois de
Boulogne. Everything is beautifully *monté* at Court—*very* quiet, and
in excellent order; I must say we are both much struck with the
difference between this and the poor King's time, when the noise,
confusion, and bustle were great. We have been to the Exposition, to
Versailles—which is most splendid and magnificent—to the Grand
Opéra, where the reception and the way in which 'God save the
Queen' was sung were *most magnificent.* Yesterday we went to the
Tuileries; in the evening *Théâtre ici*; to-night an immense ball at the
Hotel de Ville. They have asked to call a new street, which we opened,
after me!

The heat is very great, but the weather splendid, and though the
sun may be hotter, the air is certainly *lighter* than ours—and I have no
headache.—Queen Victoria, *Letters*.

THE MINUET STEP

Paris, Sept 14, 1765. I AM BUT two days old here, Madam, and I doubt
I wish I was really so, and had my life to begin, to live it here. You see
how just I am, and ready to make *amende honorable* to your ladyship.

Yet I have seen very little. My Lady Hertford has cut me to pieces, and thrown me into a caldron with tailors, periwig-makers, snuff-box-wrights, milliners, &c., which really took up but little time; and I am come out quite new, with everything but youth. The journey recovered me with magic expedition. My strength, if mine could ever be called strength, is returned; and the gout going off in a minuet step. I will say nothing of my spirits, which are indecently juvenile, and not less improper for my age than for the country where I am; which, if you will give me leave to say it, has a thought too much gravity. I don't venture to laugh or talk nonsense, but in English.—Horace Walpole, *Letters*.

GIBBON AT COURT

Borromean Islands, May 16th, 1764. I HARDLY think you will like Turin; the Court is old and dull; and in that country every one follows the example of the court. The principal amusement seems to be driving about in Your Coach in the evening & bowing to the people you meet. If you go when the royal family is there, you have the additional pleasure of stopping to salute them every time they pass. I had that advantage fifteen times one afternoon. We were presented to a Lady who keeps a public assembly, and a very mournfull one it is. The few women who go to it are each taken up by their Cicisbeo; and a poor Englishman, who can neither talk Piedmontese nor play at Faro, stands by himself, without one of their haughty nobility doing him the honor of speaking to him. . . .

The most sociable women I have met with are the King's daughters. I chatted for about a quarter of an hour with them, talked about Lausanne, and grew so very free and easy, that I drew my snuff-box, rapped it, took snuff twice (a Crime never known before in the presence-chamber,) & continued my discourse in my usual attitude of my body bent forwards, and my fore finger stretched out. As it might however have been difficult to keep up this acquaintance, I chiefly employ my time in seeing places, which fully repaid me in pleasure the trouble of my journey.—Edward Gibbon, *Letters*.

TWO MAIDEN LADIES

Hotel de la Ville, Milan, Twenty-fifth October, 1853. IT IS extraordinary that the only travellers we have encountered, since we left Paris, have been one horribly vapid Englishman and wife whom we dropped at Basle, one boring Englishman who we found (and, thank God, left) at Geneva, and two English maiden ladies, whom we found sitting on a rock (with parasols) the day before yesterday, in the most magnificent part of the Gorge of Gondo, the most awful portion of the Simplon—there awaiting their travelling chariot, in which, with their money, their parasols, and a perfect shop of baskets, they were carefully *locked up* by an English servant in sky blue and silver buttons. We have been in the most extraordinary vehicles—like swings, like boats, like Noah's arks, like barges and enormous bedsteads. After dark last night, a landlord, where we changed horses, discovered that the luggage would certainly be stolen from *questo porco d'uno carro*—this pig of a cart—his complimentary description of our carriage, unless cords were attached to each of the trunks, which cords were to hang down so that we might hold them in our hands all the way, and feel any tug that might be made at our treasures. You will imagine the absurdity of our jolting along some twenty miles in this way, exactly as if we were in three shower-baths and were afraid to pull the string.—Charles Dickens, *Letters*.

AN ANGLICAN IN ROME

Radicofani, July 5, 1740. THERE IS a horrid thing called the malaria, that comes to Rome every summer, and kills one, and I did not care for being killed so far from Christian burial.—Horace Walpole, *Letters*.

A RICH ABBEY

October 14th, 1787. TO THE benedictine abbey of St. Germain, to see pillars of African marble, &c. It is the richest abbey in France: the abbot has 300,000 liv. a year (13,125 l.) I lose my patience at such revenues being thus bestowed; consistent with the spirit of the tenth century, but not with that of the eighteenth. What a noble farm would the fourth of this income establish! what turnips, what cabbages, what potatoes, what clover, what sheep, what wool!—Are not these things better than a fat ecclesiastic? If an active English farmer was mounted behind this abbot, I think he would do more good to France with half the income than half the abbots of the kingdom with the whole of theirs. Pass the bastile; another pleasant object to make agreeable emotions vibrate in a man's bosom. I search for good farmers, and run my head at every turn against monks and state prisoners.—Arthur Young, *Travels in France*.

A FRENCH SCHOOL

Toulouse, 1864. IN THE playground the boys—dressed, all of them, in the well-known uniform of the French schoolboy—were running, shouting, and playing, with the animation of their age; but it is not by its playgrounds and means of recreation that a French lyceum, as compared with the half-dozen great English public schools, shines. The boys are taken out to walk, as the boys at Winchester used to be taken out to *hills*; but at the end of the French schoolboy's walk there are no *hills* on which he is turned loose. He learns and practises gymnastics more than our schoolboys do; and the court in which he takes his recreation is somewhat more spacious and agreeable than we English are apt to imagine a *court* to be; but it is a poor place indeed— poor in itself and poor in its resources—compared with the *playing-fields* of Eton, or the *meads* of Winchester, or the *close* of Rugby.— Matthew Arnold, *A French Eton*.

BATTLE WITH RATS

Venice (1908?). THE LAST few days I have been anchored near an empty island, Sacca Fisola, not too far away from civilisation to be out of reach of fresh water, but lonely enough for dying alone in the boat if need be. Well, to shew you how worn out I am, I frankly say that I have funked it. This is my dilemma. I'll be quite plain about it. If I stay out on the lagoon, the boat will sink, I shall swim perhaps for a few hours, and then I shall be eaten alive by crabs. At low water every mudbank swarms with them. If I stay anchored near an island, I must keep continually awake: for, the moment I cease moving, I am invaded by swarms of swimming rats, who in the winter are so voracious that they attack every man who is motionless. I have tried it. And have been bitten. Oh my dear man you can't think how artful fearless ferocious they are. I rigged up two bits of chain, lying loose on my prow and poop with a string by which I could shake them when attacked. For two nights the dodge acted. The swarms came (up the anchor rope) and nuzzled me: I shook the chains: the beasts plopped overboard. Then they got used to the noise and sneered. Then they bit the strings. Then they bit my toes and woke me shrieking and shaking with fear. . . .

My dear man, I am so awfully lonely. And tired. Is there no chance of setting me straight?—Frederick Rolfe, *Letters*.

MORNING ADVENTURE

Berlin, 11 September 1764. To PUNISH my extravagant rodomontading, and to bring up my affairs and compose my spirit, I had sitten up all night. Grievous was it to the flesh till seven in the morning, when my blood took a fine flow. I was quite drunk with brisk spirits, and about eight, in came a woman with a basket of chocolate to sell. I toyed with her and found she was with child. Oho! a safe piece. Into my closet. 'Habs er ein Man?' 'Ja, in den Gards bei Potsdam.' To bed directly. In a minute—over. I rose cool and astonished, half angry, half laughing. I sent her off. Bless me, have I now committed adultery?— Boswell, *Boswell on the Grand Tour*.

THE GOOD LIFE

Paris, 1841. SUCH A man of an engraver as I have found! I wish you could see him. He is abt. 28 has not a spark of genius: works 14 hours a day, never breakfasts except off cheese & bread in his atelier, dines in the same way, never goes out, makes about 3,000 francs a year, has a wife & child & is happy the whole day long—the whole house is like a cage of canaries, nothing but singing from night till morning. It goes to my heart to hear his little wife singing at her work—what noble characters does one light on in little nooks of this great world!—I can't tell you how this man's virtue and simplicity affects me. Bon Dieu to think of one's own beastly gormandizing egotism after this— I am trying however to correct some and yesterday walked to Ivry from the Barrier & back, and there with Isabella, & then from the Louvre, all to save 3 francs—There's virtue, my god, & think of Marvy toiling for 365 5090 hours

$$\begin{array}{r} 14 \\ \hline 1440 \\ 365 \end{array}$$

in a year, never grumbling, never exceeding, and always having a 5 franc piece—for a brother-artist in distress.

Another instance of virtue. I wouldn't drink any brandy & water yesterday.—W. M. Thackeray, *Letters*.

HOTEL FRESCOES

THE ENTRANCE to this hotel at Chiavenna is through a covered court-yard; steps lead up to the roof of the court-yard, which is a terrace where one dines in fine weather. A great tree grows in the court-yard below, its trunk pierces the floor of the terrace, and its branches shade the open-air dining-room. The walls of the house are painted in fresco, with a check pattern like the late Lord Brougham's trousers, and there are also pictures. One represents Mendelssohn. He is not called Mendelssohn, but I knew him by his legs. He is in the costume of a dandy of some five-and-forty years ago, is smoking a cigar and appears to be making an offer of marriage to his cook. Down below is a fresco of a man sitting on a barrel with a glass in his hand. A more absolutely worldly minded, uncultured individual it would be impossible to conceive. When I saw these frescoes I knew I should get along all right and not be over-charged.—Samuel Butler, *Note Books*, 1912.

SWITZERLAND

August 8th, (1846). CAFÉ IN room, off by diligence to Lucerne, vines, agreeable Swiss young lady to whom I quoted Goethe and she spouted *William Tell*, sorry to loose her, see Righi and Pilatus in the distance, walk before diligence but get in again, pass bridge over swift green stream, bureau, go to Schweizerhof, room at top of house, look out in the night and see the lake marbled with clouds, gabble of servants, bad night . . .

August 10th. Strolled about the painted bridges, M. met his friend, we bought Keller's map, off by 2 o'clock steamer to Weggis, hired a horse up the Righi, looked over and saw the little coves and wooded shores and villages under vast red ribs of rock, very fine, dismissed my horse at the Bains where we entered with an Englishman and found peasants waltzing, gave two francs to boy who had ordered bed, summit, crowd of people, very feeble sunset, tea, infernal chatter as of innumerable apes.—Lord Tennyson, *Journal*.

INDELICACY

. . . GREAT AND manifold as are the evils entailed by the scarcity of water in the bed-rooms and kitchens of Paris, there is another deficiency greater still, and infinitely worse in its effects. The want of drains and sewers is the great defect of all the cities in France; and a tremendous defect it is. That people who from their first breath of life have been obliged to accustom their senses and submit without a struggle to the sufferings this evil entails upon them,—that people so circumstanced should have less refinement in their thoughts and words than ourselves, I hold to be natural and inevitable. Thus, you see, I have come round like a preacher to his text, and have explained, as I think, very satis-factorily, what I mean by saying that the indelicacy which so often offends us in France does not arise from any natural coarseness of mind, but is the unavoidable result of circumstances, which may, and doubtless will change, as the wealth of the country and its familiarity with the manners of England increases.—Mrs Frances Trollope, *Paris and the Parisians in 1835.*

PUZZLE FOR BOTANISTS

I HAVE brought back this year some mountain auriculas and the seed of some salvia and Fusio tiger-lily, and mean to plant the auriculas and to sow the seeds in Epping Forest and elsewhere round about London. I wish people would more generally bring back the seeds of pleasing foreign plants and introduce them broadcast, sowing them by our waysides and in our fields, or in whatever situation is most likely to suit them. It is true, this would puzzle botanists, but there is no reason why botanists should not be puzzled. A botanist is a person whose aim is to uproot, kill and exterminate every plant that is at all remarkable for rarity or any special virtue, and the rarer it is the more bitterly he will hunt it down.—Samuel Butler, *Note Books*, 1912.

THE DISCOMFORTS OF VENICE

As FOR their houses they have nothing convenient at *Venice*, for the Architecture is almost all the same, one stair-case, a Hall that runs along the body of the house, and chambers on both hands, but there are no apartments, no Closets or Back-stairs; so that in houses that are of an excessive wealth, they have yet no sort of convenience; Their Bedsteads are of Iron, because of the Vermin that their moisture produces, the bottoms are of boards, upon which they lay so many quilts that it is a huge step to get up to them, their great Chairs are all upright without a stop to the back, hard in the bottom, and the wood of the arms is not covered; they mix water with their wine in their Hogsheads, so that for above half the year the wine is either dead or sour, they do not leaven their Bread, so that it is extream heavy, and the Oven is too much heated, so that the crum is as Dough, when the crust is hard as a stone, in all Inns they boil Meat first before it is roasted, and thus, as indeed they make it tender, so it is quite tasteless and insipid: And as for their land-carriage all *Lombardy* over, it is extream inconvenient, for their Coaches are fastened to the pearch, which makes them as uneasie as a Cart. . . . And thus by an enumeration of many of the innocent pleasures, and conveniences of life, it appears that the *Venetians* pursue so violently forbidden pleasures, that they know not how to find out that which is allowable.—*Dr Burnet's Travels*, 1687.

F

VOLCANO

NAPLES, Saturday, February 22nd, 1845. YESTERDAY EVENING, at four o'clock, we began (a small party of six) the ascent of Mount Vesuvius, with six saddle-horses, an armed soldier for a guard, and twenty-two guides; the latter rendered necessary by the severity of the weather, which is greater than has been known for twenty years, and has covered the precipitous part of the mountain with deep snow, the surface of which is glazed with one smooth sheet of ice from the top of the cone to the bottom. By starting at that hour I intended to catch the sunset about half way up, and night at the top, where the fire is raging. . . .

Eruption of Vesuvius

We rode to the beginning of the snow and then dismounted. Catherine and Georgina were put into two litters, just chairs with poles, like those in use in England on the 5th of November; and a fat Englishman, who was of the party, was hoisted into a third borne by eight men. I was accommodated with a tough stick, and we began to plough our way up. The ascent as steep as this line /—very nearly perpendicular. We were all tumbling at every step; and looking up and seeing the people in advance tumbling over one's very head, and looking down and seeing hundreds of feet of smooth ice below, was, I must confess, anything but agreeable. However, I knew there was little chance of another clear night before I leave this, and gave the word to get up somehow or other. . . . By prodigious exertions we passed the region of snow and came into that of fire—desolate and awful you may well suppose. It was like working one's way through a dry waterfall, with every mass of stone burnt and charred into enormous cinders, and smoke and sulphur bursting out of every chink and crevice, so that it was difficult to breathe. High before us, bursting out of a hill at the top of the mountain, shaped like this **A**, the fire was pouring out, reddening the night with flames, blackening it with smoke, and spotting it with red-hot stones and cinders that fell down again in showers. At every step everybody fell, now into a hot chink, now into a bed of ashes, now over a mass of cindered iron; and the confusion in the darkness (for the smoke obscured the moon in this part), and the quarrelling and shouting and roaring of the guides, and the waiting every now and then for somebody who was not to be found, and was supposed to have stumbled into some pit or other, made such a scene of it as I can give you no idea of. . . . The head guide, an English gentleman of the name of Le Gros . . . and your humble servant, resolved (like jackasses) to climb that hill to the brink and look into the crater itself. . . . We looked down into the flaming bowels of the mountain and came back again, alight in half a dozen places, and burnt from head to foot. You never saw such devils. And I never saw anything so awful and terrible.—Charles Dickens, *Letters*.

PASSION

1763. I HAVE no idea how anybody can live in Italy that does not give themselves wholly to passion. . . .—Lady Charlotte Burgoyne, *Portrait of a Whig Peer*.

CAROLINE LAMB

1815. AT Madame de la Tour du Pin's I kept the Fête of Madame de Maurville, with a large and pleasant party; and I just missed meeting the famous Lady C—— L——, who had been there at dinner, and whom I saw, however, crossing the Place Royale, from Madame de la Tour du Pin's to the Grand Hotel; dressed, or rather *not* dressed, so as to excite universal attention, and authorise every boldness of staring, from the General to the lowest soldier, among the military groups then constantly parading La Place,—for she had one shoulder, half her back, and all her throat and neck, displayed as if at the call of some statuary for modelling a heathen goddess. A slight scarf hung over the other shoulder, and the rest of the attire was of accordant lightness. As her Ladyship had not then written, and was not, therefore, considered as one apart, from being known as an eccentric authoress, this conduct and demeanour excited something beyond surprise, and in an

English lady provoked censure, if not derision, upon the whole English nation.—Fanny Burney, *Diary and Letters of Madame D'Arblay.*

DINNER WITH BISMARCK

Berlin, June 23rd, 1878. ON THE Monday of my return there was Congress and a grand banquet at Bismarck's; I sate on his right hand, and though he ate and drank a great deal, he talked as much: most entertaining and picturesque; a sweet and gentle voice striking from such an ogre-looking body, and recklessly frank. Then there have been other banquets: notably one at the Italian Ambassador's: but talking of dinners, the most interesting by far was my dinner with Bismarck alone. Affairs were rather critical here and I was engaged at a 'banquet' at the English Embassy, when he called on me—though he never calls on anyone—and after some time proposed that, if not engaged, I should dine with him alone and talk over matters.

He was in the bosom of his family who are interesting and devoted to him: the Princess, a daughter, 2 sons, and a married niece, pretty. After dinner he and I retired and smoked. It is the last blow to my shattered constitution, but had I refrained from smoking I should have made no way. So we spent a couple of memorable hours.— Disraeli, *The Letters of Disraeli to Lady Bradford and Lady Chesterfield.*

SIR GEORGE SITWELL

COUNTRY-HOUSES in the extreme south of Italy were exceptionally rare, but my father stayed in one that had been built for King Ferdinand the First and Fourth of the Two Sicilies. His host, a retired colonel, was most anxious to treat an English stranger well, and had determined to serve him an English breakfast, of which he had heard a good deal, and Henry had, in consequence, been obliged to carry up to his master's bedroom every morning at eight a tray on which were placed a bowl of octopus stewed in its own ink, a cup of black coffee, and a glass of the fiery local brandy.

As a rule, neither lodgings nor fare were so luxurious: for the most part they had been obliged to stay in inns that resembled tramps' doss-houses. My father paid little attention to his quarters, if he were interested in the town itself: for, after all, he could make himself uncomfortable in his own way anywhere, and had further devised a whole elaborate system towards that purpose. Wherever he went, he allowed himself, notwithstanding, one luxury, supplementing his meals with an abundant supply of cold chickens 'to keep my strength up'. . . .

Several of the *trattorie* in which he now found himself possessed no separate sleeping apartments, only dormitories in which men slept eight or ten in a room. But my father had seemed in no way taken aback at such a prospect. Henry would have to make up his bed, arranging the blankets in precisely the accustomed way, so that one or two could be pulled on or off very quickly as the mood took you, then he must sprinkle it lightly with Keating's, and proceed to hang up a mosquito-net by means of the special contrivance my father had invented,—when younger, he had invented many other things; at Eton, for example, a musical toothbrush which played 'Annie Laurie' as you brushed your teeth, and a small revolver for killing wasps. First Henry had to knock a great many nails into the wall, then from them he suspended the back of the net, and, finally, as though plumbing ocean depths, he must throw two cords with lead at the end over the side—out of window, that is—, and this would pull the whole airy contraption taut and into place. . . . Of course, occasionally, a passer-by below would complain that he had been hurt, but one really could not pay attention to that sort of thing. And it was so simple. All that you— or rather Henry—had to do now was to tuck the ends of the net in, all round, and there it was, complete! If the proprietor objected, and asked who had broken the wall by hammering nails into it, my father would always reply '*Il mio domestico*', and Henry would have to pay up. It constituted a recognised fine, as it were, for clumsy hammering; and sometimes it was not easy for him to find the money, as my father would only pay his wages once a year—or twice at the most—, and was very difficult over any small necessary advance. But, as my father said, they were not engaged in discussion over money; it was the mosquitoes that mattered, and Henry should take more care. Very inconsiderate of him to sleep without a net himself. He might be bitten by an anopheles mosquito, contract malaria and remain ill for months, and that would make things most awkward. Indeed, my father entertained a great terror of mosquitoes—and I may say at this point that I have myself seen him drive in the evening for three or four miles along the slopes of a mountain, up a road leading to a small town above, seated in an open cab, the top of which was encased in white netting, so that he should not be molested by the creatures in their flight. Thus canopied, and wearing a grey wide-awake hat and a brown covert-coat, he would eventually arrive in the piazza, peculiarly crowded as it was at this hour, looking as though he were the High Priest in *Aïda*. Only the palm-leaf fans and attendants singing in chorus seemed to be missing.—Sir Osbert Sitwell, *The Scarlet Tree*, 1946.

UNWISE PARSIMONY

Coblentz, July 24 (1820). WE DEPARTED at 5 o'clock, stopped to breakfast at the little village of Boppard, very hungry—and delighted to see an ample provision presently ready,—honey, delicious bread, and good coffee. The butter, as at Coblentz, had the appearance and somewhat the *taste* of cream-cheese:—*I* liked it, though others did not. Nothing could exceed the civility of Waiter and Landlady—the 'tout de suite', pronounced 'toute suite', the ready answer given by all attendants at the Inns whether their language be French, German or Flemish, was followed (contrary to the usual practice) by prompt performances,—which proved, however, but a preparation for charges, which rouzed our gentlemen's choler. Wm. resisted the three francs for breakfast, would only pay two and a half (which was a half a franc more than we had ever paid before). But woe is me! our Landlady and Waiter (he was Master and Post-Master also) had a better revenge in *their* power. They forced upon us an additional horse, an incumbrance, which through the friendly kindness of our Host (the post-Master) at Coblentz we had got rid of that very morning. Thus did we pay, through our hatred of extortion, in one day ten times over for our breakfasts, and no doubt the extortioners chuckled over their successful contrivance to outwit us. Mary and I walked forward during the dispute.—Dorothy Wordsworth, *Journals*.

LORD BYRON IN LOVE

Venice, November 27th, 1816. H[OBHOUSE] AND I have been some time in the north of Italy, and reached Venice about a fortnight ago, where I shall remain probably during the winter. It is a place which I like, and which I long anticipated that I should like—besides, I have fallen in love, and with a very pretty woman—so much so as to obtain the approbation of the not easily approving H., who is, in general, rather tardy in his applause of the fairer part of the creation.

She is married—so our arrangement was formed according to the incontinent continental system, which need not be described to you, an experienced voyager—and gifted withal with a modest self-confidence, which my bashful nature is not endowed with—but nevertheless I have got the woman—I do not very well know how, but we do exceedingly well together. She is not two-and-twenty, with great black eastern eyes, and a variety of subsidiary charms, &c., &c., and amongst her other accomplishments is a mighty and admirable singer—as most

of the Italians are—(though not a public one); luckily I can speak the
language fluently; and luckily (if I did not), we could employ ourselves
a little without talking.—Lord Byron, *Letters*.

CARLYLE IN GERMANY

Chelsea, 13 May, 1853. I WENT to Germany last autumn; not *seeking*
anything very definite; rather merely flying from certain troops of
carpenters, painters, bricklayers, &c., &c., who had made a lodgment
in this poor house, and have not even yet got their incalculable riot
quite concluded. . . . In Germany I found but little; and suffered, from
six weeks of sleeplessness in German beds, &c., &c., a great deal.
Indeed I seem to myself never yet to have quite recovered. The Rhine
which I honestly ascended from Rotterdam to Frankfort was, as I now
find, my chief Conquest: the beautifulest river in the Earth, I do
believe;—and my first idea of a World-river. It is many fathoms deep,
broader twice over than the Thames here at high water; and rolls along,
mirror-smooth (except that, in looking close, you will find ten thousand little eddies in it), voiceless, swift, with trim banks, through the
heart of Europe, and of the Middle Ages wedded to the Present Age:
such an image of calm *power* (to say nothing of its other properties) I
find I had never seen before. The old Cities too are a little beautiful to
me, in spite of my state of nerves; honest, kindly people too, but sadly
short of our and your *despatch-of-business* talents,— a really painful
defect in the long run. I was on two of Fritz's Battlefields, moreover:
Lobositz in Bohemia, and Kunersdorf by Frankfurt on the Oder; but
did not, especially in the latter case, make much of that. Schiller's
death-chamber, Goethe's sad Court-environment; above all, Luther's
little room in the *Wartburg* (I believe I actually had tears in my eyes
there, and *kissed* the old oak-table, being in a very flurried state of
nerves), my belief was that under the Canopy there was not at present
so *holy* a spot as that same. Of human souls I found none specially
beautiful to me at all, at all,—such my sad fate!—Thomas Carlyle,
The Correspondence of Thomas Carlyle and Ralph Waldo Emerson.

ST PETER'S

Nov. 29th, Sunday, 1840. A GREAT fuss about Pope officiating in the
Sistine Chapel—Advent Sunday. Got into a crowd, and made myself
very uncomfortable for nothing: no music worth hearing, a little
mummery with Pope and dirty cardinals. Outside and west façade of
St. Peter's certainly very fine: the inside would make a nice ball-room,
but is good for nothing else.—John Ruskin, *Praeterita*.

A BLIND LOVE

2 Rue de Perry, Le Havre, Maison Versigny: July 23, 1858. WHEN all's said and sighed, I love Italy—I love my Florence. I love that 'hole of a place', as Father Prout called it lately—with all its dust, its cob-webs, its spiders even, I love it, and with somewhat of the kind of blind, stupid, respectable, obstinate love which people feel when they talk of 'beloved native lands'. I feel this for Italy, by mistake for England. Florence is my chimney-corner, where I can sulk and be happy.—Elizabeth Barrett Browning, *Letters*.

GIBBON'S MEETING WITH VOLTAIRE

Lausanne, August the 6th, 1763. I MADE a little excursion some days ago to Geneva, not so much for the sake of the town which I had often seen before, as for a representation of Monsieur de Voltaire's. He lives now entirely at Fernay, a little place in France, but only two leagues from Geneva. He has bought the estate, and built a very pretty tho' small house upon it. After a life passed in courts and Capitals, the Great Voltaire is now become a meer country Gentleman, and even (for the honor of the profession) something of a farmer. He says he never enjoyed so much true happiness. He has got rid of most of his infirmities, and tho' very old and lean, enjoys a much better state of health than he did twenty years ago. His playhouse is very neat and well contrived, situated just by his Chappel, which is far inferior to it, tho', he says himself, *que son Christ est du meilleur faiseur de tout le pays de Gex*. The play they acted was my favourite Orphan of China. Voltaire himself acted *Gengis* and Madame Denys *Idamè*; but I do not know how it happened: either my taste is improved or Voltaire's talents are impaired since I last saw him. He appeared to me now a very ranting unnatural performer. Perhaps indeed, as I was come from Paris, I rather judged him by an unfair comparaison, than by his own independent value. Perhaps too I was too much struck with the ridiculous figure of Voltaire at seventy, acting a Tartar Conqueror with a hollow broken voice, and making love to a very ugly niece of about fifty. The play began at eight in the evening and ended (enter-tainment and all) about half an hour after eleven. The whole Company was asked to stay and set Down about twelve to a very elegant supper of a hundred Covers. The supper ended about two, the company danced till four, when we broke up, got into our Coaches and came back to Geneva just as the Gates were opened. Shew me in history or fable, a famous poet of Seventy who has acted in his own plays, and has closed the scene with a supper and ball for a hundred people. I think the last is the more extraordinary of the two.—Edward Gibbon, *Letters*.

A FAIR-WEATHER KINGDOM

Turin, June 21, 1865. As to the people, that is a long story. I have more and more come to papa's way of feeling about the Italians, and I cannot but think this a mere fair-weather kingdom. 80,000 French, English, or Germans might, I am perfectly convinced, enter this country to-morrow, overrun it in three months, and hold it forever against all the opposition they would meet with from within. The Piedmontese is the only virile element—he is like a country Frenchman—but he is a small leaven to leaven the whole lump. And the whole lump want back-bone, serious energy, and power of honest work to a degree that makes one impatient. I am tempted to take the professors I see in the schools by the collar, and hold them down to their work for five or six hours a day—so angry do I get at their shirking and inefficiency. They have all a certain refinement which they call civilisation, but a nation is really civilised by acquiring the qualities it by nature is wanting in; and the Italians are no more civilised by virtue of their refinement alone than we are civilised by virtue of our energy alone. The French detest them, and are always speaking of us and themselves together in contrast to them; and you cannot see the French soldiers in Rome without noticing in them the look of rusticity and virility, and of capacity for serious business, which is just what the Italians want—the feeling of the French towards us seems to me to be constantly getting better and better—and really the two nations have more in common than any other two modern nations. Both French and Italians dislike the Americans, and call them a *nation mal élevée*, and so they are: such awful specimens as I was in the Coliseum with! and by moonlight too. But I was much taken with a young American *attaché* at Florence; he might have been a gawky young Scotchman, and indeed he told me he had Scotch blood in him, but he has the temper and moral tone of a gentleman, and the making of a gentleman in the European sense of the word, in him; and that is what so few of his countrymen have.—Matthew Arnold, *Letters*.

A LONELY TRAVELLER

Interlaken, Switzerland, Sept. 13th, 1872. I am not enjoying myself at all. You are quite right. I do not idle well. I will try to mend. I am going up to Grindelwald this afternoon, and will go *en pension* for a fortnight at the best hotel, and there are sure to be some people there who will suit me and who will let me bore them. I have not seen a soul save waiters and chambermaids this four or five weeks, and it is not good for me. . . .—Samuel Butler, *Letters between Samuel Butler and Miss E. M. A. Savage.*

PARIS HOTEL

. . . THE *patron* swindled the customers wholeheartedly. For the most part the materials of the food were very bad, though the cooks knew how to serve it up in style. The meat was at best ordinary, and as to the vegetables, no good housekeeper would have looked at them in the market. The cream, by a standing order, was diluted with milk. The tea and coffee were of inferior sorts, and the jam was synthetic stuff out of vast, unlabelled tins. All the cheaper wines . . . were corked *vin ordinaire.* There was a rule that employees must pay for anything they spoiled, and in consequence damaged things were seldom thrown away. Once the waiter on the third floor dropped a roast chicken down the shaft of our service lift, where it fell into a litter of broken bread, torn paper and so forth at the bottom. We simply wiped it with a cloth and sent it up again. Upstairs there were dirty tales of once-used sheets not being washed, but simply damped, ironed and put back on the beds. The *patron* was as mean to us as to the customers. Throughout the vast hotel there was not, for instance, such a thing as a brush and pan; one had to manage with a broom and a piece of cardboard. And the staff lavatory was worthy of Central Asia, and there was no place to wash one's hands, except the sinks used for washing crockery.—George Orwell, *Down and Out in Paris and London,* 1933.

THE ENTRANCE INTO ITALY

April 6, 1825. THE COACH shortly after overtook us. We descended a long and steep declivity, with the highest point of Mount Cenis on our left, and a lake to the right, like a landing-place for geese. Between the two was a low, white monastery, and the barrier where we had our passports inspected, and then went forward with only two stout horses and one rider. The snow on this side of the mountain was nearly gone. I supposed myself for some time nearly on level ground, till we came in view of several black chasms or steep ravines in the side of the mountain facing us, with water oozing from it, and saw through some *galleries*, that is, massy stone-pillars knit together by thick rails of strong timber, guarding the road-side, a perpendicular precipice below, and other galleries beyond, diminished in a fairy perspective, and descending 'with cautious haste and giddy cunning' and with innumer-able windings and re-duplications to an interminable depth and distance from the height where we were. The men and horses with carts, that were labouring up the path in the hollow below, shewed like crows or flies. The road we had to pass was often immediately under that we were passing, and cut from the side of what was all but a precipice out of the solid rock by the broad, firm master-hand that traced and executed this mighty work. . . . Near the turning of one of the first galleries is a beautiful waterfall, which at this time was frozen into a sheet of green pendant ice—a magical transformation. Long after we continued to descend, now faster and now slower, and came at length to a small village at the bottom of a sweeping line of road, where the houses seemed like dove-coats with the mountains back reared like a wall behind them, and which I thought the termination of our journey. But here the wonder and the greatness began: for, advancing through a grove of slender trees to another point of the road, we caught a new view of the lofty mountain to our left. It stood in front of us, with its head in the skies, covered with snow, and its bare sides stretching far away into a valley that yawned at its feet, and over which we seemed suspended in mid-air.—William Hazlitt, *Notes of a Journey Through France and Italy.*

THE SWISS WEDDING

1846. ONE OF the farmer's people—a sister, I think—was married from here the other day. . . . The fondness of the Swiss for gunpowder on interesting occasions, is one of the drollest things. For three days before, the farmer himself, in the midst of his various agricultural duties, plunged out of a little door near my windows, about once in every hour, and fired off a rifle. I thought he was shooting rats who were spoiling the vines; but he was merely relieving his mind, it seemed, on the subject of the approaching nuptials. All night afterwards, he and a small circle of friends kept perpetually letting off guns under the casement of the bridal chamber. A Bride is always drest here in black silk; but this bride wore merino of that colour, observing to her mother when she bought it (the old lady is 82, and works on the farm), 'You know, mother, I am sure to want mourning for you, soon; and the same gown will do.'—Charles Dickens, *Letters.*

RESPECTFUL DECORUM

Paris. MADAM DE RAMBOULIET, after an acquaintance of about six weeks with her, had done me the honour to take me in her coach about two leagues out of town.—Of all women, Madame de Rambouliet is the most correct; and I never wish to see one of more virtues and purity of heart.—In our return back, Madame de Rambouliet desired me to pull the cord.—I asked her if she wanted anything?—*Rien que pour pisser*, said Madame de Rambouliet.

Grieve not, gentle traveller, to let Madame de Rambouliet p-ss on.—And ye fair mystic nymphs, go each one *pluck your rose*, and scatter them in your path,—for Madame de Rambouliet did no more.—I handed Madame de Rambouliet out of the coach; and had I been the priest of the chaste *Castalia*, I could not have served at her fountain with a more respectful decorum.—Laurence Sterne, *A Sentimental Journey Through France and Italy*, 1768.

SHELLEY ON MICHAEL ANGELO

Naples, February 25th, 1819. THE ROYAL collection of paintings in this city is sufficiently miserable. Perhaps the most remarkable is the original study of Michael Angelo of the 'Day of Judgment', which is painted in *fresco* on the Sixtine chapel of the Vatican. It is there so defaced as to be wholly indistinguishable. I cannot but think the genius of this artist highly overrated. He has not only no temperance, no modesty, no feeling for the just boundaries of art . . ., but he has no sense of beauty, and to want this is to want the sense of the creative power of mind. What is terror without a contrast with, and a connection with, loveliness . . . ? What a thing his 'Moses' is; how distorted from all that is natural and majestic, only less monstrous and detestable than its historical prototype.—Shelley, *Letters*.

CHRISTMAS IN GERMANY

Ratzeburg, 1799. THERE IS a Christmas custom here which pleased and interested me.—The children make little presents to their parents, and to each other; and the parents to the children. For three or four months before Christmas the girls are all busy, and the boys save up their pocket-money, to make or purchase these presents. What the present is to be is cautiously kept secret, and the girls have a world of contrivances to conceal it—such as working when they are out on visits and the others are not with them; getting up in the morning before day-light, and the like. Then on the evening before Christmas-day, one of the parlours is lighted up by the children, into which the parents must not go. A great yew bough is fastened on the table at a little distance from the wall, a multitude of little tapers are fastened in the bough, but so as not to catch it till they are nearly burnt out, and coloured paper hangs and flutters from the twigs. Under this bough the children lay out in great order the presents they mean for their

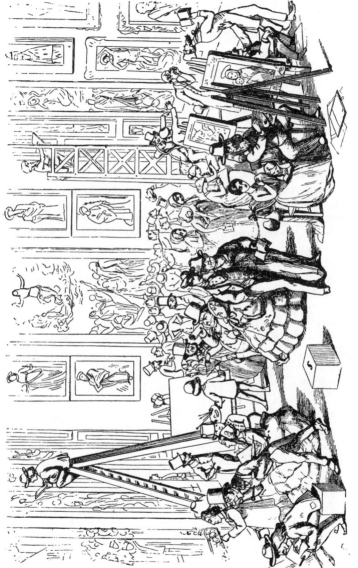

The Accademia

parents, still concealing in their pockets what they intend for each other. Then the parents are introduced, and each presents his little gift, and then bring out the rest one by one from their pockets, and present them with kisses and embraces.—S. T. Coleridge, *The Friend*.

MIRACLES

Augusta. IN THE afternoon the whole town was in motion to attend a procession in honour of St. Sebastian, one of the most favourite saints in the Sicilian calendar; he is particularly addressed in behalf of children, afflicted with hernias. The miraculous cure is performed in the following manner: the large stage, or machine, on which his effigy is placed, is crowded with diseased children, and then carried about the streets on the shoulders of the inhabitants, who frequently fight for the honour of bearing the holy burden. The poor infants seemed scared out of their wits at being hoisted so high on a tottering scaffold; this, and the awe which the pomp strikes them with, has, as I was informed by a person of note in the place, considerable efficacy in contracting the affected parts, so as to appear less than usual; but lest the motion and the fright should not act with sufficient power, the surgeon, whose province it is to inspect the children and certify the cure, always gives the little patient a smart blow on the ear before he proceeds to the examination. With these helps, appearances are generally such as are desired for the honour of the saint.—Henry Swinburne, *Travels to the Two Sicilies*, 1777–80.

THE HONEST SWISS

THE MEN are generally sincere, but heavy: they think it necessary to correct the moisture of the Air with liberal Entertainments, and they are well furnished with all necessary Ingredients for as their Soil produces good Cattel, so their Lakes abound in Fish, and their Woods in Fowl, the Wine is also light and good. The Women are generally employed in their domestick Affairs, and the Wives even of the chief Magistrates of *Bern* look into all the Concerns of the House and Kitchen as much as the Wives of the meanest Peasants. Men and Women do not converse promiscuously together; and the Women are so much amused with the Management at home, and enter so little into Intrigues, that among them, as an eminent Physician there told me, they know not what Vapours are, which he imputed to the Idleness and Intrigues that abound elsewhere, whereas he said, among them the Blood was cleansed by their Labour, and as that made them sleep well, so they did not amuse themselves with much thinking, nor did they know what Amours were. The third Adultery is punished with Death, which is also the punishment of the fifth Act of Fornication; of which I saw an instance while I was at *Bern*: for, a Woman who confessed herself guilty of many Whoredoms, and designed to be revenged on some Men that did not furnish her liberally with Money, was upon that condemned and executed: the manner was solemn; for the *Advoyer* comes into an open Bench in the middle of the Street, and for the Satisfaction of the People, the whole Process was read, and Sentence was pronounced in the hearing of all; the Counsellers both of the great and lesser Council standing about the *Advoyer*, who after Sentence took the Criminal very gently by the hand, and pray'd for her Soul: and after Execution, there was a Sermon for the Instruction of the People.—*Dr Burnet's Travels*, 1687.

OPERA DANCERS

1824. OF ALL things that I see here, it surprises me the most that the French should fancy they can dance. To dance is to move with grace and harmony to music. But the French, whether men or women, have no idea of dancing but that of moving with agility, and of distorting their limbs in every possible way, till they really alter the structure of the human form. By grace I understand the natural movements of the human body, heightened into dignity or softened into ease, each posture or step blending harmoniously into the rest. There is grace in the waving of the branch of a tree or in the bounding of a stag, because there is freedom and unity of motion. But the French Opera-dancers think it graceful to stand on one leg or on the points of their toes, or with one leg stretched out behind them, as if they were going to be shod, or to raise one foot at right angles with their bodies, and twirl themselves round like a *te-totum*, to see how long they can spin, and then stop short all of a sudden; or to skim along the ground, flat-footed, like a spider running along a cobweb, or to pop up and down like a pea on a tobacco-pipe, or to stick in their backs till another part projects out behind *comme des volails*, and to strut about like peacocks with infirm, vain-glorious steps, or to turn out their toes till their feet resemble apes, or to raise one foot above their heads, and turn swiftly round upon the other, till the petticoats of the female dancers (for I have been thinking of them) rise above their garters, and display a pair of spindle-shanks, like the wooden ones of a wax-doll, just as shapeless and as tempting.—William Hazlitt, *Notes of a Journey Through France and Italy*.

FRENCH INNS

June, 1787. HAVING NOW crossed the kingdom, and been in many French inns, I shall in general observe, that they are on an average better in two respects, and worse in all the rest, than those in England. We have lived better in point of eating and drinking beyond a question, than we should have done in going from London to the Highlands of Scotland, at double the expence. But if in England the best of every thing is ordered, without any attention to the expence, we should for double the money have lived better than we have done in France; the common cookery of the French gives great advantage. It is true, they roast every thing to a chip, if they are not cautioned: but they give such a number and variety of dishes, that if you do not like some, there are others to please your palate. The dessert at a French inn has no rival at an English one; nor are the liqueurs to be despised.—We sometimes have met with bad wine, but upon the whole, far better than such port as English inns give. Beds are better in France; in England they are good only at good inns; and we have none of that torment, which is so perplexing in England, to have the sheets aired; for we never trouble our heads about them, doubtless on account of the climate. After these two points, all is a blank. You have no parlour to eat in; only a room with two, three, or four beds. Apartments badly fitted up; the walls white-washed; or paper of different sorts in the same room; or tapestry so old, as to be a fit nidus for moths and spiders; and the furniture such, that an English innkeeper would light his fire with it. For a table, you have every where a board laid on cross bars, which are so conveniently contrived, as to leave room for your legs only at the end. —Oak chairs with rush bottoms, and the back universally a direct perpendicular, that defies all idea of rest after fatigue. Doors give music as well as entrance; the wind whistles through their chinks; and hinges grate discord. Windows admit rain as well as light; when shut they are not so easy to open; and when open not easy to shut. Mops, brooms, and scrubbing-brushes are not in the catalogue of the necessaries of a French inn. Bells there are none; the *fille* must always be bawled for; and when she appears, is neither neat, well dressed, nor handsome. The kitchen is black with smoke; the master commonly the cook, and the less you see of the cooking, the more likely you are to have a stomach to your dinner; but this is not peculiar to France. Copper utensils always in great plenty, but not always well tinned. The mistress rarely classes civility or attention to her guests among the requisites of her trade.—Arthur Young, *Travels in France.*

THE COMING OF SPRING

Florence: March 15 (1853). . . . THE SPRING has surprised us here just as we were beginning to murmur at the cold. Think of somebody advising me the other day not to send out my child without a double-lined parasol! There's a precaution for March! The sun is powerful—we are rejoicing in our Italian climate. Oh, that I could cut out just a mantle of it to wrap myself in, and so go and see you.—Elizabeth Barrett Browning, *Letters*.

THE FRENCH REVOLUTION

1791. THE ROYAL FAMILY are at perfect liberty but I do not know that they have made use of it to go without the doors of the Tuileries. They have Courts three days in the week but do not dine in public. I have seen them once going to chapel, which they do every day through a large crowd of people. If I do not get a more satisfactory view of them I must go on Sunday and be presented. The Queen you may suppose is much changed since Mr Burke and I saw her last. I think her an agreeable looking woman. She seemed to possess herself well and showed no emotion on her countenance. Mme Elizabeth, the King's sister, looked as if she was going to spit in the people's face, which I understand she is almost ready to do upon every occasion. The King himself came rolling along and looked as if he did not care a farthing about it if they would but let him alone. . . . —The Second Viscount Palmerston, *Portrait of a Whig Peer*.

ITALIAN HOSTELRY

Cosenza, Calabria, Italy, 1897. I HAD seen a good many Italian hostelries, and nourished no unreasonable expectations. The *Lion* at Paola would have seemed to any untravelled Englishman a squalid and comfortless hole, incredible as a place of public entertainment; the *Two Little Lions* of Cosenza made a decidedly worse impression. Over sloppy stones, in an atmosphere heavy with indescribable stenches, I felt rather than saw my way to the foot of a stone staircase; this I ascended, and on the floor above found a dusky room, where tablecloths and an odour of frying oil afforded some suggestion of refreshment. My arrival interested nobody; with a good deal of trouble I persuaded an untidy fellow, who seemed to be a waiter, to come down with me and secure my luggage. More trouble before I could find a bedroom; hunting for keys, wandering up and down stone stairs and along pitch-black corridors, sounds of voices in quarrel. The room itself was

G

utterly depressing—so bare, so grimy, so dark. Quickly I examined the bed, and was rewarded. It is the good point of Italian inns; be the house and the room howsoever sordid, the bed is almost invariably clean and dry and comfortable.—George Gissing, *By the Ionian Sea.*

THE JUNGFRAU

July 15, 1868. THERE ARE round one of the heights of the Jungfrau two ends or falls of a glacier. If you took the skin of a white tiger or the deep fell of some other animal and swung it tossing high in the air and then cast it out before you it would fall and so clasp and lap round anything in its way just as this glacier does and the fleece would part in the same rifts: you must suppose a lazuli under-flix to appear. The spraying out of one end I tried to catch but it would have taken hours: it was this which first made me think of a tiger-skin, and it ends in tongues and points like the tail and claws: indeed the ends of the glaciers are knotted or knuckled like talons. Above, in a plane nearly parallel to the eye, becoming thus foreshortened, it forms saddle-curves with dips and swells—*The Journals and Papers of Gerard Manley Hopkins.*

RED AND BLUE LOCUSTS

Ems, August 1, 1851. EHRENBREITSTEIN utterly disappointed me, except professionally. The lying painters paint it just three times as high as it is, and I was quite shocked to find it so small. But it is all beautiful—beautiful. That vast rushing, silent river, those yellow vine slopes, and azure hills behind, with the thunder clouds lowering over their heads—beautiful; and the air! I have felt new nerves, as well as new eyes, ever since Cologne, the wonderful freshness and transparency of the colouring, and the bracing balminess of the atmosphere, make me understand now at once why people prefer this to England; there is no denying it. It is a more charming country, and that is the best of reasons one has for thanking God that one has not the means of escaping to it from *work*. Ems is lovely, and we have got to the quiet side of it, close to the Gutenberg. . . .

The other day H. and I walked over the hills to Braubach and Marksburg, and caught unspeakable butterflies, and found—conceive my delight—some twenty-five species of plants, new to me! I cannot tell you the enjoyment of it. The scenery is certainly most lovely in every direction; and it is so delightful to think that you know it all! That thought recurs to me continually. Tell the darling children that I will bring them each home something pretty, and that the woods are full of great orange slugs, and great green lizards, and great long snakes, which bite nobody, and that I will bring them home some red and blue locusts out of the vineyards.—Charles Kingsley, *Letters*.

SIEGE

November 14th. The *Temps* gives the following details of our provisions—Beef will fail in a week, horse will then last a fortnight; salt meat a further week; vegetables, dried fruits, flour, &c., about three weeks more. In this calculation I think that the stock of flour is understated, and that if we are contented to live on bread and wine we shall not be starved out until the middle of January. The ration of fresh meat is now reduced in almost all the arrondissements to thirty grammes a head. There is no difficulty, however, in obtaining for money any quantity of it in the restaurants. In the bouillons only one portion is served to each customer. Cats have risen in the market—a good fat one now costs twenty francs. Those that remain are exceedingly wild. This morning I had a salmis of rats—it was excellent—something between frog and rabbit. I breakfasted with the correspondents of two of your contemporaries. One of them, after a certain amount of hesitation, allowed me to help him to a leg of a rat; after eating it he was as anxious as a terrier for more. The latter, however, scornfully refused to share in the repast. As he got through his portion of salted horse, which rejoiced in the name of beef, he regarded us with horror and disgust. I remember when I was in Egypt that my feelings towards the natives were of a somewhat similar nature when I saw them eating rat. The older one grows the more tolerant one becomes. If ever I am again in Africa I shall eat the national dish whenever I get a chance. During the siege of Londonderry rats sold for 7s. each, and if this siege goes on many weeks longer, the utmost which a person of moderate means will be able to allow himself will be an occasional mouse. I was curious to see whether the proprietor of the restaurant would boldly call rat, rat in my bill. His heart failed him—it figures as a salmi of game.— Henry Labouchère, *Diary of the Besieged Resident in Paris*, 1871.

FEELINGS

Hôtel Plättig, Badischer Schwarzwald, Germania, 1929. The Germans are most curious. They love things just because they think they have a sentimental reason for loving them—*das Heimatland, der Tannenbaum, das Brünnele, das Bächlein*—the very words send a German into swoon of love, which is as often as not entirely false. They make up their feelings in their heads, while their *real* feelings all go wrong. That's why Germans come out with such startling and really silly bursts of hatred. It's the result of never living from their *real* feelings, always from the feelings they invent in their heads. And that's why, as a bourgeois crowd, they are so monstrously ugly. My God, how ugly they can be! and it's because they *never* live direct from their spontaneous feeling; except in the matter of eating and drinking, God help us!—D. H. Lawrence, *Letters.*

MEREDITH IN THE TYROL

Meran, South Tyrol, July 26, 1861. MERAN IS southern in heat and luxury of growth of all kinds of fruit. The cicada goes all day like a factory wheel—poetic simile! The flies sting, and the sun is relentless. I begin to understand why Daphne fled into a laurel from the fiery fellow. Still I like sun, as you do. Anything's better than the meagre days we got last year. This land abounds in falling waters, brooks, torrents, all ice cold. We drank at the wells every ten minutes, sat over the brooks naked legged, dipped our heads desperately. Here are crucifixes at every fifty yards. You go to a well and the pipe through which the water flows is through the body of a Christ. Hear you a droning noise on the wind, it issues from a body of peasants mumbling their rosaries as they march to work. They are invariably courteous. W—— says, they remind him more of the Spaniards than do any other people, but they have not the same prolonged gravity of deportment. Nothing can be grander than the colossal mountains of porphyry and dolomite shining purple and rosy, snow-capped here and there, with some tumultuous river noising below, and that eternal stillness overhead, save when some great peak gathers the thunders and bellows for a time. Then to see the white sulphurous masks curl and cover round it, and drip moisture on the hanging meadows, would task your powers of description, O my friend!

Do our loves prosper?

> 'Life is real—life is earnest!
> Tiddle lol da lol de lol.'

—George Meredith, *Letters.*

JOURNEY WITH A DOG

1824. THERE WAS a Frenchman in the coach, who had a dog and a little boy with him, the last having a doll in his hands, which he insisted on playing with; or cried and screamed furiously if it was taken

from him. It was a true French child; that is, a little old man, like
Leonardo da Vinci's *Laughing Boy*, with eyes glittering like the glass
ones of his favourite doll, with flaxen ringlets like her's, with cheeks as
smooth and unhealthy, and a premature expression of cunning and
self-complacency. A disagreeable or ill-behaved child in a stage coach
is a common accident, and to be endured. But who but a Frenchman
would think of carrying his dog! He might as well drag his horse into
the coach after him. A Frenchman (with leave be it spoken) has no
need to take a dog with him to ventilate the air of a coach, in which
there are three other Frenchmen. It was impossible to suffer more
from heat, from pressure, or from the periodical 'exhalation of rich-
distilled perfumes'. If the French have lost the sense of smell, they
should reflect (as they are a reflecting people) that others have not.
Really, I do not see how they have a right in a public vehicle to assault
one in this way by proxy, any more than to take one literally by the
nose. One does not expect from the most refined and polished people
in Europe grossnesses that an Esquimaux Indian would have too much
sense and modesty to be guilty of.—William Hazlitt, *Notes of a
Journey Through France and Italy*.

THE BOULEVARDS

1824. A WALK on the Boulevards is not calculated to rid an Englishman
of all his prejudices or of all his spleen. The resemblance to an English
promenade afterwards makes the difference more mortifying. There is
room to breathe, a footpath on each side of the road, and trees over
your head. But presently the appearance of a Bartlemy-fair all the year
round, the number of little shabby stalls, the old iron, pastry, and
children's toys; the little white lapdogs, with red eyes, combing and
washing; the mud and the green trees, wafting alternate odours; the
old women sitting like *terra-cotta* figures; the passengers running up
against you, (most of them so taken up with themselves that they seem
like a crowd of absent people!) the noise, the bustle, the flutter, the
hurry without visible object; the vivacity without intelligible meaning;
the loud and incessant cry of '*Messieurs*' from a bawling charlatan,
inviting you to some paltry, cheating game, and a broad stare or
insignificant grin from the most ill-bred and ill-looking of the motley
set at the appearance of an Englishman among them; all this jumble of
little, teazing, fantastical, disagreeable, chaotic sensations really puts
one's patience a little to the test, and throws one a little off one's guard.
—William Hazlitt, *Notes of a Journey Through France and Italy*.

PEASANT FACES

Rome. THE ENGLISH country girls, taken collectively, are, unquestionably, the handsomest in the world. The female peasants of most other countries, indeed, are so hard worked, so ill fed, so much tanned by the sun, and so dirty, that it is difficult to know whether they have any beauty or not. Yet I have been informed by some amateurs, since I came here, that in spite of all these disadvantages, they sometimes find, among the Italian peasantry, countenances highly interesting, and which they prefer to all the cherry cheeks of Lancashire.—John Moore, *A View of Society and Manners in Italy*, 1795.

HUMAN SUFFERING

February 28, 1833. . . . OH, THE miserable creatures we saw in Sicily! I never knew what human suffering was before. Children and youths who look as if they did not know what fresh air was, though they must have had it in plenty—well, what water was—with features sunk, contracted with perpetual dirt, as if dirt was their food. The towns of Partenico and Alcamo are masses of filth; the street is a pool; but Calatafimi, where we slept!—I dare not mention facts. Suffice it to say, we found the poor children of the house slept in holes dug into the wall, which smelt not like a dog-kennel, but like a wild beast's cage, almost overpowering us in the room upstairs. I have no sleep all night from insects of prey; but this was a slight evil. The misery is increased from the custom of having the stable on the ground floor and the kitchen on the first. The dwelling is on the second floor. Yet it is pleasing to discern a better seeming class amid the misery; even at Alcamo there were tidy clean-looking women, and outside the towns much washing was going on. A great number of the Sicilians and Calabrians we have seen are a striking and bright-looking race—regular features and very intelligent. Sparkling eyes, brownish skins, and red healthy-looking cheeks. At Amalfi yesterday we were quite delighted with them.

The state of the church is deplorable. It seems as if Satan was let out of prison to range the whole earth again.—John Henry Newman, *Letters*.

ARGUMENT WITH A BAKER

Hamburg, October 3rd, (1798). I BELIEVE my letter would be more acceptable to you if, instead of speaking on this subject, I should tell you what we have seen during our fortnight's residence at Hamburg.

It is a *sad* place. In this epithet you have the soul and essence of all the information which I have been able to gather. We have, however, been treated with unbounded kindness by Mr. Klopstock, the brother of the poet; and I have no doubt this city contains a world of good and honest people, if one had but the skill to find them. I will relate to you an anecdote.[1] The other day I went into a baker's shop, put into his hand two pieces of money, for which I ought to have had five loaves, but I thought the pieces had only been worth two loaves each. I took up four loaves. The baker would not permit this, upon which I took from his hand one of the pieces, and pointed to two loaves, and then, re-offering to him the piece, I took up two others. He dashed the loaves from my hand into the basket in the most brutal manner. I begged him to return the other piece of money, which he refused to do, nor would he let me have any bread into the bargain. So I left the shop empty-handed, and he retained the money. Is there any baker in England who would have done this to a foreigner?—William Wordsworth, *Letters*.

IN PRAISE OF THE FRENCH

Keswill (Lake of Constance), Sept. 6, 1790. MY PARTIALITY to Switzerland, excited by its natural charms, induces me to hope that the manners of the inhabitants are amiable; but at the same time I cannot help frequently comparing them with those of the French, and, as far as I have had opportunity to observe, they lose very much by the comparison. We not only found the French a much less imposing people, but that politeness diffused through the lowest ranks had an air so engaging that you could scarce attribute it to any other cause than real benevolence. During the time, which was near a month, that we were in France, we had not once to complain of the smallest deficiency of courtesy in any person, much less of any positive rudeness. We had also perpetual occasion to observe that cheerfulness and sprightliness for which the French have always been remarkable.

But I must remind you that we crossed at the time when the whole nation was mad with joy in consequence of the revolution.—William Wordsworth, *Letters*.

PILGRIMAGE

Collegio Ferdinando, Pisa: March 10, 1847. EVEN NOW I walk as in a dream. We made a pilgrimage from Avignon to Vaucluse in right poetical duty, and I and my husband sate upon two stones in the midst

---

[1] It happened to his sister, not to himself.

of the fountain which in its dark prison of rocks flashes and roars and testifies to the memory of Petrarch. It was louder and fuller than usual when we were there, on account of the rains; and Flush, though by no means born to be a hero, considered my position so outrageous that he dashed through the water to me, splashing me all over, so he is baptised in Petrarch's name. The scenery is full of grandeur, the rocks sheathe themselves into the sky, and nothing grows there except a little cypress here and there, and a straggling olive tree; and the fountain works out its soul in its stony prison, and runs away in a green rapid stream. Such a striking sight it is. I sate upon deck, too, in our passage from Marseilles to Genoa, and had a vision of mountains, six or seven deep, one behind another. As to Pisa, call it a beautiful town, you cannot do less with Arno and its palaces, and above all the wonderful Duomo and Campo Santo, and Leaning Tower and Baptistery, all of which are a stone's throw from our windows. We have rooms in a great college-house built by Vasari, and fallen into desuetude from collegiate purposes; and here we live the quietest and most *tête-à-tête* of lives, knowing nobody, hearing nothing, and for nearly three months together never catching a glimpse of a paper. Oh, how wrong you were about the 'Times'!—Elizabeth Barrett Browning, *Letters*.

TACITURNITY OF THE FRENCH

July, 1787. ONE CIRCUMSTANCE I must remark on this numerous table d'hôte, because it has struck me repeatedly, which is the taciturnity of the French. I came to the kingdom expecting to have my ears constantly fatigued with the infinite volubility and spirits of the people, of which so many persons have written, sitting, I suppose, by their English fire-sides. At Montpellier, though 15 persons and some of them ladies were present, I found it impossible to make them break their inflexible silence with more than a monosyllable, and the whole company sat more like an assembly of tongue-tied quakers, than the mixed company of a people famous for loquacity. Here also, at Nismes, with a different party at every meal it is the same; not a Frenchman will open his lips. To-day at dinner, hopeless of that nation, and fearing to lose the use of an organ they had so little inclination to employ, I fixed myself by a Spaniard, and having been so lately in his country, I found him ready to converse, and tolerably communicative; but we had more conversation than thirty other persons maintained among themselves. —Arthur Young, *Travels in France*.

LAW-SUITS

Ravenna, September 25th, 1820. APROPOS OF Italian witnesses, since I have been in Italy I have had *six* law-suits, twice as plaintiff against debtors, once about horseflesh as plaintiff, twice about men's wives as defendant, and once as defendant against shopkeepers wanting to be paid *twice* over for the same bills. I gained them all but the horse-dealer; he diddled me. In the shopkeeper's one last Nov. the fellow declared positively in a court, that *I ordered in person the articles in company with my secretaries,* and when desired to describe me, described me as a *tall thin flaxen-haired man*!! Of course he was non-suited. This fellow was reckoned one of the *most respectable negocianti* in Venice.

If you can quote this you may, and I'll prove it if necessary.—Lord Byron, *Letters.*

NO INNOCENT PLEASURE

YET I must add one thing, that though *Venice* is the place in the whole World where pleasure is most studied, and where the youth have both the greatest Wealth, and the most leisure to pursue it: yet it is the place I ever saw where true and innocent pleasure is the least understood, in which I will make a little digression that perhaps will not be unpleasant. As for the pleasures of friendship or marriage they are strangers to them, for the horrible distrust, in which they all live, of one another, makes that it is very rare to find a friend in *Italy,* but most of all in *Venice*: and though we have been told of several stories of celebrated friendships there, yet these are now very rare. As for their Wives they are bred to so much ignorance, they converse so little, that they know nothing but the dull superstition on Holy-days in which they stay in the Churches as long as they can, and so prolong the little liberty they have of going abroad on those days as Children do their hours of play: They are not imployed in their domestick affairs, and generally they understand no sort of work, so that I was told that they were the insipidest creatures imaginable; they are, perhaps, as vitious as in other places; but it is among them, down-right lewdness, for they are not drawn into it by the intranglements of amour that inveigle and lead many persons much farther than they imagined or intended at first, but in them the first step without any preamble or preparative, is down-right beastliness. And an *Italian* that knew the World well, said upon this matter a very lively thing to me, he said their jealousie made them restrain their Daughters, and their Wives so much, that they could have none of those domestick entertainments of Wit, Conversation, and Friendship, that the *French* and *English* have at home: It is true those he said hazard a little the honour of their Families by that Liberty, but the *Italians* by their excessive caution, made that they had none of the true delights of a Married State; and notwithstanding all their uneasie jealousie, they were still in danger of a contraband Nobility, therefore he thought they would do much better to hazard a little, when it would produce a certain satisfaction, then to watch so anxiously, and thereby have an insipid companion instead of a lively Friend, though she might, perhaps, have some ill moments.—*Dr Burnet's Travels*, 1687.

GENTLEMEN

Paris, 1851. AT THE corner of Place de Concorde, 'Secours aux Blessés' stood painted on a signboard of a small house (police or other public house); a significant announcement; rain was now falling. Many carriages; almost all shabby. One dignitary had two servants in livery, and their coat-skirts were *hung over* the rear of the carriage, to be rightly conspicuous; the genus *gentleman* (if taken strictly) seemed to me extremely rare on the streets of Paris, or rather not discoverable at all. Perhaps owing to the *season*, all being in the country? Plenty of well-dressed men were on the streets daily; but their air was seldom or never 'gentle' in our sense: a thing I remarked.—Thomas Carlyle, *Excursion (Futile Enough) to Paris.*

THE SPELL OF VENICE

Paris, July 7, (1851). VENICE IS quite exquisite; it wrapt me round with a spell at first sight, and I longed to live and die there—never to go away. The gondolas, and the glory they swim through, and the silence of the population, drifted over one's head across the bridges, and the fantastic architecture and the coffee-drinking and music in the Piazza San Marco, everything fitted into my lazy, idle nature and weakness of body, as if I had been born to the manner of it and to no other.—Elizabeth Barrett Browning, *Letters.*

NIGHT STROLL

July 6, 1868. BUT BASEL at night! with a full moon waking the river and sending up straight beams from the heavy clouds that overhung it. We saw this from the bridge. The river runs so strong that it keeps the bridge shaking. . . . We went through great spacious streets and places dead still and came to fountains of the clearest black water through which pieces of things at the bottom gleamed white. We got up to a height where a bastion-shaped vertical prominence shaded with chestnut trees looked down on the near roofs, which then in the moonlight were purple and velvety and edged along with ridges and chimneys of chalk white. A woman came to a window with a candle and some mess she was making, and then that was gone and there was no light anywhere but the moon. We heard music indoors about. We saw the courtyard of a charming house with some tree pushing to the windows and a fountain. A church too of immensely high front all dead and flush to the top and next to it three most graceful flamboyant windows. Nothing could be more taking and fantastic than this stroll.—*The Journals and Papers of Gerard Manley Hopkins.*

THE PRUSSIANS

EXCESSIVELY GOOD people are—speaking socially—angular. Take, for instance, the Prussians; they are saints compared with the French. They have every sort of excellence: they are honest, sober, hardworking, well-instructed, brave, good sons, husbands, and fathers; and yet all this is spoilt by one single fault—they are insupportable. Laugh at the French, abuse them as one may, it is impossible to help liking them. Admire, respect the Prussians as one may, it is impossible to help disliking them. I will venture to say that it would be impossible to find 100 Germans born south of the Main who would declare, on their honour, that they prefer a Prussian to a Frenchman. The only Prussian I ever knew who was an agreeable man was Bismarck. All others with whom I have been thrown—and I have lived for years in Germany—were proud as Scotchmen, cold as New Englanders, and touchy as only Prussians can be. I once had a friend among them. His name was Buckenbrock. Inadvertently I called him Butterbrod. We have never spoken since.—Henry Labouchère, *Diary of the Besieged Resident in Paris,* 1871.

A NOBLE SIGHT

1824. WE CAME to the brow of the hill overlooking Florence, which lay under us, a scene of enchantment, a city planted in a garden, and resembling a rich and varied suburb. The whole presented a brilliant amphitheatre of hill and vale, of buildings, groves, and terraces. The circling heights were crowned with sparkling villas; the varying landscape, above or below, waved in an endless succession of olive-grounds. The olive is not unlike the common willow in shape or colour, and being still in leaf, gave to the middle of winter the appearance of a grey summer. In the midst, the Duomo and other churches raised their heads; vineyards and olive-grounds climbed the hills opposite till they joined a snowy ridge of Apennines rising above the top of Fesole; one plantation or row of trees after another fringed the ground, like rich lace; though you saw it not, there flowed the Arno; every thing was on the noblest scale, yet finished in the minutest part—the perfection of nature and of art, populous, splendid, full of life, yet simple, airy, embowered.—-William Hazlitt, *Notes of a Journey Through France and Italy.*

PAINTED LADIES

Paris, October 12, 1763. I SHALL only mention one particular dress essential to the fashion in this country, which seems to me to carry human affectation to the very farthest verge of folly and extravagance; that is, the manner in which the faces of the ladies are primed and painted. When the Indian chiefs were in England every body ridiculed their preposterous method of painting their cheeks and eye-lids; but this ridicule was wrong placed. Those critics ought to have considered, that the Indians do not use paint to make themselves agreeable; but in order to be the more terrible to their enemies. It is generally supposed, I think, that your sex make use of *fard* and vermilion for very different purposes; namely, to help a bad or faded complexion, to heighten the graces, or conceal the defects of nature, as well as the ravages of time. I shall not enquire at present, whether it is just and honest to impose in this manner on mankind: if it is not honest, it may be allowed to be artful and politic, and shews, at least, a desire of being agreeable. But to lay it on as the fashion in France prescribes to all the ladies of condition, who indeed cannot appear without this badge of distinction, is to disguise themselves in such a manner, as to render them odious and detestable to every specatator, who has the least relish left for nature and propriety. As for the *fard*, or *white*, with which their necks and shoulders are plaistered, it may be in some measure excusable, as their skins are naturally brown, or sallow; but the *rouge*, which is daubed on their faces, from the chin up to the eyes, without the least art or dexterity, not only destroys all distinction of features, but renders the aspect really frightful, or at best conveys nothing but ideas of disgust and aversion. You know, that without this horrible masque no married lady is admitted at court, or in any polite assembly; and that it is a mark of distinction which no bourgeoise dare assume. Ladies of fashion only have the privilege of exposing themselves in these ungracious colours. As their faces are concealed under a false complexion, so their heads are covered with a vast load of false hair, which is frizzled on the forehead, so as exactly to resemble the wooly heads of the Guinea negroes. As to the natural hue of it, this is a matter of no consequence, for powder makes every head of hair of the same colour; and no woman appears in this country, from the moment she rises till night, without being compleatly whitened. Powder or meal was first used in Europe by the Poles, to conceal their scald heads; but the present fashion of using it, as well as the modish method of dressing the hair, must have been borrowed from the Hottentots, who grease their wooly heads with mutton suet, and then paste it over with the powder called *buchu*. In like manner, the hair of our fine ladies is frizzled into the appearance of negroes wool, and stiffened with an abominable paste of hog's grease, tallow, and white powder. The present fashion, therefore, of painting the face, and adorning the head, adopted by the beau monde in France, is taken from those two polite nations the Chickesaws of America and the Hottentots of Africa. On the whole, when I see one of those fine creatures sailing along, in her taudry robes of silk and gauze, frilled, and flounced, and furbelowed, with her false locks, her false jewels, her paint, her patches, and perfumes; I cannot help looking upon her as the vilest piece of sophistication that art ever produced.—Tobias Smollett, *Travels Through France and Italy.*

YARDS OF TENDERNESS

Italy is so tender—like cooked macaroni—yards and yards of soft tenderness ravelled round everything.—D. H. Lawrence, *Sea and Sardinia*, 1923.

A BEASTLY TOWN

Coblentz, July 31, 1830. Cologne as the guide book saith had at one time 365 churches and this the waiter & some gentlemen at the table d'hote told me was exactly the no of days in the year. It had likewise 11000 virgins who were destroyed by the Romans & whose unfortunate bones have been used to decorate a Church. The town is beastly—the Cathedral unfinished, the weather was hot beyond all bearing—& I was consequently in my own room a great part of the day employing myself between sleeping smoking reading, & eating raw herring & onions.—W. M. Thackeray, *Letters.*

POVERTY

Palazzo Mocenigo-Corner, Venice (1908?). I LIVE and sleep in the open landing of a stair in this barrack of a palace. I have walked the city many nights, wet and fine, before I found this refuge—have been six consecutive days without food, half-starved for weeks together on two rolls (at three centesimi each) a day, and endured all extremes of penury short of prison and the Asili dei Senza Tetto. All my pawn-tickets of the Monte di Pietà have expired, save one. Now and then I contrive to get a job as a private gondogliere: at present I chop and saw and carry logs, work a cream separator, light fires, and fill boilers. My mother in England works for a living at 75: my sister has become blind; and we have not met for three years.—Frederick Rolfe, *Letters*.

A KING'S GREETING

Paris, May, 1765. OH! BY the bye, I suppose my sister has told you how well we were received at Marli, & how we luckily saw the King and Royal Family, but she has not told you the Paris story which says that he embrac'd me twice, and that one of the Seigneurs said, '*En verité c'est trop, Sire.*' '*Je ne sais si c'est trop, mais je sais que ça me plaît,*' says the King. Is it not charming? Now don't go & repeat this nonsense to everybody I beg. Adieu.—Lady Sarah Lennox, *Life and Letters*.

ROMANCE

Milan, August 16, 1861. WELL, I walked the Lido every day, and bathed with my little man in the tepid Adriatic, and floated through the streets in my gondola, and received charming salutes from barred windows: from one notably where a very pretty damsel, lost in langour, hung with her loose-robed bosom against the iron, and pressed amorously to see me pass, till she could no further: I meantime issued order to Lorenzo, my gondolier, to return, and lo, as I came slowly into view she as slowly arranged her sweet shape to be seen decently, and so stood, but half a pace in the recess, with one dear hand on one shoulder, her head slightly lying on her neck, her drooped eyelids mournfully seeming to say: 'No, no; never! tho' I am dying to be wedded to that wish of yours and would stake my soul I have divined it!'—wasn't it charming? This too, so intensely human from a figure vaporous, but half discernible!—George Meredith, *Letters*.

WORDSWORTH'S JOURNEY

Toulon, 8th April, 1837. . . . I WILL just mention what pleased me most. The day at Vaucluse, where I was enchanted with the power and beauty of the stream, and the wildness and grandeur of the rocks, and several minor beauties which Mr. R. has not noticed, and which I should have particularised but for this blinding cold. I was much pleased with Nismes, with Marseilles, but most of all with the drive between Marseilles and Toulon, which is singularly romantic and varied. From a height above Toulon, as we approached, we had a noble view of the purple waters of the Mediterranean, purple no doubt from the state of the atmosphere; for at Marseilles, where we first saw it, the colour was not different from the sea of our own island. At Nismes the evening was calm, the atmosphere unusually clear, and the air warm, not from its own temperature, but from the effect of the sun. I there first observed the stars, as appearing brighter and at a greater variety of depths, i.e. advancing one before the other more than they do with us. . . . One of the few promises of summer which we have had is the peach-blossom abundantly scattered over some parts of the country, and very beautiful, especially when neighboured by the cypress. . . .—William Wordsworth, *Letters*.

VILLAGE LIFE

Brescia, Sept. 1 (1747). I WALK and read much, but have very little company except that of a neighbouring convent. I do what good I am able in the village round me, which is a very large one; and have had so much success, that I am thought a great physician, and should be esteemed a saint if I went to mass.—Lady Mary Wortley Montagu, *Letters*.

WRETCHED CASTRATOS

Rome. THE PROHIBITION of female performers renders the amusement of the Roman theatre very insipid, in the opinion of some unrefined Englishmen of your acquaintance who are here. In my own poor opinion, the natural sweetness of the female voice is ill supplied by the artificial trills of wretched castratos; and the awkward agility of robust sinewy fellows dressed in women's clothes is a most deplorable substitution for the graceful movements of elegant female dancers. Is not the horrid practice which is encouraged by this manner of supplying the place of female singers, a greater outrage on religion and morality,

than can be produced by the evils which their prohibition is intended
to prevent? Is it possible to believe, that purity of sentiment will be
preserved by producing eunuchs on the stage? I should fear it would
have a different effect.—John Moore, *A View of Society and Manners
in Italy,* 1795.

THE TUMULT OF SIGHT-SEEING

Rome: March 7, 1833. . . . I SHALL stop as long as I can, and see all
that can be grasped in the time, for I sincerely hope never to go abroad
again. I never loved home so well as now I am away from it—and the
exquisite sights which foreign countries supply both to the imagination
and the moral taste are most pleasurable in *memory*, but scarcely
satisfactory as a present enjoyment. There is far too much of tumult in
seeing the places one has read so much about all one's life, to make it
desirable for it to continue.—John Henry Newman, *Letters.*

THE DAILY ROUND

La Celle, M. de Vindé's Country House, June 4th, 1820. WE HAVE
coffee brought to us in our rooms about eight o'clock, and the family
assemble at breakfast in the dining-room about ten: this breakfast has
consisted of mackerel stewed in oil; cutlets; eggs, boiled and poached,
au jus; peas stewed; lettuce stewed, and rolled up like sausages;
radishes; salad; stewed prunes; preserved gooseberries; chocolate
biscuits; apricot biscuits—that is to say, a kind of flat tartlet, sweet-
meat between paste; finishing with coffee. There are sugar-tongs in
this house, which I have seen nowhere else except at Madame Gautier's.
Salt-spoons never to be seen, so do not be surprised at seeing me take
salt and sugar in the natural way when I come back.

Carriages about twelve, and drive about seeing places in the
neighbourhood—afterwards go to our own rooms or to the salon, or
play billiards or chess. Dinner at half-past five; no luncheon and no
dressing for dinner. I will describe one dinner—*Bouilli de bœuf*—
large piece in the middle, and all the other dishes round it—*rôtie de
mouton: ris de veau piqué—maquereaux—pâtés de cervelle*—salad.
Second service; *œufs aux jus—petits pois*—lettuce stewed—*gâteaux
de confitures*—prunes. Dessert; *gâteaux, cerises—confiture d'abricot et
de groseille.*

Wash hands at side table; coffee in the saloon: men and women all
gathering round the table as of yore. But I should observe, that a great
change has taken place; the men huddle together now in France as they

used to do in England, talking politics with their backs to the women in a corner, or even in the middle of the room, without minding them in the least, and the ladies complain and look very disconsolate, and many ask, 'if this be Paris?' and others scream *ultra* nonsense or *liberal* nonsense, to make themselves of consequence and to attract the attention of the gentlemen.—Maria Edgeworth, *Letters*.

THE CUSTOMS

Calabria, Italy, 1897. BUT, FIRST of all, the *dazio*. This time it was a serious business; impossible to convince the rather surly officer that certain of the contents of my portmanteau were not for sale. What in the world was I doing with *tanti libri?* Of course I was a commercial traveller; ridiculous to pretend anything else. After much strain of courtesy, I clapped to my luggage, locked it up, and with resolute face cried 'Avanti!' And there was an end to it. In this case, as so often, I have no doubt that simple curiosity went for much in the man's pertinacious questioning. Of course the whole *dazio* business is ludicrous and contemptible; I scarce know a baser spectacle than that of uniformed officials groping in the poor little bundles of starved peasant women, mauling a handful of onions, or prodding with long irons a cartload of straw. Did any one ever compare the expenses with the results?—George Gissing, *By the Ionian Sea*.

SWEETNESS AND HORROR

1814. HUMAN LIFE in Paris was matter of farce. In the Jardin des Plantes a gentleman dropped a five-franc piece into the bear court. An old grenadier early the next morning crept down to get it. A bear was awake, rushed out, killed him and ate a great part of him. In England the bear would have been shot, a deodand levied, and subscriptions raised for the man's widow. In France they caricatured the incident and called the bear by the veteran's name. Everybody was asking, with a joke: 'Which is the bear which ate the moustache?' and servant girls and children were perpetually calling out for Martin, clapping their hands and flinging him buns for his dexterity. . . .

And yet everything, however abominable, was done by the women with such grace and sweetness, that residence among them would soon have rendered me as insensible as themselves. The lowest servant took your hat and gloves as if you did her a favour. Nothing struck us English more in the manners of the French than the sweetness of address in all classes. A little beggar bored Wilkie for money; he rather

H

Arrival at Cologne (Customs)

pettishly repulsed him. In London the boy's pride would have fired up, and provoked some rough retort; but the little fellow in Paris made a bow, saying, '*Pardon, Monsieur; une autre occasion . . .*'

On my landing at Dover, an old man cautioned me not to lean against one of the machines by which the cavalry were landing their horses, or I should get 'squeezed as flat as a pancake'. I remember very perfectly being astounded. In Paris they would have let me be squeezed first and punned on me afterwards. Yet, after all, such is the intoxicating gaiety of French manners, such the liveliness and sweetness of French society, such the fascination of French amusement, so easy is admission to all their public places, libraries and collections, that, though most men enter Paris with disgust, no man ever left it with disappointment. —B. R. Haydon, *Autobiography.*

SPA

Stretton, 10th May, 1785. I AM sorry my information about Spa, where I passed a summer 18 years ago, will be of so little use to you, for I'm told '*que tout est changé*' so compleatly there, that I should scarce know it: however you shall hear what it was. The place did consist of 6 or 7 largish houses, & the rest a neat village of houses containing an entry & staircase, with 4 rooms of about 9 or 12 feet square, one of them a kitchen, one for the landlord only (for they are chiefly widows), & the 2 others for you with bedchambers over them; all plain white-washed walls & wooden chairs, *very clean*. Farmhouse windows, at which everybody (*for the world lives in the great street*) peeps in as you sit at breakfast, so that if you have not a backroom or a large house, you are at the receipt of custom all day. If it rains, Spa is detestable. If it's *fine*, & your *health* admits of it, 'tis impossible to resist entering into the goodhumoured idleness of the whole place, particularly as it is easily done without expence. You need never ask a *soul to eat*, but dine at 2 or 3 o'clock in peace. You may walk out *in the street* or in a promenade close by all the morning, buy your own greens & fruit, read the papers at the booksellers, go a shopping, or make parties for the evening; after dinner you go on *foot* to the rooms, play ball, or walk, make your own party, & *walk* home (or in a chair if sick) at 9, 10, 11, 12 o'clock. In *my* time all was shut up at that hour; but now I hear late hours, parties at home, & dinners are the fashion. *My system was (et je m'en suis très bien trouvé)* to *cut* all the tiresome English, to join the agreable ones if asked; if not, I comforted myself with chusing my own society among the forreigners, which I always found civil, chearfull, obliging, & very often agreable. I am afraid the mere eating

& drinking is expensive; but your very delightful servant will remedy that very much by his care. Your dress need not cost you nothing but a French lutestring for dress, as the great perfection of Spa is that it is a perfect masquerade, & that as you will probably chuse to dress French, you may do it cheap. A lady who left Paris last autumn told me that the *Queen and everybody* wore white linnen levettes & night-gowns *all day long*, no apron, & a chip or straw hat with ribbons, & that when she went to the great milliner for a *cap* to bring home, she told her there was no such thing except a *court cap*, & she sold her a straw hat for 5 shillings, & the lady could not get the same in London under 10 shillings, tho' Mad Bertin the miliner get hers from England: this is an *annecdote in dress* worth your notice. Take gauze handker-chiefs in plenty of an ell square; I get them reasonable at a shop I will look for the dirrection of, & add it. I know nothing of men's dress, but that a Bruxelle camlet is a stronger kind of Irish popplin, & much worn there for habbits & coats. There are riding horses to be hired that carry you creeping up the hill to the fountain at 6 or 7 in the morning, for it's 2 miles or more off. An English saddle would be usefull, & by the bye, if Mr. O'Brien has an easy poney he likes, he had better carry it. It saves a post horse, & can always be well sold. If you love riding, & mean to carry 2 menservants, your horse will be of use, as there are places within 50 miles round well worth seing, & parties often made.—Lady Sarah Lennox, *Life and Letters.*

A FRIVOLOUS PLACE

Naples: February 19, 1833. WE HAVE fallen on bad weather at Naples. The books tell us that a perpetual spring is here; but more piercing winds, and more raw, wretched rains, I have scarcely ever felt. For invalids the place is emphatically bad; especially when they don't see the harm of linen wet from the wash. . . . On Thursday evening we went to the Opera. In spite of my reasonings, which I continue to think sound, I felt so great a repugnance to going, that, had I been alone, I should not have gone. There was nothing there to offend me, however, more than that the whole city offends me. It is a frivolous, dissipated place. This is carnival time, and all sorts of silly saturnalia between King and people are going on. Religion is turned into a mere occasion of worldly gaiety—as in the history of the Israelites—and the sooner we are out of so bad a place the better.—John Henry Newman, *Letters.*

THE MARCH OF THE BUGS

MY HOTEL was called the Hôtel des Trois Moineaux. It was a dark, rickety warren of five storeys, cut up by wooden partitions into forty rooms. The rooms were small and inveterately dirty, for there was no maid, and Madame F., the *patronne*, had no time to do any sweeping. The walls were as thin as matchwood, and to hide the cracks they had been covered with layer after layer of pink paper, which had come loose and housed innumerable bugs. Near the ceiling long lines of bugs marched all day like columns of soldiers, and at night came down ravenously hungry, so that one had to get up every few hours and kill them in hecatombs. Sometimes when the bugs got too bad one used to burn sulphur and drive them into the next room; whereupon the lodger next door would retort by having *his* room sulphured, and drive the bugs back. It was a dirty place, but homelike, for Madame F. and her husband were good sorts. The rent of the rooms varied between thirty and fifty francs a week.—George Orwell, *Down and Out in Paris and London*, 1933.

QUEEN OF MARBLE AND MUD

1849. I WENT through so much hard, dry, mechanical, toil there, that I quite lost before I left it, the charm of the place. . . . I have got all the right feeling back now, however; and hope to write a word or two about Venice yet, when I have got the mouldings well out of my head —and the mud. For the fact is, with reverence be it spoken, that whereas Rogers says 'There is a glorious city in the Sea', a truthful person must say 'There is a glorious city in the Mud'. It is startling at first to say so, but it goes well enough with marble, 'Oh Queen of Marble and Mud'.—John Ruskin, *The Order of Release*.

SHELLEY'S ARRIVAL IN ITALY

Milan, April, 1818. BEHOLD US arrived at length at the end of our journey—that is, within a few miles of it—because we design to spend the summer on the shore of the Lake of Como. Our journey was somewhat painful from the cold—and in no other manner interesting until we passed the Alps: of course I except the Alps themselves; but no sooner had we arrived at Italy, than the loveliness of the earth and the serenity of the sky made the greatest difference in my sensations. I depend on these things for life; for in the smoke of cities, and the tumult of human kind, and the chilling fogs and rain of our own country, I can hardly be said to live. With what delight did I hear the woman, who conducted us to see the triumphal arch of Augustus at Susa, speak the clear and complete language of Italy, though half unintelligible to me, after that nasal and abbreviated cacophony of the French! A ruined arch of magnificent proportions in the Greek taste, standing in a kind of road of green lawn, overgrown with violets and primroses, and in the midst of stupendous mountains, and a *blonde* woman, of light and graceful manners, something in the style of Fuseli's Eve, were the first things we met in Italy.—Shelley, *Letters*.

THE GONDOLA

Este, October 8, 1818. THE GONDOLAS themselves are things of a most romantic and picturesque appearance; I can only compare them to moths of which a coffin might have been the chrysalis.—Shelley, *Letters*.

THREE LUSTY HUSSIES

Paris, October 12th, 1763. THERE ARE three young lusty hussies, nieces or daughters of a blacksmith, that lives just opposite to my windows, who do nothing from morning till night. They eat grapes and bread from seven till nine, from nine till twelve they dress their hair, and are all the afternoon gaping at the window to view passengers. I don't perceive that they give themselves the trouble either to make their beds, or clean their apartment. The same spirit of idleness and dissipation I have observed in every part of France, and among every class of people.—Tobias Smollett, *Travels Through France and Italy*.

VERSAILLES

Oct 23rd, 1787. AGAIN TO Versailles. In viewing the king's apartment, which he had not left a quarter of an hour, with those slight traits of disorder that shewed he *lived* in it, it was amusing to see the blackguard figures that were walking uncontrouled about the palace, and even in his bed-chamber; men whose rags betrayed them to be in the last stage of poverty, and I was the only person that stared and wondered how the devil they got there. It is impossible not to like this careless indifference and freedom from suspicion. One loves the master of the house, who would not be hurt or offended at seeing his apartment thus occupied, if he returned suddenly; for if there was danger of this, the intrusion would be prevented. This is certainly a feature of that *good temper* which appears to me so visible every where in France. I desired to see the queen's apartments, but I could not. Is her majesty in it? No. Why then not see it as well as the king's? *Ma foi, Mons. C'est une autre chose.* Ramble through the gardens, and by the grand canal, with absolute astonishment at the exaggerations of writers and travellers. There is magnificence in the quarter of the orangerie, but no beauty any where; there are some statues good enough to wish them under-cover. The extent and breadth of the canal are nothing to the eye; and it is not in such good repair as a farmer's horse-pond. The menagerie is well enough, but nothing great. Let those who desire that the buildings and establishments of Louis XIV. should continue the impression made by the writings of Voltaire, go to the canal of Lanquedoc, and by no means to Versailles.—Arthur Young, *Travels in France.*

MERCILESS HEAT

Florence: August 24, 1848. So WE went to Ancona, a striking sea city, holding up against the brown rocks and elbowing out the purple tides, beautiful to look upon. An exfoliation of the rock itself, you would call the houses that seem to grow there, so identical is the colour and character. I should like to visit Ancona again when there is a little air and shadow; we stayed a week as it was, living upon fish and cold water. Water, water, was the cry all day long, and really you should have seen me (or you should not have seen me) lying on the sofa, and demoralised out of all sense of female vanity, not to say decency, with dishevelled hair at full length, and 'sans gown, sans stays, sans shoes, sans everything', except a petticoat and white dressing wrapper. I said something feebly once about the waiter; but I don't think I meant it for earnest, for when Robert said, 'Oh, don't mind, dear', certainly I didn't mind in the least. People *don't,* I suppose, when they are in ovens, or in exhausted receivers. Never before did I guess what heat was—that's sure.—Elizabeth Barrett Browning, *Letters.*

A DIRTY SCRUBBY PLACE

Paris, 1851. FINALLY INTO Bois de Boulogne, which is also a dirty scrubby place (one long road mainly of two miles or so, with paltry bits of trees on each hand, and dust in abundance); there we careered along at a sharp trot, and had almost all to ourselves, for nobody else except a walker or two, a cab-party or two at long intervals were seen. Ugly unkept grass on each side; cross-roads, one or two, turning off into one knew not what; I found it an extremely sober 'Park'!— Thomas Carlyle, *Excursion (Futile Enough) to Paris.*

MALMAISON

La Celle, M. de Vindé's Country House, June 4th, 1820. MAL MAISON was Josephine's, and is still Beauharnais's property, but is now occupied only by his steward. The place is very pretty—profusion of rhododendrons, as underwood in the groves, on the grass, beside the rivers, everywhere, and in the most luxuriant flower. Poor Josephine! Do you remember Doctor Marcet telling us that when he breakfasted with her, she said, pointing to her flowers: 'These are my subjects; I try to make them happy.'

The grounds are admirably well taken care of, but the solitude and silence and the continual reference to the dead were strikingly melancholy, even in the midst of sunshine and flowers, and the song of nightingales. In one pond we saw swimming in graceful desolate dignity two black swans, which, as rare birds, were once great favourites. Now they curve their necks of ebony in vain. . . .

You may imagine the feelings that made us walk in absolute silence through the library, which was formerly Napoleon's: the gilt Ns and Js still in the arches of the ceilings: busts and portraits all round—that of Josephine admirable.—Maria Edgeworth, *Letters*.

LANDING IN CALABRIA

Italy, Paola, 1897. AT LAST my portmanteau was dropped down on to a laden boat; I, as best I could, managed to follow it; and on the top of a pile of rope and empty flour-sacks we rolled landward. The surf was high; it cost much yelling, leaping, and splashing to gain the dry beach. Meanwhile, not without apprehension, I had eyed the group awaiting our arrival; that they had their eyes on me was obvious, and I knew enough of southern Italians to foresee my reception. I sprang into the midst of a clamorous conflict; half a dozen men were quarrelling for possession of me. No sooner was my luggage on shore than they flung themselves upon it. By what force or authority I know not, one of the fellows triumphed; he turned to me with a satisfied smile, and—presented his wife.

'*Mia sposa, signore!*'

Wondering, and trying to look pleased, I saw the woman seize the portmanteau (a frightful weight), fling it on to her head, and march away at a good speed. The crowd and I followed to the *dogana*, close by, where as rigorous a search was made as I have ever had to undergo. I puzzled the people; my arrival was an unwonted thing, and they felt sure I was a trader of some sort. Dismissed under suspicion, I allowed the lady to whom I had been introduced to guide me townwards. Again she bore the portmanteau on her head, and evidently thought it a trifle, but as the climbing road lengthened, and as I myself began to perspire in the warm sunshine, I looked at my attendant with uncomfortable feelings. It was a long and winding way, but the woman continued to talk and laugh so cheerfully that I tried to forget her toil.—George Gissing, *By the Ionian Sea*.

TRISTES ANGLAIS

1814. ROUEN WAS well worth investigating. On the pedestal of the statue of the Maid of Orleans in the Place aux Vaux was still visible '*Liberté, Égalité, Fraternité*', but nearly obliterated by dripping rain. In the Hall for trials were some more specimens of revolutionary cant and sentiment, and blue velvet hangings lettered with N.N.N. covered the sides of a small committee room. 'You ought to take those out', said I, 'now you have dishonoured him.' 'Every one does as he likes in his own house', said our cicerone, quite touchy. . . .

We went to hear service in their massy and eternal cathedral, built by the English. Our faculties were overwhelmed by the ceremonies of their expressive religion. . . .

As we walked along we saw many in side-chapels totally abstracted in devotion. This absorption, in conjunction with their richly coloured dresses, darkly illumined by the religious light of the magnificent windows, filled our minds with grand sensations. Yet after kneeling all the morning at the cathedral, and praying and singing hymns, so as to make us, heretics as we were, thoughtful for the day, the scene in the evening was like Barthelmy Fair. The quay was covered with booths and merry-andrews and monkeys; the men all chatting, and the women all coquetting with their delicious black eyes and tripping gaiety of walk, and so contagious was their fun that even we, *tristes Anglais*, were infected, and rushed away to the theatre with the crowd.—B. R. Haydon, *Autobiography*.

FRENCH INN

France, 1820. July. *Half-past* 10. THE PARTY gone to bed. This Salle, where I sit, how unlike a parlour in an English inn! Yet the history of a sea-fight, or a siege, painted on the walls, with the costumes of Philip the Second, or even of our own time, would have better suited my associations, with the names of Gravelines and Dunkirk, than the story of Cupid and Psyche now before my eyes, as large as life, on French paper! The paper is in pannels, with big mirrors between, in gilt frames. With all this taste and finery, and wax candles, and Brussels carpet, what a mixture of troublesome awkwardness! They brought us a ponderous teapot that would not pour out the tea: the latches (with metal enough to fasten up a dungeon) can hardly, by unpractised hands, be made to open and shut the doors. I have seen the diligence come into the yard and unload—heavy, dirty, dusty— a lap-dog walking about the top, like a panther in its cage, and viewing the gulph below. A monkey was an outside passenger when it departed. —Dorothy Wordsworth, *Journals*.

PARADE AND POVERTY

Paris, Oct. 3, 1765. WHAT STRIKES me the most upon the whole is, the total difference of manners between them and us, from the greatest object to the least. There is not the smallest similitude in the twenty-four hours. It is obvious in every trifle. Servants carry their lady's train, and put her into her coach with their hat on. They walk about the streets in the rain with umbrellas to avoid putting on their hats; driving themselves in open chaises in the country without hats, in the rain too, and yet often wear them in a chariot in Paris when it does not rain. The very footmen are powdered from the break of day, and yet wait behind their master, as I saw the Duc of Praslin's do, with a red pocket-handkerchief about their necks. Versailles, like everything else, is a mixture of parade and poverty, and in every instance exhibits something most dissonant from our manners. In the colonnades, upon the staircase, nay in the antechambers of the royal family, there are people selling all sorts of wares. While we were waiting in the Dauphin's sumptuous bedchamber, till his dressing-room door should be opened, two fellows were sweeping it, and dancing about in sabots to rub the floor.—Horace Walpole, *Letters*.

MONEY TROUBLE

France, 1802. THOUGH Valenciennes lace is very pretty we bought none, recollecting that though Coventry is famous for ribbons, and Tewkesbury for stockings, yet only the worst ribbons, and the worst stockings, are to be had at Coventry and Tewkesbury. Besides we are not expert at counting Flemish money, which is quite different from French, and puzzling enough to drive the seven sages of Greece mad. Even the natives cannot count it without rubbing their foreheads, and counting in their hands, and repeating '*ça fait*', '*cela fait*'. For my part I fairly gave the point up, and resolved to be cheated rather than go distracted. But indeed the Flemish are not cheats, as far as I have seen of them. They would go to the utmost borders of honesty for a couronne de Brabant, or a demi-couronne, or a double escalin, or a single escalin, or a plaquet, or a livre, or a sous, or a liard, or for any the vilest denomination of their absurd coin, yet I do not believe they would go beyond the bounds of honesty with any but an English Milor: they are privileged dupes. A maid at the hotel at Dunkirk said to me, '*Ah! Madame, nous autres nous aimons bien de voir rouler les Anglais*'. Yes, because they think the English roll in gold.—Maria Edgeworth, *Letters*.

FIRST THOUGHTS ON CALAIS

July, 1814. EXHAUSTED WITH sickness and fatigue, I walked over the sands with my companions to the hotel. I heard for the first time the confused buzz of voices speaking a different language from that to which I had been accustomed; and saw a costume very unlike that

Channel Crossing

worn on the opposite side of the channel; the women with high caps and short jackets; the men with earrings, ladies walking about with high bonnets or *coiffures* lodged on the top of the head, the hair dragged up underneath, without any stray curls to decorate the temples or cheeks. There is, however, something very pleasing in the manners and appearance of the people of Calais, that prepossesses you in their favour. A national reflection might occur, that when Edward III took

Calais, he turned out the old inhabitants, and peopled it almost entirely with our own countrymen; but unfortunately the manners are not English.—Shelley, *History of a Six Weeks' Tour*.

HOPELESS VICE

Baveno, July 12th, 1841. I HAVE more feeling for Italy than ever, but it makes me deeply sad. The vines and pasture about this place make it a Paradise; the people are fine-featured, and singularly graceful in motion; but there is every appearance of hopeless vice. Four men have been playing cards and drinking, without stirring, in the inn-yard since twelve o'clock (noon). I had come in from an evening walk, and the gardens and enclosed spots of ground are foul as dunghills. The Isola Bella is fast going to decay—all the stucco of it green, damp, shattered, covered with weeds and dead leaves; yet the flowers and foliage of surpassing beauty.—John Ruskin, *Praeterita*.

DOUBLE TALK IN ITALY

The wine of Airolo and its songs, how greatly they refreshed me! To see men with answering eyes and to find a salute returned; the noise of careless mouths talking all together; the group at cards, and the laughter that is proper to mankind; the straight carriage of the women, and in all the people something erect and noble as though indeed they possessed the earth. I made a meal there, talking to all my companions left and right in a new speech of my own, which was made up, as it were, of the essence of all the Latin tongues, saying—

'*Ha! Si jo a traversa li montagna no erat facile! Nenni! Il san Gottardo? Nil est! pooh! poco! Ma hestérna jo ha voulu traversar in Val Bavona, e credi non ritornar, nam fredo, fredo erat in alto! La tourmente ma prise . . .*'

And so forth, explaining all fully with gestures, exaggerating, emphasising, and acting the whole matter, so that they understood me without much error. But I found it more difficult to understand them, because they had a regular formed language with terminations and special words.—Hilaire Belloc, *The Path to Rome*, 1902.

FRENCH GALLANTRY

Paris, October 12th, 1763. I SHALL not even deny, that the French are by no means deficient in natural capacity; but they are at the same time remarkable for a natural levity, which hinders their youth from cultivating that capacity. This is reinforced by the most preposterous education, and the example of a giddy people, engaged in the most frivolous pursuits. A Frenchman is by some Jesuit, or other monk, taught to read his mother tongue, and to say his prayers in a language he does not understand. He learns to dance and to fence, by the masters of those noble sciences. He becomes a compleat connoisseur in dressing hair, and in adorning his own person, under the hands and instructions of his barber and valet de chambre. If he learns to play upon the flute or the fiddle, he is altogether irresistible. But he piques himself upon being polished above the natives of any other country by his conversation with the fair sex. In the course of this communication, with which he is indulged from his tender years, he learns like a parrot, by rote, the whole circle of French compliments, which you know are a set of phrases, ridiculous even to a proverb; and these he throws out indiscriminately to all women, without distinction, in the exercise of that kind of address, which is here distinguished by the name of gallantry: it is no more than his making love to every woman who will give him the hearing. It is an exercise, by the repetition of which he becomes very pert, very familiar, and very impertinent. Modesty, or diffidence, I have already said, is utterly unknown among them, and therefore I wonder there should be a term to express it in their language. —Tobias Smollett, *Travels Through France and Italy.*

SNOBBISHNESS

Paris, Sept, 22, 1765. THERE ARE swarms of English here, but most of them are going, to my great satisfaction.—Horace Walpole, *Letters.*

ILLNESS IN SICILY

1833. How I dreaded the long nights, lying without sleep, as it seemed, all through the darkness. I wanted to get some one to sit up with me, but did not succeed. Indeed, it was with difficulty I got nurses. The principal one said to Gennaro (as he told me afterwards), and he to her, 'Well, we must go through with it, and if we catch the fever, we catch it.' Gennaro slept in the room. I got the muleteer to sit up with me. The heat, too, was miserable. I suspect I ought to have been quite cool. I was reduced to the lowest conceivable weakness, not being able to raise my hand to my head, nor to swallow. I had macaroni, &c., but nothing agreed; biscuits, some I liked. (When I first got there, there were some camomile flowers on the table near the bed, which were most refreshing, and I begged they might not be removed.) I continually had most oppressive almost faintings; I suspect the heat had much to do with it. They had nothing but vinegar to relieve me, which the muleteer with his great bullet tips of fingers (so I recollect I called them, while he administered it with them) applied to my nose in the middle of the night. When I got better I used to watch for the day, and when light appeared through the shutter, for there was no blind or curtain, I used to soliloquise: 'O sweet light! God's best gift', &c. . . .

What distressed me most was the daily Mass bell (I suppose it was in a neighbouring church). I used quite to writhe about, and put my head under the bed-clothes, and asked Gennaro if it could be stopped. He answered with a laugh of surprise that it should not annoy me, and of encouragement, as if making light of it. I have since thought they might suppose it was a heretic's misery under a holy bell. . . . The master of the house was very civil. He heard I liked music, and he got some performers to play to me in the next room. It was very beautiful, but too much for me.—John Henry Newman, *Letters*.

THE TARANTELLA

1777. . . . IT IS rare to hear any agreeable sounds in the streets of Naples, though it is the nursery of musical professors: a school, where the greatest masters have imbibed their principles, and acquired that knowledge of composition, which has enchanted the ears of all Europe. There is no such thing as a national music, unless we give that name to a monotonous drawling seguidilla, that serves the nurses as a lullaby to put their children to rest, and seems borrowed from the Spaniards, who, I believe, learnt it of the Moors. I never resided in any Italian town where there was a less musical turn in the populace: few songs, guittars, vielles, or organs, enliven the evenings, as in the northern states of Italy, unless they be sent for to entertain the parties that in summer sup on the shore of Posilipo.

They do not even dance to music, but perform the Tarantella to the beating of a kind of tambourine, which was in use among their ancestors, as appears by the pictures of Herculaneum. The Tarantella is a low dance, consisting of turns on the heel, much footing and snapping of the fingers. It seems the delight of their soul, and a constant holiday diversion of the young women, who are, in general, far from handsome, although they have fine eyes and striking features. Their hands and feet are clumsy, their shapes neglected, their necks flabby, and their skins discoloured by living so much in the sun without bonnets.—Henry Swinburne, *Travels to the Two Sicilies*, 1777–80.

BARROW-WOMAN'S TOUCH

THE MANNER in which an old barrow-woman will tie up her sous' worth of cherries for her urchin customers might give a lesson to the most skilful decorator of the supper-table. A bunch of wild violets, sold at a price that may come within reach of the worst-paid *soubrette* in Paris, is arranged with a grace that might make a duchess covet them; and I have seen the paltry stock-in-trade of a florist, whose only pavilion was a tree and the blue heavens, set off with such felicity in the mixture of colours, and the gradations of shape and form, as made me stand to gaze longer and more delightedly than I ever did before Flora's own palace in the King's Road.—Mrs Frances Trollope, *Paris and the Parisians in 1835.*

Misery

SICILIAN ADVENTURE

Syracuse: April 27, 1833. IN ENGLAND we have no idea what a Sicilian flea is.—John Henry Newman, *Letters.*

MARTHA AND MARY

Thursday, January 3, 1838–39. I MUST say that the accounts which I had heard of Naples are very incorrect. There is far less beggary than at Rome, and far more industry. Rome is a city of priests. It reminded me of the towns in Palestine which were set apart to be inhabited by the Levites. Trade and agriculture seem only to be tolerated as subsidiary to devotion. Men are allowed to work; because, unless somebody works, nobody can live; and, if nobody lives, nobody can pray. But, as soon as you enter Naples, you notice a striking contrast. It is the difference between Sunday and Monday. Here the business of civil life is evidently the great thing, and religion is the accessory. A poet might introduce Naples as Martha, and Rome as Mary. A Catholic may think Mary's the better employment; but even a Catholic, much more a Protestant, would prefer the table of Martha. I must ask many questions about these matters. At present, my impressions are very favourable to Naples. It is the only place in Italy that has seemed to me to have the same sort of vitality which you find in all the great English ports and cities. Rome and Pisa are dead and gone; Florence is not dead, but sleepeth; while Naples overflows with life.—Lord Macaulay, *Letters.*

DREGS OF ANCIENT ROME

Rome, 1824. IN LONDON there is a look of wealth and populousness which is to be found nowhere else. In Rome you are for the most part lost in a mass of tawdry, fulsome *common-places.* It is not the contrast of pig-styes and palaces that I complain of, the distinction between the old and new; what I object to is the want of any such striking contrast, but an almost uninterrupted succession of narrow, vulgar-looking streets, where the smell of garlick prevails over the odour of antiquity, with the dingy, melancholy flat fronts of modern-built houses, that seem in search of an owner. A dunghill, an outhouse, the weeds growing under an imperial arch offend me not; but what has a greengrocer's stall, a stupid English china warehouse, a putrid *trattoria,* a barber's sign, an old clothes or old picture shop or a Gothic palace, with two or three lacqueys in modern liveries lounging at the gate, to do with ancient Rome?—William Hazlitt, *Notes of a Journey Through France and Italy.*

EXPLORING ITALY

Florence, June 20th, 1764. EVERY STEP I take in Italy, I am more and more sensible of the obligation I have to my father in allowing me to undertake the tour. Indeed, Dear Madam, this tour is one of the very few things that exceed the most sanguine and flattering hopes. I do not pretend to say that there are no disagreeable things in it: bad roads, and indifferent inns, taking very often a good deal of trouble to

see things which do not deserve it, and especially the continual converse one is obliged to have with the vilest part of mankind—inn-
keepers, post-masters, and custom house officers, who impose upon
you without any possibility of preventing it,—all these are far from
being pleasing. But how amply is a traveller repaid for those little
mortifications by the pleasure and knowledge he finds in almost every
place. The actual beauties are always the very great singularity of the
country, the different pieces of antiquity either dispersed or collected
into cabinets, and the variety of master-pieces of sculpture and painting
have already made me pass some of the most entertaining days I have
yet known, and I have before me the pleasing reflexion that what I
have yet seen is far inferior to what I shall find in this place as well as
Rome and Naples. I flatter myself, that the works of the greatest
artists, which I have continually before my eyes, have already begun to
form my taste for the fine arts. I shall however endeavour not to become
a Coxcomb, nor to take the knowledge of a few terms for real science.
I shall perhaps bring back to England an unaffected taste for those arts,
I am afraid without the judgment of a connoisseur, and I hope without
the ridiculous part of that character.—Edward Gibbon, *Letters*.

ROME

January 1854, Italy. IF I HAD to write a book about Rome what on
airth could I say? I might as well be at Jericho or Islington.—W. M.
Thackeray, *Letters*.

I

Part III

THE MIDDLE DISTANCE

PLEASURING IN THE SUN

Lisbon, July 16, 1809. I AM very happy here, because I love oranges, and talk bad Latin to the monks, who understand it, as it is like their own, and I goes into society (with my pocket-pistols), and I swims in the Tagus all across it once, and I rides on an ass or a mule, and swears Portuguese, and have got a diarrhoea and bites from the mosquitoes. But what of that? Comfort must not be expected by folks that go a pleasuring.—Lord Byron, *Letters*.

A MELANCHOLY EVENING

Utrecht, 23 September 1763. I ARRIVED at Utrecht on a Saturday evening. I went to the Nouveau Château d'Anvers. I was shown up to a high bedroom with old furniture, where I had to sit and be fed by myself. At every hour the bells of the great tower played a dreary psalm tune. A deep melancholy seized upon me. I groaned with the idea of living all winter in so shocking a place. I thought myself old and wretched and forlorn. I was worse and worse next day. All the horrid ideas that you can imagine, recurred upon me. I was quite unemployed and had not a soul to speak to but the clerk of the English meeting, who could do me no good. I sunk quite into despair. I thought that at length the time was come that I should grow mad. I actually believed myself so. I went out to the streets, and even in public could not refrain from groaning and weeping bitterly. I said always, 'Poor Boswell! is it come to this? Miserable wretch that I am! what shall I do?'—O my friend, pause here a little and figure to yourself what I endured. I took general speculative views of things; all seemed full of darkness and woe. Tortured in this manner, I determined to leave Utrecht, and next day returned to Rotterdam in a condition that I shudder to recollect. But I must not be downhearted.—Boswell, *Boswell in Holland*.

AN IRREVERENT MORNING IN CHURCH

HOLAR WAS the seat of a bishopric, and I spent the next morning in the church, which is as ugly as most protestant places of worship. The only relic of the past is the carved altar piece. I strummed on the harmonium, and balanced books and hassocks on the altar candlesticks, and stood on the altar in my socks and struck matches trying to photograph the carving. Mysterious violent figures rise out of the background slashing at prisoners without looking at them. Impassive horses survey another world than theirs. One of the thieves has his head thrown right back and on his forehead dances a bear holding a child. Serried figures, the Queen of Heaven with a tower, St. Peter with no back to his head etc., rise like a Greek Chorus, right and left of the main panel. After lunch we got a couple of rather obstinate horses and started up the valley intending to visit the glacier at its head. It was a brilliant sunny day and we didn't get half way, but lay on the grass dozing and teasing a couple of bell spiders with a straw. —W. H. Auden and Louis MacNeice, *Letters from Iceland,* 1937.

JOURNEY THROUGH POLAND

Cracow, *Aug.* 2, 1758. YOU SEE, by the date of my letter, that I am arrived in Poland. When will my wanderings be at an end? When will my restless disposition give me leave to enjoy the present hour? When at Lyons, I thought all happiness lay beyond the Alps; when in Italy, I found myself still in want of something, and expected to leave solitude behind me by going into Roumelia; and now you find me turning back, still expecting ease everywhere but where I am. It is now seven years since I saw the face of a single creature who cared a farthing whether I was dead or alive. Secluded from all the comforts of confidence, friendship, or society, I feel the solitude of a hermit, but not his ease. . . .

When I consider myself in the country which was once so formidable in war, and spread terror and desolation over the whole Roman empire, I can hardly account for the present wretchedness and pusillanimity of its inhabitants; a prey to every invader; their cities plundered without an enemy; their magistrates seeking redress by complaints, and not by vigour. Everything conspires to raise my compassion for their miseries, were not my thoughts too busily engaged by my own. The whole kingdom is in strange disorder; when our equipage, which consists of the prince and thirteen attendants, had arrived at some towns, there were no conveniences to be found, and we were obliged to have girls to conduct us to the next. I have seen a woman travel thus on horseback before us for thirty miles, and think herself highly paid, and make twenty reverences, upon receiving, with ecstacy, about twopence for her trouble. In general, we were better served by the women than the men on those occasions. The men seemed directed by a low sordid interest alone; they seemed mere machines, and all their thoughts were employed in the care of their horses. If we gently desired them to make more speed, they took not the least notice; kind language was what they had by no means been used to. It was proper to speak to them in the tones of anger, and sometimes it was even necessary to use blows, to excite them to their duty. How different these from the common people of England, whom a blow might induce to return the affront sevenfold. . . .

The enthusiasm of liberty an Englishman feels is never so strong as when presented by such prospects as these. I must own, in all my indigence, it is one of my comforts (perhaps, indeed, it is my only boast) that I am of that happy country; though I scorn to starve there; though I do not choose to lead a life of wretched dependence, or be an object for my former acquaintance to point at. While you enjoy all the ease and elegance of prudence and virtue, your old friend wanders over the world, without a single anchor to hold by, or a friend, except you, to confide in.—Oliver Goldsmith, *The Bee and Other Essays*.

A SCHOOLMASTER IN CYPRUS

SIGMA GAMMA was the appropriate title of the Girls' Sixth, and here I began my ministrations at seven each day, entering the large unheated classroom with a shiver. They rose politely enough and repeated a prayer under the prompting of the head girl. Then I read out their names from the register—like the dramatis personae to a Greek tragedy: 'Electra, Io, Aphrodite, Iolanthe, Penelope, Chloe'. Like the boys, they were a mixed group in the social sense; Electra's father was a gardener in Kythrea, Io's father a judge, Penelope the daughter of a shoemaker. They comprised a cross-section of Nicosia and the surrounding districts. But they were uncomfortably united in one thing, besides Enosis, and that was a passionate, heart-rending determination to marry their English teacher. Every morning my desk bore half a dozen offerings—Electra brought black roses and white, Chloe a special kind of meat ball made by her grandmother, Aphrodite a volume of poems I had mentioned. If their devotion had been accompanied by greater self-control in class life would have been easier; but no sooner had I opened the proceedings than each started to do work of her own. One sewed secretively, another made darts, a third made a catapult from a paper-clip, a fourth decided to enter up her diary for the day. ('Today he looks cross, my teacher, his jaw is set, his brow grim, but I love him all the more.') Reprisals were always accompanied by agonizing tears as the expelled creature betook herself to the library where she ran the risk of being found by the headmistress. Heaven alone knows what punishments a girl-student might be liable to undergo. I never dared to ask. I maintained throughout a decorous reserve which always hovered on the edge of laughter. Aphrodite, appropriately enough, was the most spirited and most difficult of the girls. Her father was a rich confectioner of the town and she had all the confidence and repose which comes of never having been short of money. She was indeed as beautiful as her counterpart in myth was supposed to be; but she was something more—she was a writer. She read poetry to herself in a low murmuring voice and behaved for most of the time as if she was succumbing to ether. But these dreamy Chopinesque moods alternated with moods of anarchy. Invited to the blackboard, she had a habit of passing behind the back row of girls and with one flowing movement, invisible as a conjuror's pass, of tying their pigtails together—so that by the time I was study-ing her blackboard technique a riot had broken out among the back benches, where six girls found themselves yoked like oxen. Invited to write an essay on her favourite historical character she never failed to delight me with something like this: 'I have no historical character but in the real life there is one I love. He is writer. I dote him and he dotes me. How pleasure is the moment when I see him came at the door. My glad is very big. How pleasure is that moment. As all people are dreamed so am I', and so on. Her essays were a perpetual delight; but they were not the only ones. Dimitra also wrote some which were memorable, though she always verged upon self-pity. 'I am orphan and have never been enjoyed', was the beginning to one. She also was afflicted by the verb 'dote', as indeed the whole class was. This was the unfortunate fruit of a day when Aphrodite asked me slyly why English had only one word for 'love' when Greek had several; in my attempt not to let the Empire down I produced 'adore' and 'dote'. The latter stuck like a burr. But unfortunately each girl elected to marry it to a different preposition so that my essays the next day were full of heart-rending examples. Electra described the King and Queen of Greece 'doting at each other'; while Chloe wrote: 'When they married they were in a great dote. He was so excitement and she was so excitement. They were both excitement.' Which was fair enough I suppose; only it was difficult to see how on earth to correct such work intelligibly. Driving home in the afternoon I used to brood on these problems, mentally conjugating 'dote' like a Bach fugue, 'I dote, thou dotest, he dotes. . . .'—Lawrence Durrell, *Bitter Lemons*, 1957.

A SMALL TASTE OF HOLLAND

Amsterdam, June 12, 1859. A SMALL taste of Holland is sufficient, one place is so exactly like another. . . . The climate is detestable. When the sun shines, the exhalations from the canals make an atmosphere which is the closest and the most unwholesome I ever breathed, and when the sun does not shine, the weather is raw, gray, and cold. The general impression Holland, curious as it is, makes on me, is one of mortal *ennui*. I know no country and people where that word seems to me to apply with such force. You have the feeling which oppresses you so in Suffolk and Norfolk, that it all leads nowhere, that you are not even on the way to any beautiful or interesting country. The Hague is a town of 70,000 people, with a number of streets of excellent houses, bordered with fine trees. I never saw a city where the well-to-do classes seemed to have given the whole place so much their own air of wealth, finished cleanliness, and comfort; but I never saw one, either, in which my heart would have so sunk at the thought of living. —Matthew Arnold, *Letters*.

SPANISH GIRLS

Rodrigo, Spain, 1811. WE INVITED the villagers, every evening, to a dance at our quarters alternately. A Spanish peasant girl has an address about her which I have never met with in the same class of any other country; and she at once enters into society with the ease and confidence of one who had been accustomed to it all her life. We used to flourish away at the bolero, fandango, and waltz, and wound up early in the evening with a supper of roasted chestnuts.

Our village *belles*, as already stated, made themselves perfectly at home in our society, and we, too, should have enjoyed theirs for a season; but, when month after month, and year after year, continued to roll along, without producing any change, we found that the cherry cheek and sparkling eye of rustic beauty furnished but a very poor apology for the illuminated portion of Nature's fairest works, and ardently longed for an opportunity of once more feasting our eyes on a *lady*.—Captain Sir John Kincaid, *Adventures in the Rifle Brigade*.

ICELAND JOURNAL

Brunnar. So ON we stumble: great lumps of lava sticking up here and there above the loose stones and sand, Skialdbrei never changing, and the hills we are making for looking as if they were going back from us. Certainly this is what I came out for to see, and highly satisfactory I find it, nor indeed to-day did it depress me at all. At last we turn the corner of a big black sand-hill, and are off the stones on to sand thickly be-sprinkled with flowers, then these presently disappear, and we ride under the sand-hills over smooth black sand, that stretches far into the distance, getting quite purple at last, till a low bank of sand along a stream side stops it : in which bank is suddenly a scarped place which is deep Indian red. Past the sand hills we get into lava again but of the solid manageable kind : the weather has cleared by now, and we are coming near our supper and bed, and at last can see a patch of green on a little slope side which is verily it. My pony was tired and I had been tailing for some time when I saw the sight; so now I push on at my best, and at last coming over the brow of a shaly slope see it lying before me, a little swampy river and over that a shallow valley, marshy at the bottom but with slopes of firmer grass. I scuttle across the stream and the marsh, and up into the hollow on the slope side where the horses are halted, which is on the edge of a little gully of sand and loam which is handy to make our fire in; and so straightway Magnússon and I go to work with some birch-boughs we have brought from Hawkdale, which we eke out with the resinous crowberry branches, and soon have a fire, whereon we fry a joint (nondescript, Magnússon's butchering, but partaking of the nature of a leg) of lamb parboiled yesterday in the Sigher, then we make a great pot of cocoa, and are very happy in spite of the rain which again comes peppering on our tents: the guides creep under a very primitive tent that Sigurd of Hawkdale has brought with him, and so presently to sleep after a nine hours' ride over much the roughest road I met with in Iceland: Faulkner in good condition.—William Morris, *Journals of Travel in Iceland, 1871–1873.*

LISBON NIGHTS

Lisbon, 29th June, 1787. THESE DAYS and nights of glowing temperature, which oppress me beyond endurance, are the delight and boast of the inhabitants of this capital. The heat seems not only to have new venomed the stings of the fleas and the musquitoes, but to have drawn out, the whole night long, all the human ephemera of Lisbon. They frisk, and dance, and tinkle their guitars from sunset to sunrise. The dogs, too, keep yelping and howling without intermission; and what with the bellowing of litanies by parochial processions, the whizzing of fireworks, which devotees are perpetually letting off in honour of some member or other of the celestial hierarchy, and the squabbles of bullying rake-hells, who scour the streets in search of adventures, there is no getting a wink of sleep, even if the heat would allow it.

As to those quiet nocturnal parties, where ingenuous youths rest their heads, not on the lap of earth, but on that of their mistresses, who are soothingly employed in delivering the jetty locks of their lovers from too abundant a population, I have nothing to say against them, nor am I much disturbed by the dashing sound of a few downfalls from the windows; but these dog-howlings exceed every annoyance of the kind I ever endured, and give no slight foretaste of the infernal regions.—William Beckford, *Italy, Spain, and Portugal.*

SPANISH TUSKES

1620. THE MOST penurious Peasants in the World be heere, whose Quotidian moanes, might draw teares from stones. Their Villages stand as wast like as the Sabunck, Garamont, or Arabian Pavilleons, wanting Gardens, Hedges, Closses, Barnes, or Backe-sides: This sluggish and idle husbandry, being a natural instinct of their neighbour or paternal Moores.

As for industrious Artes, Inventions, and Vertues, they are as dull thereof, as their late Predecessours: and truely I confesse for the Spanish Nunne, she is more holy then the Italian; the former are onely Reserved to the Friers, and Priests: The latter being more Noble, have most affinity, with Gentle-men. The Spaniard is of a spare dyet and temperate, if at his owne cost he spend; but if given Gratis, he hath the longest Tuskes that ever stroke at Table.—William Lithgow, *Rare Adventures and Painfull Peregrinations.*

MARTYRDOM

December, 1795. OTHER PLACES attract the eye of a traveller, but Coruña takes his attention by the nose. My head, still giddy from the motion of the ship, is confused by the multiplicity of novel objects . . . the dress of the people . . . the projecting roofs and balconies of the houses . . . the filth of the streets, so strange and so disgusting to an Englishman: but, what is most strange, is to hear a language which conveys to me only the melancholy reflection, that I am in a land of strangers.

We are at the Navio (*the Ship*) a POSADA, kept by an Italian. Forgive me for using the Spanish name, that I may not commit blasphemy against all English pot-houses. Our dinner was a fowl fried in oil, and served up in an attitude not unlike that of a frog, taken suddenly with a fit of the cramp. With this we had an omelet of eggs and garlic, fried in the same execrable oil; for execrable it is in this land of olives, as the fruit is suffered to grow rancid before the juice is expressed. Our only drink was wine, not the same *vino generoso* with which Spain supplies us in England, but the meagre beverage which the labourers in the vineyard reserve for themselves.

... It is now Monday morning. Oh, the misery of the night! I have been so *flead*, that a painter would find me an excellent subject for the martyrdom of St. Bartholomew. Jacob's pillow of stone was a down cushion, compared to that which bruised my head last night; and my bed had all possible varieties of hill and vale, in whose recesses the fleas lay safe; for otherwise, it was so hard that I should inevitably have broken their bones by rolling over them. Our apartment is indeed furnished with windows; and he who takes the trouble to examine, may convince himself that they have once been glazed. The night air is very cold, and I have only one solitary blanket, but it is a very pretty one, with red and yellow stripes. Add to this catalogue of comforts, that the cats were saying soft things in most vile Spanish: and you may judge what refreshment I have received from sleep.—Robert Southey, *Letters Written during a Journey in Spain and a Short Residence in Portugal.*

GARDEN OF HESPERIDES

Lisbon, Oct. 19th, 1787. MY HEALTH improves every day. The clear exhilarating weather we now enjoy calls forth the liveliest sense of existence. I ride, walk, and climb, as long as I please, without fatiguing myself. The valley of Collares affords me a source of perpetual amusement. I have discovered a variety of paths which lead through chestnut copses and orchards to irregular green spots, where self-sown bays and citron-bushes hang wild over the rocky margin of a little river, and drop their fruit and blossoms into the stream. . . .

The mossy fragments of rock, grotesque pollards, and rustic bridges you meet with at every step, recall Savoy and Switzerland to the imagination; but the exotic cast of the vegetation, the vivid green of the citron, the golden fruitage of the orange, the blossoming myrtle, and the rich fragrance of a turf, embroidered with the brightest-coloured and most aromatic flowers, allow me, without a violent stretch of fancy, to believe myself in the garden of the Hesperides, and to expect the dragon under every tree. I by no means like the thoughts of abandoning these smiling regions, and have been twenty times on the point this very day of revoking the orders I have given for my journey. Whatever objections I may have had to Portugal seem to vanish, since I have determined to leave it; for such is the perversity of human nature, that objects appear the most estimable precisely at the moment when we are going to lose them.—William Beckford, *Italy, Spain, and Portugal.*

ON FIRST SEEING PORTUGAL

'The Hermes', December 13, 1832. I HAVE had before my eyes the last two hours visions such as I can hardly believe to be real: the Portuguese coast, in all that indescribable peculiarity of foreign scenery which paintings attempt. . . . The cliffs are high, composed of sandstone. They form a natural architecture—pyramids, and these in groups. The water, which is beautifully calm, breaks in high foam; the sun is bright and casts large shadows on the rocks and downs. Above, all is exposed, barren, or poorly cultivated; an immense plain, irregularly surfaced, slopes down to the brink of the cliffs, a beautiful pale reddish-brown. Through the glass we see houses, flocks of sheep, windmills with sails like a spider's web, martello towers with men lounging about the walls, woods of cork-trees with very long stems, all as clear and as unnaturally bright as you can fancy. To the south the town Mafra, which we are passing; above the magnificent heights of Torres Vedras. Cintra is to the south, and we are expecting it. It is so very tantalising that we cannot land and really determine that it *is* a country. It is like a vision. It is the first foreign soil I have come near.—John Henry Newman, *Letters*.

THE SIESTA

AND ON the bed? What cool quiet shade in the watered light of jalousie and curtain, of rattan Spanish blind and striped Venetian shutter! There is such burning power outside that each infusion holds a luminescence of its own, as though phosphorus was laid there, original light powdered on the shutters and diffused in green reflection round the room. No sleep at first, the pillow white and cool, the one light-weary fly exhausting the circuit of the walls to drop and buzz itself to death on the tiled floor; and as relaxation takes its course, sheets kicked away and body naked for the shadow's cooling touch, cool as the tiled floor—then what calligraphies astound the walls! What memories come back—for this is the nearest we will ever get to those long-lost hours of childhood's afternoon rest, even to earlier silk-fringed moments in the pram. A prismic jewel stabs the wall by the wardrobe, the shape and size exactly of a rainbow medal-ribbon. The window-covering traces its soft grey pattern on the ceiling, a ribbing of shutters, a tracery of lace, the ghost-grey tasselling of a pelmet huge as a nursery dream. And all these images, with a silent vegetable stealth, moving quietly, slowly round. The room is never still. New shadows wink and play about the chairs, and in the furthest corners. A white jug softly comes to life, stays, withdraws itself. Sometimes, if there is a street outside, the open window-glass and shutter-frame will play a strange projection on the wall—the passing car, and cart, and passer-by will all appear, upside down in silhouette and moving in a soundless swimming way, to show the dreamlife of a world somewhere out and far away continuing. And it is better so. If the room were too precisely still, rest would never seem so precious. It is good to know that else-where there is rest—the old lady in the *comestibles* nodding cool in her rocking-chair, the labourer slumped like a lord in carob-shade, the town-clerk sweating off his rice and wine, coat off and feet up, secure till four o'clock: but it is good also to know that *something* goes on, a tram or an insect, to rarefy this moment stolen from between two of our northern childhoods, the first in the canopied pram, the second allowed only after sixty years of afternoon effort. All afternoons, in the north as well, should surely know the grace of Forty Winks: the financier with his black eye-band knows the value of the couch's half-hour, the Sunday joint is a right-of-way to the armchair by the fire. But for most of our working years this necessary relaxation is energeti-cally denied—at, of course, the cost of energy.—William Sansom, *Blue Skies, Brown Studies,* 1961.

FILTHY TOYS

September 29th, 1815. BRUSSELS HAS been too much modernized, too much Frenchified in all respects. As a specimen of the leprous filthiness with which the French have infected these countries, I saw some toys in a shop window representing men with their loins ungirt, in the attitude of the *Deus Cacaturiens*, each with a piece of yellow metal, like a sham coin, inserted behind. The persons who exhibit such things as these for sale deserve the pillory or the whipping post—the very mob in England would not tolerate them. And where these are exposed, it may easily be guessed what sort of ware is to be found within.—Robert Southey, *Journal of a Tour in the Netherlands.*

IN PRAISE OF MADRID

Circa 1835. I HAVE visited most of the principal capitals of the world, but upon the whole none have ever so interested me as this city of Madrid, in which I now found myself. I will not dwell upon its streets, its edifices, its public squares, its fountains, though some of these are remarkable enough; but Petersburg has finer streets, Paris and Edin-burgh more stately edifices, London far nobler squares, whilst Shiraz can boast of more costly fountains, though not cooler waters. But the population! Within a mud wall, scarcely one league and a half in circuit, are contained two hundred thousand human beings, certainly forming the most extraordinary vital mass to be found in the entire world; and be it always remembered that this mass is strictly Spanish. . . . Here are no colonies of Germans, as St. Petersburg; no English factories, as at Lisbon; no multitudes of insolent Yankees lounging through the streets, as at the Havannah, with an air which seems to say, the land is our own whenever we choose to take it; but a population which, however strange and wild, and composed of various elements, is Spanish, and will remain so as long as the city itself shall exist. Hail, ye aguadores of Asturia! who, in your dress of coarse duffel and leathern skull-caps, are seen seated in hundreds by the fountain sides, upon your empty water casks, or staggering with them filled to the topmost stories of lofty houses. Hail, ye caleseros of Valencia! who, lolling lazily against your vehicles, rasp tobacco for your paper cigars whilst waiting for a fare. Hail to you, beggars of La Mancha! men and women, who, wrapped in coarse blankets, demand charity indifferently at the gate of the palace or the prison. Hail to you, valets from the mountains, mayordomos and secretaries from Biscay and Guipuscoa, toreros from Andalusia, riposteros from Galicia, shopkeepers from Catalonia! Hail to ye, Castilians, Estremenians, and Aragonese, of whatever calling! And lastly, genuine sons of the capital, rabble of Madrid, ye twenty thousand manolos, whose terrible knives, on the second morning of May, worked such grim havoc amongst the legions of Murat!—George Borrow, *The Bible in Spain*.

SWEET CADIZ

Gibraltar, August 6, 1809. CADIZ, SWEET Cadiz!—it is the first spot in the creation.—The beauty of its streets and mansions is only excelled by the loveliness of its inhabitants. For, with all national prejudice, I must confess the women of Cadiz are as far superior to the English women in beauty as the Spaniards are inferior to the English in every quality that dignifies the name of man.—Lord Byron, *Letters*.

A FINE TALE TO TELL

Sunday 11 December (1763). YESTERDAY YOU did very well. You read an immensity of Greek. You was *retenu* yet cheerful at table. It was a dismal day and you eat too much wild duck, so was a little gloomy. However, you said not a word of it, nor have you said a word of it

near these three months. . . . Take long walk to-day to brace you, and
do so every day. Eat less. . . .

Monday 12 December. Yesterday you did delightfully. You did not
commit one fault in any respect the whole day. . . . You was *retenu* at
dinner. You admired *la Comtesse* in church, but not imprudently. You
supped happy and cheerful. In short, for all yesterday you enjoyed
tranquillitatem animi. There is a fine tale to tell. Persist. Relax not
propriety, yet torment not yourself with trifles to be an old woman. . . .
Go to bed exact at twelve. Pick teeth with wood; make toothpicks. At
six Madame Maleprade. Be easy and gay. Approach not love. . . .
—Boswell, *Boswell in Holland*.

FAREWELL TO MADRID

January, 1796. FAREWELL MADRID! I shall say of thee with the Portu-
gueze poet,

> He who likes thee does not know thee;
> He who knows thee does not like thee.

—Robert Southey, *Letters Written during a Journey in Spain and a
Short Residence in Portugal*.

AMUSEMENTS

Hague, July 13, 1728. THIS PLACE, though empty in comparison of
what it is in the winter, is not yet without its recreations. I played at
blind man's buff till past three this morning; we have music in the
Wood; parties out of town; besides the constant amusements of
quadrille and scandal, which flourish and abound. We have even
attempted two or three balls, but with very moderate success; the
ladies here being a little apt to quarrel with one another, insomuch,
that before you can dance down three couples, it is highly probable
that two of them are sat down in a huff. Upon these occasions I show
the circumspection of a minister, and observe a strict neutrality; by
which means I have hitherto escaped being engaged in a war.—Lord
Chesterfield, *Letters*.

THE DUKE AT A CONCERT

Brussels, 1815. OUR LAST entertainment here was a concert in the public
and fine room appropriated for music or dancing. The celebrated
Madame Catalani had a benefit, at which the Queen of the Netherlands
was present, not, however, in state, though not incognita; and the

king of warriors, Marshal Lord Wellington, surrounded by his staff and all the officers and first persons here, whether Belgians, Prussians, Hanoverians, or English. I looked at Lord Wellington watchfully, and was charmed with every turn of his countenance, with his noble and singular physiognomy and his eagle eye. He was gay even to sportiveness all the evening, conversing with the officers around him. He never was seated, not even a moment, though I saw seats vacated to offer to him frequently. He seemed enthusiastically charmed with Catalani, ardently applauding whatsoever she sung, except the Rule, Britannia; and there, with sagacious reserve, he listened in utter silence. Who ordered it I know not, but he felt it was injudicious in every country but our own to give out a chorus of 'Rule, Britannia! Britannia, rule the Waves!'

And when an encore began to be vociferated from his officers, he instantly crushed it by a commanding air of disapprobation, and thus offered me an opportunity of seeing how magnificently he could quit his convivial familiarity for imperious dominion when occasion might call for the transformation.—Fanny Burney, *Diary and Letters of Madame D'Arblay*.

SHIP A-HOY ON THE ROAD

THE HABITS of all Spaniards when on the road are remarkably gregarious; a common fear acts as a cement, while the more they are in number the merrier. It is hail! well met, fellow-traveller! and the being glad to see each other is an excellent introduction. The sight of passangers bound our way is like speaking a strange sail on the Atlantic, *Hola Camara!* ship a-hoy. This predisposition tends to make all travellers write so much and so handsomely of the lower classes of Spaniards, not indeed more than they deserve, for they are a fine, noble race. Something of this arises, because on such occasions all parties meet on an equality; and this levelling effect, perhaps unperceived, induces many a foreigner, however proud and reserved at home, to unbend, and that unaffectedly. He treats these accidental acquaintances quite differently from the manner in which he would venture to treat the lower orders of his own country, who, probably, if conciliated by the same condescension of manner, would appear in a more amiable light, although they are inferior to the Spaniard in his Oriental goodness of manner, his perfect tact, his putting himself and others into their proper place, without either self-degradation or vulgar assumption of social equality or superior physical powers.—Richard Ford, *Gatherings from Spain*, 1846.

K

FRIGHTENING PEOPLE

Byglandssommerhjemmet, Soetersdalen, Norway, Aug. 12th, 1899. You would be amused with the country-people here. Soetersdalen is the most remote, unfriended, melancholy and slow province of Norway, and the only one now where the ancient dress is habitually worn. It is not like the tourist-haunted places where waitresses put on a scarlet bodice and call it their 'costume'. You wander here high up among the woods, and you hear a tinkle of bells, and three kids and a lamb gallop out, and suddenly there stands at your side a being as dark as an Indian and dressed like a hoplite, with a kind of white fustinella showing her long black legs, and a fringe of black shawl waving like feathers about her iron forehead. She is not at all shy—it is you who are shy, and she comes quite close to you and asks questions in a loud, harsh voice and a strange Norrona-dialect as old as the hills. They are the kindest people in Europe, but they frighten me to death.
—*The Life and Letters of Sir Edmund Gosse.*

TURKISH BATH

Adrianople, April 1, O.S. (1717). I won't trouble you with a relation of our tedious journey; but I must not omit what I saw remarkable at Sophia, one of the most beautiful towns in the Turkish empire, and famous for its hot baths, that are resorted to both for diversion and health. I stopped here one day on purpose to see them. Designing to go *incognita*, I hired a Turkish coach. These voitures are not at all like ours, but much more convenient for the country, the heat being so great that glasses would be very troublesome. They are made a good deal in the manner of the Dutch coaches, having wooden lattices painted and gilded; the inside being painted with baskets and nosegays of flowers, inter-mixed commonly with little poetical mottoes. They are covered all over with scarlet cloth, lined with silk, and very often richly embroidered and fringed. This covering entirely hides the persons in them, but may be thrown back at pleasure, and the ladies peep through the lattices. They hold four people very conveniently, seated on cushions, but not raised.

   In one of these covered waggons, I went to the bagnio about ten o'clock. It was already full of women. It is built of stone, in the shape of a dome, with no windows but in the roof, which gives light enough. ... I was in my travelling habit, which is a riding dress, and certainly appeared very extraordinary to them. Yet there was not one of them that shewed the least surprise or impertinent curiosity, but received me with all the obliging civility possible. I know no European court where the ladies would have behaved themselves in so polite a manner to a stranger. I believe in the whole, there were two hundred women, and yet none of those disdainful smiles, or satiric whispers, that never fail in our assemblies when any body appears that is not dressed exactly in the fashion. They repeated over and over to me, 'Uzelle, pék uzelle', which is nothing but Charming, very charming.—The first sofas were covered with cushions and rich carpets, on which sat the ladies; and on the second, their slaves behind them, but without any distinction of rank by their dress, all being in the state of nature, that is, in plain English, stark naked, without any beauty or defect concealed. Yet there was not the least wanton smile or immodest gesture amongst them. They walked and moved with the same majestic grace which Milton describes of our general mother. There were many amongst them as exactly proportioned as ever any goddess was drawn by the pencil of Guido or Titian,—and most of their skins shiningly white, only adorned by their beautiful hair divided into many tresses, hanging on their shoulders, braided either with pearl or ribbon, perfectly representing the figures of the Graces. . . .

In short, it is the women's coffee-house, where all the news of the town is told, scandal invented, &c.—They generally take this diversion once a-week, and stay there at least four or five hours, without getting cold by immediate coming out of the hot bath into the cold room, which was very surprising to me. The lady that seemed the most considerable among them, entreated me to sit by her, and would fain have undressed me for the bath. I excused myself with some difficulty. They being all so earnest in persuading me, I was at last forced to open my shirt, and shew them my stays; which satisfied them very well, for, I saw, they believed I was so locked up in that machine, that it was not in my power to open it, which contrivance they attributed to my husband.—I was charmed with their civility and beauty, and should have been very glad to pass more time with them.—Lady Mary Wortley Montagu, *Letters*.

MISERY

Lisbon, 1796. . . . YOU CANNOT pass a street without being sickened by some huge tumour, some misshapen member, or uncovered wound, carefully exposed to the public eye. These people should not be suffered to mangle the feelings and insult the decency of the passenger: if they will not accept the relief of the hospital, they should be compelled to endure the restraint of the prison. Perhaps you may think I express myself too harshly against these miserable beings: if I were to describe some of the disgusting objects that they force upon observation, you would agree with me in the censure. I do not extend it to the multitude of beggars who weary you at every corner with supplications for the love of God and the Virgin; these wretches, so many and so miserable, do indeed occasion harsh and indignant feelings, not against them, but against that mistaken system of society which disinherits of happiness so large a proportion of the civilized world.— Robert Southey, *Letters Written during a Journey in Spain and a Short Residence in Portugal.*

A BAD START

August 2nd, (1846). UP AT 4 to go by 'Princess Maude'. Picturesque sunrise from the pier. Bruges. Englishman with moustache told us of festival at Bruges. I go down into fore-cabin and get the very worst breakfast I ever had in my life. Arrival at Ostende. Order from Belgian king that no passports need be shown. Inhuman conduct and supererogatory fury of porters. We lose our presence of mind and run for it, but there is plenty of time. Arrive at Bruges, walk to Hôtel de Blé, recommended by moustached Englishman, missing the conveyance thitherward, which, marked with gilt letters Fleur de Blé, rolls by us as we near our hotel. . . . Horsemen riding in a circle for prize. High tower and clock in great square, picturesque groups in Cathedral, motioned from the seats we had taken opposite pulpit, depart to F. de Blé, dinner in salle—affected Englishwoman whom I took for Belge or German opposite, hot nervous night with me. Man 'hemmed' overhead enough to shake the walls of Jericho.—Lord Tennyson, *Journal.*

NOSTALGIA

FOR THE first time in my life I have become a wireless fan. I suppose it is due to being alone in a foreign country. I listen to everything from England, even the cricket matches and the Stock Exchange quotations. —W. H. Auden and Louis MacNeice, *Letters from Iceland,* 1937.

THE DIGNITY OF HUMAN NATURE

Circa 1835. YET TO the honour of Spain be it spoken, it is one of the few countries in Europe where poverty is never insulted nor looked upon with contempt. Even at an inn, the poor man is never spurned from the door, and if not harboured, is at least dismissed with fair words, and consigned to the mercies of God and his mother. This is as it should be. I laugh at the bigotry and prejudices of Spain; I abhor the cruelty and ferocity which have cast a stain of eternal infamy on her history; but I will say for the Spaniards, that in their social intercourse no people in the world exhibit a juster feeling of what is due to the dignity of human nature, or better understand the behaviour which it behoves a man to adopt towards his fellow-beings. I have said that it is one of the few countries in Europe where poverty is not treated with contempt, and I may add, where the wealthy are not blindly idolised. In Spain the very beggar does not feel himself a degraded being, for he kisses no one's feet, and knows not what it is to be cuffed or spitten upon; and in Spain the duke or the marquis can scarcely entertain a very over-weening opinion of his own consequence, as he finds no one, with perhaps the exception of his French valet, to fawn upon or flatter him.—George Borrow, *The Bible in Spain.*

A MEMORY OF THE SPANISH CIVIL WAR

ON THE night before the Spanish army's crossing of the Sigre, the most impressive thing I ever saw in my life, when the whole army knelt at Mass before dawn in those icy highlands, and then plunged chest-deep into the ice-cold water to victory, it was uncanny to hear before lights-out the sultry sound of a *fado*, which I had never imagined could be sung outside of a crowded café in a smoke-filled atmosphere, but even there, transposed so far out of its element amongst the snow-peaks, it seemed to gain rather than lose that weird piercing and hypnotic magic that it has in a crowd, in a smoky, wine-fuming *boîte-de-nuit*, which is its true atmosphere. When next day I stumbled over several armless, discarded torsos of guitars plugged with bullet-holes, they seemed almost as human and pathetic as the dead around them, who had also lost their voices so suddenly after all the cheering, singing, and shouting of the advance. Guitars have, owing to their lovely female curves, always been popular subjects for still-lives. Even to this day, in Lisbon, when I am in the crowded Luso, Mesquita, Tipoia, or Faia, or other *fado* 'joints', with British friends who wish to hear the *fado*, I never see a Portuguese guitar without recalling that strangest and stillest of 'still-lives' composed by dead guitars and men in the icy haunts of the eagle, the bear, and the wolf, on the slopes of the Pyrenees, so utterly and oppositely different from the scene of their origin.—Roy Campbell, *Portugal,* 1957.

BED FELLOWS

December, 1795. AT MIDNIGHT we heard the arrival of a post from Madrid, who awoke the people of the house by cracking his whip. I cannot say he awoke me, for I, like Polonius, was at supper, not where I eat, but where I was eaten. The ingenious gentleman who communicated his discovery to the public, in the Encyclopaedia, that ninety millions of mites' eggs amount exactly to the size of one pigeon's egg, may, if he please, calculate what quantity of blood was extracted from my body, in the course of seven hours; the bed being six feet two and a half, by four feet five, and as populous as possible in that given space. —Robert Southey, *Letters Written during a Journey in Spain and a Short Residence in Portugal.*

STATION SCENE

'THIS IS Zagreb!' cried the Germans and took all their luggage down from the racks. Then they broke into excessive cries of exasperation and distress because it was not Zagreb, it was Zagreb-Sava, a suburb three or four miles out of the main town. I leaned out of the window. Rain was falling heavily, and the mud shone between the railway tracks. An elderly man, his thin body clad in a tight-fitting, flimsy overcoat, trotted along beside the train, crying softly, 'Anna! Anna! Anna!' He held an open umbrella not over himself but at arm's length. He had not brought it for himself, but for the beloved woman he was calling. He did not lose hope when he found her nowhere in all the long train, but turned and trotted all the way back, calling still with anxious sweetness, 'Anna! Anna! Anna!' When the train steamed out he was trotting along it for a third time, holding his umbrella still further away from him. A ray of light from an electric standard shone on his white hair, on the dome of his umbrella, which was streaked with several rents, and on the strong spears of the driving rain. I was among people I could understand.—Rebecca West, *Black Lamb and Grey Falcon*, 1946.

NO RIGHT TO EXIST

Paris, Sunday, June 19, 1859. WHAT WOUNDS one's feelings in Holland is the perpetual consciousness that the country has no business there at all. You see it all below the level of the water, soppy, hideous, and artificial; and because it exists against nature, nobody can exist there except at a frightful expense, which is very well for the natives, who may be thankful to live on any terms, but disagreeable for foreigners, who do not like to pay twice as much as elsewhere for being half as comfortable. .... It was a dull, cold, blustering day,—unluckily, we have too many of them in England,—and when we finally landed and looked back across the broad Maas at the cloudy plains and trees of Holland, I felt that we had got into the real world again, though I dislike Belgium, and think the Belgians, on the whole, the most contemptible people in Europe.—Matthew Arnold, *Letters*.

MEETING WITH A GOATHERD

Circa 1835. UPON THE shoulder of the goatherd was a beast, which he told me was a lontra, or otter, which he had lately caught in the neighbouring brook; it had a string round its neck, which was attached to his arm. At his left side was a bag, from the top of which peered the heads of two or three singular-looking animals, and at his right was squatted the sullen cub of a wolf, which he was endeavouring to tame; his whole appearance was to the last degree savage and wild. After a little conversation such as those who meet on the road frequently hold, I asked him if he could read, but he made me no answer. I then inquired if he knew anything of God or Jesus Christ; he looked me fixedly in the face for a moment, and then turned his countenance towards the sun, which was beginning to sink in the west, nodded to it, and then again looked fixedly upon me. I believe that I understood the mute reply, which probably was, that it was God who made that glorious light which illumines and gladdens all creation; and gratified with that belief, I left him and hastened after my companions, who by this time were a considerable way in advance.—George Borrow, *The Bible in Spain*.

ADVICE

Tuesday 18 October (1763). YOU WAS a little irregular yesterday, but it was but for one day to see the Utrecht concert. You don't like it, and you're not to go any more. ....—Boswell, *Boswell in Holland*.

THE LORDLY LIFE

Athens, January 20th, 1811. I AM living in the Capuchin Convent, Hymettus before me, the Acropolis behind, the Temple of Jove to my right, the Stadium in front, the town to the left; eh, Sir, there's a situation, there's your picturesque! nothing like that, Sir, in Lunnun, no, not even the Mansion House. And I feed upon Woodcocks and Red Mullet every day, and I have three horses (one a present from the Pasha of the Morea), and I ride to Piraeus, and Phalerum, and Munychia, which however don't look quite so magnificent after the harbours

of Cadiz, Lisbon, Constantinople and Gibraltar, not forgetting Malta.
I wish to be sure I had a few books, one's own works for instance, any
damned nonsense on a long Evening.—Lord Byron, *Letters*.

ON EXPECTING NOTHING

LET NOT the traveller expect to find too much; if he reckons on finding
nothing he will seldom be disappointed; so let him not look for five
feet in a cat, '*no busces cinco pies al gato*'. Spain, as the East, is not to be
enjoyed by the over-fastidious in the fleshly comforts: there, those who
over analyze, who peep too much behind the culinary or domestic
curtains, must not expect to pass a tranquil existence.—Richard Ford,
Gatherings from Spain, 1846.

THACKERAY IN ATHENS

1844. I SWEAR solemnly that I would rather have two hundred a year
in Fleet Street, than be King of the Greeks, with Basileus written before
my name round their beggarly coin; with the bother of perpetual
revolutions in my huge plaster-of-Paris palace, with no amusement but
a drive in the afternoon over a wretched arid country, where roads are
not made, with ambassadors (the deuce knows why, for what good can
the English, or the French, or the Russian party get out of such a
bankrupt alliance as this?) perpetually pulling and tugging at me, away
from honest Germany, where there is beer and aesthetic conversation,
and operas at a small cost. The shabbiness of this place actually beats
Ireland, and that is a strong word. The palace of the Basileus is an
enormous edifice of plaster, in a square containing six houses, three
donkeys, no roads, no fountains (except in the picture of the inn);
backwards it seems to look straight to the mountain—on one side is a
beggarly garden—the King goes out to drive (revolutions permitting)
at five—some four-and-twenty blackguards saunter up to the huge
sandhill of a terrace, as his Majesty passes by in a gilt barouche and an
absurd fancy dress; the gilt barouche goes plunging down the sand-
hills; the two dozen soldiers, who have been presenting arms, slouch
off to their quarters; the vast barrack of a palace remains entirely
white, ghastly, and lonely; and, save the braying of a donkey now and
then (which long-eared minstrels are more active and sonorous in
Athens than in any place I know), all is entirely silent round Basileus's
palace. How could people who knew Leopold fancy he would be so
'jolly green' as to take such a berth? It was only a gobemouche of a
Bavarian that could ever have been induced to accept it.—W. M.
Thackeray, *A Journey from Cornhill to Cairo*.

TURKISH DIET

1809–1810. EVERY READER is sufficiently acquainted with the Turks, to know the sort of viands usual at their tables: but I must say of them, that many are very palatable to an English taste, much more so, indeed, than those to be met with in Portuguese and Spanish cookery. There is a dish of chopped mutton, rolled up with rice highly seasoned, called *ypraik*, and a large thin pasty of fowl, or spinach sprinkled with sugar; both of which are very commendable. Oil is not often used, but butter, which, it must be confessed, is now and then very strong, and would be called by us, grease. The *sherbet* is but a very poor liquor, being only sweet water sometimes coloured with marygold flowers, and a few blanched almonds swimming on the top of it. It is handed round at the conclusion of the dinner, and either drunk out of the bowl, or sipped with large horn spoons. The boiled and roast are always done to rags, to suit not only the taste, but the convenience of a people, who do not eat with knives and forks, but with their fingers, making use of a thin crumplet instead of a plate, and each man tearing off his portion from the joint before him, with his right hand only, for his left is supposed to be employed on services that render it very unfit to be thrust into a plate containing common stock.—J. C. Hobhouse, *A Journey Through Albania and Provinces of Turkey in Europe and Asia.*

PUBLIC-HOUSE MANNERS

Villa Leonardi, Riva, Sud Tirol, Austria. . . . AUSTRIA IS funny—so easygoing. The officials are all Chocolate Soldiers. They let you walk through the Customs with a good day. At Trient there was a great crowd at the ticket office—and the train came. So a man—a high station official—sauntered up and told them to buck up. It made no difference. You know the free-and-easy manners of men in a pub— the Austrians have always got 'em—their jolly public-house manners. —D. H. Lawrence, *Letters*, 1932.

SPOTLESS ROTTERDAM

Rotterdam, Friday, Aug 3, O.S. (1716). . . . MY ARRIVAL at Rotterdam presented me a new scene of pleasure. All the streets are paved with broad stones, and before the meanest artificers' doors seats of various-coloured marbles, and so neatly kept, that, I will assure you, I walked almost all over the town yesterday, *incognita*, in my slippers, without receiving one spot of dirt; and you may see the Dutch maids washing the pavement of the street with more application than ours do our bed-chambers. . . . Here is neither dirt nor beggary to be seen. One is not shocked with those loathsome cripples, so common in London, nor teazed with the importunities of idle fellows and wenches, that choose to be nasty and lazy. The common servants and little shop-women here are more nicely clean than most of our ladies; and the great variety of neat dresses (every woman dressing her head after her own fashion) is an additional pleasure in seeing the town.—Lady Mary Wortley Montagu, *Letters*.

BELLS

(Near Liège), Oct. 6, 1815. THE CHURCH bells were very loud, frequent and troublesome—this annoyance alone would have told us that we were in a Catholic country.—Robert Southey, *Journal of a Tour in the Netherlands*.

RAPTURE

Circa 1835. THE DAY was intensely hot, notwithstanding the coldness of the preceding nights; and the brilliant sun of Portugal now illumined a landscape of entrancing beauty. Groves of cork trees covered the farther side of the valley and the distant acclivities, exhibiting here and there charming vistas, where various flocks of cattle were feeding; the soft murmur of the stream, which was at intervals chafed and broken by huge stones, ascended to my ears and filled my mind with delicious feelings. I sat down on the broken wall and remained gazing, and listening, and shedding tears of rapture; for, of all the pleasures which a bountiful God permitteth His children to enjoy, none are so dear to some hearts as the music of forests and streams, and the view of the beauties of His glorious creation. An hour elapsed, and I still main-tained my seat on the wall; the past scenes of my life flitting before my eyes in airy and fantastic array, through which every now and then peeped trees and hills and other patches of the real landscape which I was confronting; the sun burnt my visage, but I heeded it not; and I believe that I should have remained till night, buried in these reveries, which, I confess, only serve to enervate the mind, and steal many a minute which might be most profitably employed, had not the report of a gun of a fowler in the valley, which awakened the echoes of the woods, hills, and ruins, caused me to start on my feet, and remember that I had to proceed three leagues before I could reach the hostelry where I intended to pass the night.—George Borrow, *The Bible in Spain*.

SPANISH MANNERS

Gibraltar, August 6, 1809. WE LODGED in the house of two Spanish unmarried ladies, who possess *six* houses in Seville, and gave me a curious specimen of Spanish manners. They are women of character, and the eldest a fine woman, the youngest pretty, but not so good a figure as Donna Josepha. The freedom of manner, which is general here, astonished me not a little; and in the course of further observation, I find that reserve is not the characteristic of the Spanish belles, who are, in general, very handsome, with large black eyes, and very fine forms. The eldest honoured your *unworthy* son with very particular attention, embracing him with great tenderness at parting (I was there but three days), after cutting off a lock of his hair, and presenting him with one of her own, about three feet in length, which I send, and beg you will retain till my return. Her last words were, 'Adios, tu hermoso! me gusto mucho.'—'Adieu, you pretty fellow! you please me much.' She offered me a share of her apartment, which my *virtue* induced me to decline; she laughed, and said I had some English 'amante' (lover), and added that she was going to be married to an officer in the Spanish army.—Lord Byron, *Letters*.

A SPANISH HOUSEHOLD

Spain, December 10th, 1787. WE DINED at a village called Brabo, not in the least worth mentioning, and arrived in due tiresome course, about six in the evening, at Santa Olaya, where my courier had procured us an admirable lodging in the house of a veteran colonel. The principal apartment, in which I pitched my bed, was a lofty gallery, with large folding glazed doors, gilt and varnished, its white walls almost covered with saintly pictures and small mirrors, stuck near the ceiling, beyond the reach of mortal sight, as if their proprietor was afraid they would wear out by being looked into. On low tables, to the right and left of the door, stood glass cases, filled with relics and artificial flowers. Stools covered with velvet, and raised not above a foot from the floor, were stationed all round the room. On one of these I squatted like an Oriental, warming my hands over a brazier of coals.

The old lady of the house, followed by a train of curtseying handmaids and sniffling lapdogs, favoured me with her company the best part of the evening. Her spouse, the colonel, being indisposed, did not make his appearance. Whilst she was entertaining me with a most flourishing detail of the excellent qualities and wonderful acquisitions of the Infant Don Louis, who died about two years ago at his villa in this neighbourhood, some very grotesque figures entered the ante-chamber, and tinkling their guitars, struck up a seguidilla, that in a minute or two set all the feet in the house in motion. Amongst the dancers, two young girls, whose jetty locks were braided with some degree of elegance, shone forth in a fandango, beating the ground and snapping their fingers with rapturous agility.

This sport lasted a full hour, before they showed the least sign of being tired; then succeeded some langourous tirannas, by no means so delightful as I expected. I was not sorry when the ball ceased, and my kind hostess, moving off with all her dogs and dancers, left me to sup and sleep in tranquillity.—William Beckford, *Italy, Spain, and Portugal.*

ALBANIAN ROBBERS

1834. . . . 'IT IS no use resisting; we are caught; there are too many of them.' So I bolted the locks of the four barrels of my pistol carefully, hoping that the bolts would form an impediment to my being shot with my own weapon after I had been robbed of it. The place was so narrow that there were no hopes of running away, and there we sat on horseback, looking silly enough, I dare say. There was a good deal of talking and chattering among the robbers, and they asked the Albanian various questions to which I paid no attention, all my faculties being engrossed in watching the proceedings of the party in front, who were examining the effects in the panniers of the baggage mule. First they pulled out my bag of clothes, and threw it upon the ground; then out came the sugar and the coffee, and whatever else there was. Some of the men had hold of the poor muleteer, and a loud argument was going on between him and his captors. I did not like all this, but my rage was excited to a violent pitch when I saw one man appropriating to his own use the half of a certain fat tender cold fowl, whereof I had eaten the other half with much appetite and satisfaction. 'Let that fowl alone, you scoundrel!' said I in good English; 'put it down, will you? if you don't, I'll——!' The man, surprised at this address in an unknown tongue, put down the fowl, and looked up with wonder at the explosion of ire which his actions had called forth. 'That is right', said I, 'my good fellow, it is too good for such a dirty brute as you.'—Hon. Robert Curzon, *Monasteries of the Levant.*

THE RETIRED GENERAL

. . . THE BRITISH colony lived what appeared to be a life of blameless monotony, rolling about in small cars, drinking at the yacht club, sailing a bit, going to church, and suffering agonies of apprehension at the thought of not being invited to Government House on the Queen's birthday. One saw the murk creeping up over Brixton as one listened to their conversations. No doubt Malta and Gibraltar have similar colonies. How often they have been described and how wearisome they are. Yet my compatriots were decent, civil folk, who had been brought here, not by any desire to broaden minds cumbered only by the problems of indolence and trade, but by a perfectly honourable passion for sunlight and low income tax. How sad it is that so many of our national characteristics are misinterpreted! Our timidity and lack of imagination seem to foreigners to be churlishness, our taciturnity the deepest misanthropy. But are these choking suburbanisms with which we seem infused when we are abroad any worse than the tireless dissimulation and insincerity of the Mediterreanean way of life? I doubt it. Yet Manoli the chemist lived in a perpetual ferment of indignation about British manners, British standoffishness and so on. His particular hate was General Envy. He would perform a little dance of rage as he saw the old soldier sauntering down the main street, patronizing not only the poor Cypriots but the very morning air by the self-confident sweep of his tobacco-stained moustache. 'Look at him', he would say. 'I could throw a tomato at him.' Then one day the General asked him how to pronounce the Greek for 'potato' and shyly showed him a shopping list which he had laboriously made out in Greek. After that Manoli would flush with annoyance if ever he heard a word spoken against the old fellow. He became, for Manoli at least, a saint; and yet the General, as all who remember him will agree, was a vile old bore with scarce manners and little enough consideration for the world around him. 'Such a good, kind man', Manoli would say after the General's canonization, rolling his dark eyes and nodding. 'Such a *worthy* and *respected* man.' This is what happened whenever Briton and Cypriot met, even to exchange the merest civility.—Lawrence Durrell, *Bitter Lemons*, 1957.

THE MAGIC TINKLE

THE SOUND principles in Spanish sight-seeing are few and simple, but, if observed, they will generally prove successful; first, persevere; never be put back; never take an answer if it be in the negative; never lose temper or courteous manners; and lastly, let the tinkle of metal be heard at once; if the chief or great man be inexorable, find out privately who is the wretched sub who keeps the key, or the crone who sweeps the room; and then send a discreet messenger to say that you will pay to be admitted, without mentioning 'nothing to nobody'. Thus you will always obtain your view, even when an official order fails. On our first arrival at Madrid, when but young in these things of Spain, we were desirous of having daily permission to examine a royal gallery, which was only open to the public on certain days in the week. In our grave dilemma we consulted a sage and experienced diplomatist, and this was the oracular reply:—'Certainly, if you wish it, I will make a request to Señor Salmon (the then Home Secretary), and beg him to give you the proper order, as a personal favour to myself. By the way, how much longer shall you remain here?'—'From three to four weeks.'—'Well, then, after you have been gone a good month, I shall get a courteous and verbose epistle from his Excellency, in which he will deeply regret that, on searching the archives of his office, there was no instance of such a request having ever been granted, and that he is compelled most reluctantly to return a refusal, from the fear of a precedent being created. My advice to you is to give the porter a dollar, to be repeated whenever the door-hinges seem to be getting rusty and require oiling.' The hint was taken, as was the bribe, and the prohibited portals expanded so regularly, that at last they knew the sound of our footsteps. Gold is the Spanish *sesame*.—Richard Ford, *Gatherings from Spain*, 1845.

BAGGAGE

Albania, 1809–1810. . . . OUR BAGGAGE was weighty; but, I believe, we could not have done well with less, as a large quantity of linen is necessary for those who are much at sea, or travel so fast as not to be able to have their clothes washed. Besides four large leathern trunks, weighing about eighty pounds when full, and three smaller trunks, we had a canteen, which is quite indispensable; three beds, with bedding, and two light wooden bedsteads. The latter article some travellers do not carry with them; but it contributes so much to comfort and health, as to be very recommendable. We heard, indeed, that in Asiatic Turkey you cannot make use of bedsteads, being always lodged in the hans or inns; but in Europe, where you put up in cottages and private houses, they are always serviceable, preserving you from vermin, and the damp of mud floors, and possessing advantages which overbalance the evils caused by the delays of half an hour in packing and taking them to pieces.—J. C. Hobhouse, *A Journey Through Albania and Provinces of Turkey in Europe and Asia*.

OLD TURKISH HOUSE

Herzegovina, 1937. 'COME IN, come in', cried the man in the frock-coat, placing himself between us and Trebinye. 'I will show you all, old Turkish house, where the great pasha kept his harem, all very fine.' He drove us up the stairs, and shepherded us through the main door into a little room, which in its day had been agreeable enough. Pointing at the latticed windows he said richly, 'The harem was here, beautiful Turkish women wearing the beautiful Turkish clothes.' He opened a cupboard and took out a collection of clothes such as may be found in any old-clothes shop in those provinces of Yugoslavia that were formerly occupied by the Turks. 'Very fine, all done by hand', he said of the gold-braided jackets and embroidered bodices. 'And look, trousers!' He held up before us a garment of white lawn, folded at the ankle into flashy gold cuffs, which can never have been worn by any lady engaged in regular private harem work. 'Transparent', he said. It was evident that he was affected by a glad pruritis of the mind. Coyly he sprang to another cupboard and brought out a mattress. 'The bed was never left in the room', he said; 'they took it out when it was needed.' There was unluckily a third cupboard, with a tiled floor and an ewer. 'This was the bathroom, here is where the Turkish lady kept herself clean, all Turkish ladies were very clean and sweet.' He assumed a voluptuous expression, cocked a hip forward and put a hand on it, lifted the ewer upside-down over his head, and held the pose.— Rebecca West, *Black Lamb and Grey Falcon*, 1946.

THE PROTESTANT EYE

(Near Liège), 1815. THEY BROUGHT us grapes and Gruyère cheese at breakfast. The butter was marked with the I.H.S.—a mark of devotion I believe—not the initials of the vendor.—Robert Southey, *Journal of a Tour in the Netherlands*.

Part IV

WIDER HORIZONS

LUGGAGE

MY PROVISIONS were prepared for me by the Bovril Company after instructions furnished by me, with a view to the severe Tibetan climate and the altitudes we should find ourselves in. They contained a vast amount of fat and carbonaceous food, as well as ingredients easily digestible and calculated to maintain one's strength even in moments of unusual stress. I had them packed in tin cases and skin bags. I carried in a water-tight box 1000 cartridges for my .256 Männlicher rifle, besides 500 cartridges for my revolver, and a number of hunting knives, skinning implements, wire traps of several sizes for capturing small mammals, butterfly nets, bottles for preserving reptiles in alcohol, insect-killing bottles (cyanide of potassium), a quantity of arsenical soap, bone nippers, scalpels, and all other accessories necessary for the collection of natural history specimens. . . . I had two sets of instruments for astronomical observation and for use in surveying (one of which had been furnished me by the Royal Geographical Society), such as the six-inch sextant, hypsometrical apparatus for measuring heights, with boiling-point thermometers specially constructed for very great altitudes; two aneroids, one to 20,000 feet, the other to 25,000 feet; three artificial horizons (one mercury, the others plate-glass with levels); a powerful telescope with astronomical eyepiece and stand; a prismatic, a luminous, a floating, and two pocket compasses; maximum and minimum thermometers, a case of drawing instruments, protractors, parallel rules, tape rules, a silver water-tight half-chronometer watch and three other watches, section paper in books and in large sheets, Raper's and the Nautical Almanac for 1897 and 1898.—Henry Savage-Landor, *In the Forbidden Land*, 1899.

THE ALMIGHTY DOLLAR

1832. I HEARD an Englishman, who had been long resident in America, declare that in following, in meeting, or in overtaking, in the street, on the road, or in the field, at the theatre, the coffee-house, or at home, he had never overheard Americans conversing without the word DOLLAR being pronounced between them. Such unity of purpose, such sympathy of feeling, can, I believe, be found nowhere else, except, perhaps, in an ants' nest. The result is exactly what might be anticipated. This sordid subject, for ever before their eyes, must inevitably produce a sordid tone of mind, and worse still, it produces a seared and blunted conscience on all questions of probity.—Mrs Frances Trollope, *Domestic Manners of the Americans.*

A MEAL IN THE WEST INDIES

St. Thomas, West Indies, 1859. A HOT climate, it is generally thought, interferes with the appetite, affects the gastric juices with lassitude, gives to the stomach some of the apathy of the body, and lessens at any rate the consumption of animal food. That charge cannot be made against the air of St. Thomas. To whatever sudden changes the health may be subject, no lingering disinclination for food affects it. Men eat there as though it were the only solace of their life, and women also. Probably it is so.

They never talk at meals. A man and his wife may interchange a word or two as to the dishes; or men coming from the same store may whisper a syllable as to their culinary desires; but in an ordinary way there is no talking. I myself generally am not a mute person at my meals; and having dined at sundry tables d'hôte have got over in a great degree that disinclination to speak to my neighbour which is attributed—I believe wrongly—to Englishmen. But at St. Thomas I took it into my head to wait till I was spoken to, and for a week I sat, twice daily, between the same persons without receiving or speaking a single word.

I shall not soon forget the stout lady who sat opposite to me, and who was married to a little hooked-nosed Jew, who always accompanied her. Soup, fish, and then meat is the ordinary rule at such banquets; but here the fashion is for the guests, having curried favour with the waiters, to get their plates of food brought in and put round before them in little circles; so that a man while taking his soup may contemplate his fish and his roast beef, his wing of fowl, his allotment of salad, his peas and potatoes, his pudding, pie, and custard, and whatever other good things a benevolent and well-fee'd waiter may be able to collect for him. This somewhat crowds the table, and occasionally it becomes necessary for the guest to guard his treasures with an eagle's eye. . . .

This stout lady was great on such occasions. 'A bit of that', she would exclaim, with head half turned round, as a man would pass behind her with a dish, while she was in the very act of unloading within her throat a whole knifeful charged to the hilt. The efforts which at first affected me as almost ridiculous advanced to the sublime as dinner went on. There was no shirking, no half measures, no slackened pace as the breath became short. The work was daily done to the final half-pound of cheese. Anthony Trollope, *The West Indies and the Spanish Main,* 1860.

BREAKFAST MANNERS

1861. ONE IS in a free country and has come from a country in which one has been brought up to hug one's chains,—so at least the English traveller is constantly assured—and yet in an American inn one can never do as one likes. A terrific gong sounds early in the morning, breaking one's sweet slumbers, and then a second gong sounding some thirty minutes later, makes you understand that you must proceed to breakfast, whether you be dressed or no. You certainly can go on with your toilet and obtain your meal after half an hour's delay. Nobody actually scolds you for so doing, but the breakfast is, as they say in this country, 'through'. You sit down alone, and the attendant stands immediately over you. Probably there are two so standing. They fill your cup the instant it is empty. They tender you fresh food before that which has disappeared from your plate has been swallowed. They begrudge you no amount that you can eat or drink; but they begrudge you a single moment that you sit there neither eating nor drinking. This is your fate if you are too late, and therefore as a rule you are not late.... Then the dinner comes early; at least it always does so in New England, and the ceremony is much of the same kind. You came there to eat, and the food is pressed on you almost *ad nauseam.* But as far as one can see there is no drinking. In these days, I am quite aware, that drinking has become improper, even in England. We are apt at home to speak of wine as a thing tabooed, wondering how our fathers lived and swilled. I believe that as a fact we drink as much as they did; but nevertheless that is our theory. I confess, however, that I like wine.... After dinner, if all that I hear be true, the gentlemen occasionally drop into the hotel bar and 'liquor up'. Or rather this is not done specially after dinner, but without prejudice to the hour at any time that may be found desirable. I also have 'liquored up', but I cannot say that I enjoy the process. I do not intend hereby to accuse Americans of drinking much, but I maintain that what they do drink, they drink in the most uncomfortable manner that the imagination can devise.—Anthony Trollope, *North America.*

A VISIT TO MOSCOW

WE ARRIVED at the season of the year in which this city is most interesting to strangers. *Moscow* is in every thing extraordinary; as well in disappointing expectation, as in surpassing it; in causing wonder and derision, pleasure and regret. Let the Reader be conducted back again to the gate by which we entered, and thence through the streets. Numerous spires, glittering with gold, amidst burnished domes and painted palaces, appear in the midst of an open plain, for several versts before you reach this gate. Having passed, you look about, and wonder what is become of the city, or where you are; and are ready to ask, once more, How far is it to *Moscow?* They will tell you, 'This is *Moscow!*' and you behold nothing but a wide and scattered suburb, huts, gardens, pig-sties, brick walls, churches, dunghills, palaces, timber-yards, warehouses, and a refuse, as it were, of materials sufficient to stock an empire with miserable towns and miserable villages. One might imagine all the States of EUROPE and ASIA had sent a building, by way of representative to *Moscow*: and under this impression the eye is presented with deputies from all countries, holding congress: timber-huts from regions beyond the ARCTIC; plastered palaces from SWEDEN and DENMARK, not white-washed since their arrival; painted walls from the TIROL; mosques from CONSTAN-TINOPLE; Tahtar temples from BUCHARIA; pagodas, pavilions, and virandas, from CHINA; cabarets from SPAIN; dungeons, prisons, and public offices, from FRANCE; architectural ruins from ROME; terraces and trellisses from NAPLES; and warehouses from WAPPING.—E. D. Clarke, *Travels in Various Countries of Europe, Asia and Africa,* 1810–23.

STORM

Vailima, Christmas Eve, 1890. YESTERDAY, WHO could write? My wife near crazy with ear-ache; the rain descending in white crystal rods and playing hell's tattoo, like a *tutti* of battering rams, on our sheet-iron roof; the wind passing high overhead with a strange dumb mutter, or striking us full, so that all the huge trees in the paddock cried aloud, and wrung their hands, and brandished their vast arms. The horses stood in the shed like things stupid. The sea and the flagship lying on the jaws of the bay vanished in sheer rain. All day it lasted; I locked up my papers in the iron box, in case it was a hurricane, and the house might go. We went to bed with mighty uncertain feelings; far more than on shipboard, where you only have drowning ahead—whereas here you have a smash of beams, a shower of sheet-iron, and a blind race in the dark and through a whirlwind for the shelter of an unfinished stable—and my wife with ear-ache! Well, well, this morning, we had word from Apia; a hurricane was looked for, the ships were to leave the bay by 10 a.m.; it is now 3.30, and the flagship is still a fixture and

the wind round in the blessed east, so I suppose the danger is over.
But heaven is still laden; the day dim, with frequent rattling bucketfuls
of rain; and just this moment (as I write) a squall went overhead,
scarce striking us, with that singular, solemn noise of its passage,which
is to me dreadful. I have always feared the sound of wind beyond
everything. In my hell it would always blow a gale.—R. L. Stevenson,
Letters.

CANADIAN INN

1861. I HAVE said that the Canadians hereabouts are somewhat slow.
As we were driving back to Sherbrooke it became necessary that we
should rest for an hour or so in the middle of the day, and for this
purpose we stopped at a village inn. It was a large house, in which
there appeared to be three public sitting-rooms of ample size, one of
which was occupied as the bar. In this there were congregated some
six or seven men, seated in arm-chairs round a stove, and among these
I placed myself. No one spoke a word either to me or to any one else.
No one smoked, and no one read, nor did they even whittle sticks. I
asked a question first of one and then of another, and was answered
with monosyllables. So I gave up any hope in that direction, and sat
staring at the big stove in the middle of the room, as the others did.
Presently another stranger entered, having arrived in a waggon as I
had done. He entered the room and sat down, addressing no one, and
addressed by no one. After a while, however, he spoke. 'Will there be
any chance of dinner here?' he said. 'I guess there'll be dinner by-and-
by', answered the landlord, and then there was silence for another ten
minutes, during which the stranger stared at the stove. 'Is that dinner
any way ready?' he asked again. 'I guess it is', said the landlord. And
then the stranger went out to see after his dinner himself. When we
started at the end of an hour nobody said anything to us. The driver
'hitched' on the horses, as they call it, and we started on our way,
having been charged nothing for our accommodation. That some
profit arose from the horse provender is to be hoped.—Anthony
Trollope, *North America*.

HOSPITALITY

Gulahek (Persia), June 18, 1892. WELL IN this country the men wear
flowing robes of green and white and brown, the women lift the veil
of a Raphael Madonna to look at you as you pass; wherever there is
water a luxuriant vegetation springs up and where there is not there is
nothing but stone and desert. Oh the desert round Teheran! miles and

miles of it with nothing, *nothing* growing; ringed in with bleak bare mountains snow crowned and furrowed with the deep courses of torrents. I never knew what desert was till I came here; it is a very wonderful thing to see; and suddenly in the middle of it all, out of nothing, out of a little cold water, springs up a garden. Such a garden! trees, fountains, tanks, roses and a house in it, the houses which we heard of in fairy tales when we were little: inlaid with tiny slabs of looking-glass in lovely patterns, blue tiled, carpeted, echoing with the sound of running water and fountains. Here sits the enchanted prince, solemn, dignified, clothed in long robes. He comes down to meet you as you enter, his house is yours, his garden is yours, better still his tea and fruit are yours, so are his kalyans (but *I* think kalyans are a horrid form of smoke, they taste to me of charcoal and paint and nothing else). By the grace of God your slave hopes that the health of your nobility is well? It is very well out of his great kindness. Will your magnificence carry itself on to this cushion? Your magnificence sits down and spends ten minutes in bandying florid compliments through an interpreter while ices are served and coffee, after which you ride home refreshed, charmed, and with many blessings on your fortunate head. And all the time your host was probably a perfect stranger into whose privacy you had forced yourself in this unblushing way. Ah, we have no hospitality in the west and no manners. I felt ashamed almost before the beggars in the street—they wear their rags with a better grace than I my most becoming habit, and the veils of the commonest women (now the veil is the touchstone on which to try a woman's toilette) are far better put on than mine. A veil should fall from the top of your head to the soles of your feet, of that I feel convinced, and it should not be transparent.

Say, is it not rather refreshing to the spirit to lie in a hammock strung between the plane trees of a Persian garden and read the poems of Hafiz—in the original mark you!—out of a book curiously bound in stamped leather which you have bought in the bazaars. That is how I spend my mornings here; a stream murmurs past me which Zoroastrian gardeners guide with long handled spades into tiny sluices leading into the flower beds all around. The dictionary which is also in my hammock is not perhaps so poetic as the other attributes—let us hide it under our muslin petticoats!—Gertrude Bell, *Letters*.

POWERFUL NATURE

Calcutta, 1784. HAVING FROM my earliest youth been of an amorous disposition I began to feel the effects of a long continence. I therefore one night sent for a native woman, but the moment I lay myself down upon the bed all desire ceased, being succeeded by disgust. I could think of nothing but her I had for ever lost, and the bitter recollection rendered me so miserable that I sent off my Hindostanee companion untouched. The same circumstance occurred to me three successive times. Nature, however, at last proved too powerful to be surmounted, and I subsequently ceased to feel the horror that at first prevailed at the thought of a connection with black women, some of whom are indeed very lovely, nor is it correct to call them black, those that come from the Upper Provinces being very fair.—William Hickey.

THE HOLY MAN

AT PESHAWAR we were seized with one of our periodical financial panics. Money, in this country, slips rapidly between the fingers, particularly between the fingers of the tourist. Great wads of it have to be handed out every time one gets into the train; for fares are high and distances enormous. No place in India seems to be less than three hundred miles from any other place; the longer journeys have to be measured in thousands. Financial panics are justifiable. We decided to travel second class as far as Lahore.

For the first hour or so we were alone in our compartment. We congratulated ourselves on having secured all the comfort and privacy of first-class travelling at exactly half the price. In future, we decided, we would always travel second. But Nature abhors a vacuum, and our compartment was evidently the object of her special abhorrence. When the train stopped at Campbellpur, we were invaded. In the twinkling of an eye our luxurious emptiness was filled to overflowing with luggage and humanity. And what queer specimens of humanity! The leader of the party which now entered the compartment was a middle-aged man wearing a yellow robe and, on his head, a kind of quilted bonnet with hanging ear-flaps. He was profusely garlanded with yellow chrysanthemums, and had been followed on to the platform by a large crowd of flower-bearing admirers and devotees. Our ignorance of the language did not permit us to discover who this exalted person might be. But he was evidently some kind of high priest, some Hindu pope of considerable holiness, to judge by the respect which was paid him by his numerous retinue and his admirers. His passage along the line must have been well advertised; for at every station our compartment was invaded by a swarm of devotees who came to kiss the great man's feet and to crave a blessing, which in most cases he seemed too lazy to give. Even the guards and ticket-collectors and stationmasters came in to pay their respects. The enthusiasm of one ticket-collector was so great

that he travelled about thirty miles in our already packed compartment, simply in order to be near the holy man. He, meanwhile, passed
the time by counting his money, which was contained in a large brass-
bound box, by loudly eating, and, later, dozing. Even at the stations
he did not take the trouble to rouse himself, but reclined with closed
eyes along his seat, and passively permitted the faithful to kiss his feet.
When one is as holy as he evidently was, it is unnecessary to keep up
appearances, behave decently, or do anything for one's followers.
Office and hereditary honour claim the respect of a believing people
quite as much as personal merit. . . .

Meanwhile, the crowd in our compartment increased. The day, as
it advanced, grew hotter. And suddenly the holy man woke up and
began to hoick and spit all over the compartment. By the time we
reached Rawal Pindi we had decided that the twenty-two rupees we
should economize by remaining seven hours longer among our second-
class brothers were not enough. We had our luggage transferred into a
first-class carriage and paid the difference. The only other occupant of
the compartment was an English official of the Kashmir State, bound
for his winter headquarters at Jammu. He was a dim little man; but at
any rate his linen was clean, and he was not in the least holy. Nobody
came in to kiss his feet.—Aldous Huxley, *Jesting Pilate*, 1926.

A DINNER IN RIO

Rio Janeiro, Dec. 15th, (1806). I DINED in what they call a cooking-
house. The host showed us into a miserable back room looking into
the kitchen, where was a black fellow cooking. My stomach was not
yet turned. No glass in the window (but that is the case with all the
houses, except those of the grandees), and the light shining through the
pantiles over our heads. We had for dinner first some macaroni soup,
half oil, and scraped cheese to eat with it; afterwards some mutton
chops swimming in grease, pork chops in a similar way, a pair of fowls
we could scarcely pull to pieces, not an atom of flesh on their bones.
There was also a piece of thin beef rolled up with the stuffing in it and
roast—a famous dish for a hungry mastiff dog. These being removed,
we then had a cold plum-pudding, which was very good. We drank at
dinner bad American bottled ale, afterwards some decent port wine.
When we called for our bill, we were all amazingly astonished. It came
to 4880—*whats*, we could not tell. We afterwards found it was about
six dollars. They give you always their bills in that way in some
imaginary coin about half a farthing value.—Sir Harry Smith, *Autobiography*.

GHOST TOWN

October 6th, 187–. ONTONAGAN IS a name which the Indian translated
for me in two different ways: firstly, 'the-place-where-a-young-girl-
cried-because-she-dropped-her-panniken-into-the-water';   secondly,
'the-place-where-a-man-shot-a-man-through-a-place-without-seeing-
him',—I suppose he meant that one gentleman had fired through the
bush in the direction in which he supposed another gentleman to be,
and had bagged him. . . . The black desolation of the spot is not to be
described. It was only after a long search that a spark of life could be
discovered, but then it was bright enough. A scientific watchmaker
from Brighton, who sells specimens which are never bought, publishes
a monthly gazette, and drinks lager beer, a young lady who teaches
music but has no pupils, and rears canary birds, and a German gentleman who sells lager beer, and everything else, in the neatest and tidiest
wooden cottages, and reads a monthly gazette, are the most prominent,
if not the only inhabitants. A vast wooden hotel, the whitened sepulchre
of many thousands of dollars, looms high above the surrounding level,
its flagstaff blown down, its halls deserted. . . . All is desolation; stores
have descended into hotels, hotels have descended into Hades, their
signs hanging askew for want of the nail which it would not pay to
expend on them. Vast wharves, crumbling and falling piece-meal into
the water, masses of valuable machinery rusting and sinking by their
own weight into the mud, utter bankruptcy. One boarding-house there
is, conducted on temperance principles, probably because the landlord,
Mr. Paul, feels that he would be obliged to drink himself to death with
his own liquor if he had any. In addition to the few miners who are
still left, and some explorers who are still hungrily seeking after
wealth, it has a permanent clustage consisting of the telegraph clerk,
who, the wires being broken, enjoys a sinecure, and the gentleman
who assists in the store. It is comfortable and clean, and there is a
sufficiency of well-cooked food, which Mr. Paul dispenses to us, three
times a day, with his own hands, relieving his labours by occasionally
stalking about the room and spitting as heavily as if he thought we all
had evil eyes.—George Henry Kingsley, *Notes on Sport and Travel*.

HOTEL ROOM

Herat (Afghanistan), November 26th, 1933. As I shall probably be
here for the rest of my life (which won't last long at this rate), I have
had my room cleaned out. I must describe it, and indeed the whole
hotel. Downstairs three large rooms with glass fronts give on to the

street. The first is the kitchen, indicated by a pool of blood and a decapitated cock's head on the pavement. The second and third are filled with marble-topped tables, and hung with European scenes painted on glass by an Indian familiar with the early numbers of the *Illustrated London News*. . . . Adjoining the kitchen, an outside staircase leads up to a long corridor lit by skylights, which has rooms on either side. My room is at the back, where it avoids part of the coppersmiths' din: a square box, with a ceiling of bare poles and laths, white walls, and a sky-blue dado. The floor is paved with tiles, whose interstices secrete a cloud of dust and straw; half of it is covered with a carpet, and half the rest with my bedding and waterproof sheets. Two Windsor chairs and a table draped in white American cloth are the furniture. On the table stands a vase of blue and white spirals adorned with a pink glass rose—the kind you win at hoop-la—in which Seyid Mahmud has placed a tight round posy of yellow chrysanthemums enclosing a ring of chocolate red ones enclosing a centre of yellow button daisies. A pewter basin and a graceful ewer enable me to wash on the bare part of the floor. My bedding consists of a green flea-bag, yellow sheepskin coat, and an Afghan quilt of scarlet chintz. Beside it, my lamp, Boswell, clock, cigarettes, and a plate of grapes are conveniently disposed on a despatch-case . . . . I have had a nail put in for my ties, another for my hat, and a third for my looking-glass. If the door and the window were not opposite one another, if the door would shut and the window had its full complement of panes, I should be comfortable enough. But the draught is like a storm at sea. All the refuse goes out of the window into the garden of the Municipality.

I caught my breath just now as I stepped into the moonlit corridor. Four rifles menaced my stomach, aimed by four ghostly figures cloaked in white, who were squatting in the room opposite. I could see the glitter of their eyes in the dark beneath their dim white turbans. Four others had their backs to me and their rifles pointing out of the window. No doubt it was just a pleasant evening party. But the Muntazim-i-Telegraph had been croaking again this morning about the coming upheaval, and I wondered for a moment if Amanullah had actually arrived.—Robert Byron, *The Road to Oxiana*.

THE PASHA'S HANDKERCHIEF

Egypt, 1834. WE DISCOURSED for three quarters of an hour about the possibility of laying a railway across the Isthmus of Suez, which was the project then uppermost in the Pasha's mind; but the circumstance which most strongly recalls this audience to my memory, and which struck me as an instance of manners differing entirely from our own, was, in itself, a very trivial one. The Pasha wanted his pocket handkerchief, and looked about and felt in his pocket for it, but could not find it, making various exclamations during his search, which at last were answered by an attendant from the lower end of the room—'Feel in the other pocket', said the servant. 'Well, it is not there', said the Pasha. 'Look in the other, then.' 'I have not got a handkerchief', or words to that effect, were replied to immediately—'Yes, you have'; —'No, I have not';—'Yes, you have.' Eventually this attendant, advancing up to the Pasha, felt in the pocket of his jacket, but the handkerchief was not to be found; then he poked all round the Pasha's waist, to see whether it was not tucked into his shawl: that would not do. So he took hold of his Sovereign and pushed him half over on the divan, and looked under him to see whether he was sitting on the handkerchief; then he pushed him over on the other side. During all which manœuvres the Pasha sat as quietly and passively as possible. The servant then, thrusting his arm up to the elbow in one of the pockets of his Highness's voluminous trousers, pulled out a snuff-box, a rosary, and several other things, which he laid upon the divan. That would not do, either; so he came over to the other pocket, and diving to a prodigious depth he produced the missing handkerchief from the recesses thereof; and with great respect and gravity, thrusting it into the Pasha's hand, he retired again to his place at the lower end of the hall.—Hon. Robert Curzon, *Monasteries of the Levant.*

SEA-SICKNESS

Bahia, or San Salvador, Brazil, (February 8, 1832). IN THE Bay of Biscay there was a long and continuous swell, and the misery I endured from sea-sickness is far beyond what I ever guessed at. I believe you are curious about it. I will give you all my dear-bought experience. Nobody who has only been to sea for twenty-four hours has a right to say that sea-sickness is even uncomfortable. The real misery only begins when you are so exhausted that a little exertion makes a feeling of faintness come on. I found nothing but lying in my hammock did me any good. I must especially except your receipt of raisins, which is the only food that the stomach will bear.—Charles Darwin, *Letters.*

GERTRUDE BELL AND THE ARABS

Bagdad, Feb. 16th, 1922. I WANT to tell you, just you, who know and understand everything, that I'm acutely conscious of how much life has given me. I've gone back now to the wild feeling of joy in existence—

I'm happy in feeling that I've got the love and confidence of a whole nation, a very wonderful and absorbing thing—almost too absorbing perhaps. You must forgive me if it seems to preoccupy me too much— it doesn't really divide me from you, for one of the greatest pleasures is to tell you all about it, in the certainty that you will sympathise. I don't for a moment suppose that I can make much difference to our ultimate relations with the Arabs and with Asia, but for the time I'm one of the factors in the game. I can't think why all these people here turn to me for comfort and encouragement; if I weren't here they would find someone else, of course, but being accustomed to come to me, they come. And in their comfort I find my own. I remember your saying to me once that the older one grows the more one lives in other people's lives. Well, I've got plenty of lives to live in, haven't I? And perhaps after all, it has been best this way.—Gertrude Bell, *Letters.*

AFRICAN MUSIC

I KNOW I am no musician, so I own to loving African music, bar that Fernandian harp! Like Benedick, I can say, 'Give me a horn for my money when all is done', unless it be a tom-tom. The African horn, usually made of a tooth of ivory, and blown from a hole in the side, is an instrument I unfortunately cannot play on. I have not the lung capacity. It requires of you to breathe in at one breath a whole S.W. gale of wind and then to empty it into the horn, which responds with a pre- liminary root-too-toot before it goes off into its noble dirge bellow. It is a fine instrument and should be introduced into European orchestras, for it is full of colour. But I think that even the horn, and certainly all other instruments, savage and civilised, should bow their heads in homage to the tom-tom, for, as a method of getting at the inner soul of humanity where are they compared with that noble instrument! You doubt it. Well go and hear a military tattoo or any performance on kettle drums up here and I feel you will reconsider the affair; but even then, remember you have not heard all the African tom-tom can tell you. I don't say it's an instrument suited for serenading your lady-love with, but that is a thing I don't require of an instrument.—Mary Kingsley, *West African Studies,* 1899.

WEIRD AUSTRALIA

Thirroul, South Coast, N.S.W., 22nd June, 1922. IF YOU want to know what it is to feel the 'correct' social world fizzle to nothing, you should come to Australia. It *is* a weird place. In the *established* sense, it is socially nil. Happy-go-lucky, don't-you-bother, we're-in-Australia. But also there seems to be no inside life of any sort: just a long lapse and drift. A rather fascinating indifference, a *physical* indifference to what we call soul or spirit. It's really a weird show. The country has an extraordinary hoary, weird attraction. As you get used to it, it seems so *old*, as if it had missed all this Semite-Egyptian-Indo-European vast era of history, and was coal age, the age of great ferns and mosses. It hasn't got a consciousness—just none—too far back. A strange effect it has on one. Often I hate it like poison, then again it fascinates me, and the spell of its indifference gets me. I can't quite explain it: as if one resolved back almost to the plant kingdom, before souls, spirits and minds were grown at all: only quite a live, energetic body with a weird face.—D. H. Lawrence, *Letters*.

FEROCIOUS WOMEN

1861. FOR MYSELF, I have entertained on sundry occasions that sort of feeling for an American woman which the close vicinity of an unclean animal produces. I have spoken of this with reference to street cars, because in no position of life does an unfortunate man become more liable to these anti-feminine atrocities than in the centre of one of these vehicles. The woman, as she enters, drags after her a misshapen, dirty mass of battered wirework, which she calls her crinoline, and which adds as much to her grace and comfort as a log of wood does to a donkey when tied to the animal's leg in a paddock. Of this she takes much heed, not managing it so that it may be conveyed up the carriage with some decency, but striking it about against men's legs, and heaving it with violence over people's knees. The touch of a real woman's dress is in itself delicate; but these blows from a harpy's fins are loathsome. If there be two of them they talk loudly together, having a theory that modesty has been put out of court by women's rights. But, though not modest, the woman I describe is ferocious in her propriety. She ignores the whole world around her, and as she sits with raised chin and face flattened by affectation, she pretends to declare aloud that she is positively not aware that any man is even near her. She speaks as though to her, in her womanhood, the neighbourhood of men was the same as that of dogs or cats.—Anthony Trollope, *North America*.

SLAUGHTER-HOUSE

1832. IT SEEMS hardly fair to quarrel with a place because its staple commodity is not pretty, but I am sure I should have liked Cincinnati much better if the people had not dealt so very largely in hogs. The immense quantity of business done in this line would hardly be believed by those who had not witnessed it. I never saw a newspaper without remarking such advertisements as the following:

'Wanted, immediately, 4,000 fat hogs.'

'For sale, 2,000 barrels of prime pork.'

But the annoyance came nearer than this; if I determined upon a walk up Main Street, the chances were five hundred to one against my reaching the shady side without brushing by a snout fresh dripping from the kennel; when we had screwed our courage to the enterprise of mounting a certain noble-looking sugar-loaf hill, that promised pure air and a fine view, we found the brook we had to cross, at its foot, red with the stream from a pig slaughter-house; while our noses, instead of meeting 'the thyme that loves the green hill's breast', were greeted by odours that I will not describe, and which I heartily hope my readers cannot imagine; our feet, that on leaving the city had expected to press the flowery sod, literally got entangled in pigs' tails and jaw-bones; and thus the prettiest walk in the neighbourhood was interdicted for ever.—Mrs Frances Trollope, *Domestic Manners of the Americans*.

TIPPLING

1817–1819. THERE IS one thing in the Americans, which. . . I have reserved, or rather *kept back*, to the last moment. It has presented itself several times; but I have turned from the thought, as men do from thinking of any mortal disease that is at work in their frame. It is not covetousness; it is not niggardliness; it is not insincerity; it is not enviousness; it is not cowardness, above all things: it is DRINKING. Aye, and that too, amongst but too many men who, one would think, would loath it. You can go into hardly any man's house, without being asked to drink wine, or spirits, even *in the morning*. They are quick at meals, are little eaters, seem to care little about what they eat, and never talk about it. This, which arises out of the universal abundance of good and even fine eatables, is very amiable. You are here disgusted with none of those *eaters* by *reputation* that are found, especial *amongst the Parsons*, in England: fellows that *unbutton* at it. Nor do the Americans *sit and tope much after dinner*, and talk on till they get into nonsense and *smut*, which last is a sure mark of a silly and, pretty generally, even of a base mind. But, they *tipple*: and the infernal spirits they tipple, too! The scenes that I witnessed at Harrisburgh I shall never forget.— William Cobbett, *A Year's Residence in America*.

WATER OF THE EUPHRATES

Circa 1909. THE WATER of the Euphrates is much esteemed by the inhabitants of its banks. It is, I think, an acquired taste; the newcomer will be apt to look askance at the turgid liquid that issues from the spout of his teapot and to question whether a decoction of ancient dust can be beneficial to the European constitution. Gertrude Bell, *Amurath to Amurath.*

ARRIVAL OF THE DALAI LHAMA

ON THE 25th October, 1906, Mr. Ridley and I rode out to Sining to see the Dalai Lhama arrive. The roads were lined with the grotesque Chinese soldier, with his straw hat and pink coat of cotton cloth which hangs on him like a sack, and his very ancient gun. The Chinese onlookers had come out of their town partly because they had nothing else to do, and partly because Chinamen must see everything that is going on; but no one was overpleased with their guest, whom they had to supply with enforced hospitality. In fact, for months before the Mandarin of Sining had been collecting pots and pans, and even tables, from the cottages of the poor.

As is the case at most functions of this sort, we waited for a long time for any sign of the Dalai Lhama's coming. At last, in the far distance, we heard the shrieking of a Chinese band, then, as the diabolical noise came closer, amidst a great cloud of dust some five or six Chinamen emerged, shuffling along in a gait which was neither a walk nor a run. They were dressed as they liked, played as they liked, and shuffled where they liked. Next came the Standard Bearers, in the same order, who were in considerable danger of being run down by the horsemen behind them. They carried long poles with red flags, and all manner of curiously designed spears which you see outside the Chinese Yamens, and are emblems of authority and justice. Now came the mounted Tibetans, in wonderful long yellow coats and curious hats made of gilded wood, riding rough, high-spirited little ponies, which did not lend dignity to the spectacle. Suddenly a distinguished looking Tibetan galloped out of the crowd and shouted to the on-lookers to kow-tow. We dismounted from our ponies, but refused to do more, so he left us and harangued the Chinese, who were quite indifferent and only laughed and said rude things, as our English crowd sometimes does to our respected metropolitan police, who have learnt to take it better than our irate friend.—J. W. Brooke, *Through China to Tibet in 1906.*

M

PARADISE

IN THE South Seas the Creator seems to have laid Himself out to show what He *can* do. Imagine an island with the most perfect climate in the world, tropical, yet almost always cooled by a breeze from the sea. No malaria or other fevers. No dangerous beasts, snakes, or insects. Fish for the catching, and fruits for the plucking. And an earth and sky and sea of immortal loveliness. What more could civilisation give? Umbrellas? Rope? Gladstone bags? . . . Any one of the vast leaves of the banana is more waterproof than the most expensive woven stuff. And from the first tree you can tear off a long strip of fibre that holds better than any rope. And thirty seconds' work on a great palm-leaf produces a basket-bag which will carry incredible weights all day, and can be thrown away in the evening. A world of conveniences. And the things which civilisation has left behind or missed by the way are there, too, among the Polynesians: beauty and courtesy and mirth. I think there is no gift of mind or body that the wise value which these people lack. A man I met in some other islands, who had travelled much all over the world, said to me, 'I have found no man, in or out of Europe, with the good manners and dignity of the Samoan, with the possible exception of the Irish peasant'. A people among whom an Italian would be uncouth, and a high-caste Hindu vulgar, and Karsavina would seem clumsy, and Helen of Troy a frump.—Rupert Brooke, *Letters from America*, 1916.

SINGULAR COSTUMES

Afghanistan, 1933. ENGROSSED BY the contrast with Persia, I return the people's stare. The appearance of the ordinary Persian, as dressed by Marjoribanks's [1] sumptuary laws, is a slur on human dignity; impossible, one thinks, for this swarm of seedy mongrels to be really the race that have endeared themselves to countless travellers with their manners, gardens, horsemanship, and love of literature. How the Afghans may endear themselves remains to be seen. Their clothes and their walk are credential enough to begin with. A few, the officials, wear European suits, surmounted by a dashing lambskin hat. The townsmen too sport an occasional waistcoat in the Victorian style, or the high-collared frock-coat of the Indian Mussulman. But these importations, when accompanied by a turban as big as a heap of

[1] R. Byron's name for the Shah of Persia.

bed-clothes, cloak of parti-coloured blanket, and loose white peg-topped trousers reaching down to gold-embroidered shoes of gondola shape, have an exotic gaiety, like an Indian shawl at the Opera. This is the southern fashion, favoured by the Afghans proper. The Tajiks, or Persian element, prefer the quilted gown of Turkestan. Turcomans wear high black boots, long red coats, and busbies of silky black goats' curls. The most singular costume is that of the neighbouring highlanders, who sail through the streets in surtouts of stiff white serge, dangling false sleeves, almost wings, that stretch to the back of the knee and are pierced in patterns like a stencil. Now and then a calico bee-hive with a window at the top flits across the scene. This is a woman.

Hawk-eyed and eagle-beaked, the swarthy loose-knit men swing through the dark bazaar with a devil-may-care self-confidence. They carry rifles to go shopping as Londoners carry umbrellas.—Robert Byron, *The Road to Oxiana*.

HOMESICKNESS

Sydney, January, 1836. I MUST feed upon the future, and it is beyond bounds delightful to feel the certainty that within eight months I shall be residing once again most quietly in Cambridge. Certainly, I never was intended for a traveller; my thoughts are always rambling over past or future scenes; I cannot enjoy the present happiness for anticipating the future, which is about as foolish as the dog who dropped the real bone for its shadow.—Charles Darwin, *Letters*.

BEAUTY OF THE CAMEL

WHEN the sun was setting, we saw another camel troop not far off. The herdsmen trotting round upon some of their lighter beasts were driving-in the great cattle to a sheltered place between two hills; for this night closed starless over our heads with falling weather. When we came to them the young men had halted their camels and were hissing to them to kneel,—*ikh-kh-kh!* The great brutes fall stiffly, with a sob, upon one or both their knees, and underdoubling the crooked hind legs, they sit ponderously down upon their haunches. Then shuffling forward one and the other fore-knee, with a grating of the harsh gravel under their vast carcase-weight, they settle themselves, and with these pains are at rest; the fore-bulk-weight is sustained upon the ẓôra;[1] so they lie still and chaw their cud, till the morning sun. The

[1] The pillar-like stay under the camel's chest.

camel leaves a strange (reptile-like) print (of his knees, of the *ǵóra*, and of the sharp hind quarters), which may be seen in the hard wilderness soil after even a year or two. The smell of the camel is muskish and a little dog-like, the hinder parts being crusted with urine; yet is the camel more beautiful in our eyes than the gazelles, because man sees in this creature his whole welfare. . . .—Charles Doughty, *Travels in Arabia Deserta*, 1888.

DEPRESSING CHRISTMAS

(Cawnpore), Monday (Christmas Day), Dec. 25, 1837. I DON'T know why, but I am particularly *Indianly* low to-day. There is such a horrid mixture of sights and sounds for Christmas. The servants have hung garlands at the doors of our tents, and (which is very wrong) my soul recoiled when they all assembled, and in their patois wished us, I suppose, a happy Christmas.

Somehow a detestation of the Hindustani language sounding all round us, came over me in a very inexplicable manner.

Then, though nothing could be better than the way in which Mr. Y. performed the service, still it was in a tent, and unnatural, and we were kneeling just where the Prince of Lucknow and his son, and their turbaned attendants, were sitting on Saturday at the durbar, and there was nobody except G.[1] with whom I felt any real communion of heart and feelings. So, you see, I just cried for you and some others, and I daresay I shall be better after luncheon.—Emily Eden, *Up the Country*.

RUSSIAN TYRANNY

THE PICTURE of Russian manners varies little with reference to the Prince or the peasant. The first nobleman in the empire, when dismissed by his Sovereign from attendance upon his person, or withdrawing to his estate in consequence of dissipation and debt, betakes himself to a mode of life little superior to that of brutes. You will then find him, throughout the day, with his neck bare, his beard lengthened, his body wrapped in a sheep's skin, eating raw turnips, and drinking *quass*; sleeping one half of the day, and growling at his wife and family the other. The same feelings, the same wants, wishes, and gratifications, then characterize the nobleman and the peasant; and the same system of tyranny, extending from the throne downwards, through all the

---

[1] G.—George Eden, Earl of Auckland and Governor-General, Emily's brother.

bearings and ramifications of society, even to the cottage of the lowest
boor, has entirely extinguished every spark of liberality in the breasts
of a people composed entirely of slaves. They are all, high and low,
rich and poor, alike servile to superiors; haughty and cruel to their
dependants; ignorant, superstitious, cunning, brutal, barbarous, dirty,
mean. The Emperor canes the first of his grandees; princes and nobles
cane their slaves; and the slaves, their wives and daughters. Ere the sun
dawns in Russia, flagellation begins; and throughout its vast empire,
cudgels are going, in every department of its population, from morning
until night.—E. D. Clarke, *Travels in Various Countries of Europe,
Asia and Africa,* 1810–23.

TIBET CAMP

1849–51.ON ASCENDING a low hill, we came in sight of the Tibet camp
at the distance of a mile, when the great mastiffs that guarded it
immediately bayed; and our ponies starting off at full gallop, we soon
reached an enclosure of stone dykes, within which the black tents were
pitched. The dogs were of immense size, and ragged, like the yaks,
from their winter coat hanging to their flanks in great masses; each
was chained near a large stone, on and off which he leapt as he gave
tongue; they are very savage, but great cowards, and not remarkable
for intelligence.

The people were natives of Gearee and Kambajong, in the adjacent
province of Dingcham, which is the loftiest, coldest, most windy and
arid in Eastern Tibet. . . . Both men and women were indescribably
filthy; as they never wash, their faces were perfectly black with smoke
and exposure, and the women's with a pigment of grease as a protection
from the wind. The men were dressed as usual, in the blanket-cloak,
with brass pipes, long knives, flint, steel, and amulets; the women
wore similar, but shorter cloaks, with silver and copper girdles,
trowsers, and flannel boots. Their head-dresses were very remarkable.
A circular band of plaited yak's hair was attached to the back hair, and
encircled the head like a saint's glory, at some distance round it. A
band crossed the forehead, from which coins, coral, and turquoises
hung down to the eyebrows, while lappets of these ornaments fell over
the ears. Their own hair was plaited in two tails, brought over the
shoulders, and fastened together in front; and a little yellow felt cap,
traversely elongated, so as not to interfere with the shape of the glory,
was perched on the head. Their countenances were pleasing, and their
manners timid.

The children crawled half-naked about the tent, or burrowed like
moles in an immense heap of goats' and sheep-droppings, piled up for

fuel, upon which the family lounged. An infant in arms was playing with a 'coral', ornamented much like ours, and was covered with jewels and coins. This custom of decorating children is very common amongst half-civilised people; and the coral is, perhaps, one of the last relics of a barbarous age that is retained amongst ourselves. One mother was nursing her baby, and churning at the same time, by rolling the goat-skin of yak-milk about on the ground. Extreme poverty induces the practice of nursing the children for years; and in one tent I saw a lad upwards of four years of age unconcernedly taking food from his aunt, and immediately afterwards chewing hard dry grains of maize.—Sir Joseph Dalton Hooker, *Himalayan Journals*.

RICE TABLE

MY GASTRONOMIC experiences in Holland led me to expect a no less fabulous profusion in Colonial Java. But I was disappointed, or perhaps relieved, to find that the hotels catered not for giants but for men and women only about twice life size. The only truly Rabelaisian feature of Javanese diet is the Rice Table. The Rice Table must be seen, and eaten, to be believed. Without the co-operation of the gullet, faith cannot swallow it. I do not even expect those who have never eaten a Rice Table to believe my description. Marco Polo, when he returned from the court of the Great Khan, full of true stories and correct statistics, was by his compatriots derisively nicknamed 'Marco Milione'. For the sake of the truth about Rice Tables, I am prepared with old Mark Million to be thought a liar; here then it is—the truth, literal but unbelievable.

It is lunch time. You enter the dining-room of the hotel. A little old yellow waiter, looking less like a man than a kindly orang-utan, shaved and with a batik handkerchief tied round its head, shows you to your place, asks what you will eat. You push aside the menu of the commonplace European lunch.

'Ane Rice Tafel for mich', you say, combining German and Lowland Scotch into what you believe, quite erroneously, to be the language of Holland. The kindly little monkey-man trots off, smiling; it seems to please him when his clients decide on the Rice Table. You wait. In a little while the monkey-man's embassy to the kitchen has its effect. A waiter appears at your elbow with an enormous cauldron of rice; you heap your plate with it. He moves away. Immediately another waiter takes his place, offering fish soup. You damp your rice; the soup man goes. A dish of chops at once replaces the tureen. Looking round, you see that the chop carrier is standing at the head of a long procession of Javanese waiters, extending in unbroken line from your table right across the dining-room to the kitchen door. Each time you help yourself, the procession advances a step and a new dish is presented. I took the trouble one day to count the number of dishes offered me. Twenty-six actually appeared before me; but it was a busy day for the waiters and I do not think I got all the dishes I was entitled to. They included after the chops, two other kinds of meat, two kinds of bird, a species of sausage; fish, both fresh and dried; roast bananas; several kinds of vegetables, plain and curried; two varieties of salads; fried nuts; numerous pickles; jam; a queer kind of unleavened bread, and various other things which I cannot at the moment remember. All these articles are thoroughly stirred in with the rice on your plate —a trough would be more suitable receptacle—the napkin is tucked firmly into place beneath the chin, and leaning forward you shovel the immense and steaming mound of food down your throat.—Aldous Huxley, *Jesting Pilate*, 1926.

A FORD IN TURKESTAN

Maimena, May 22, 1934. THREE CARS stood in the Governor's garden at Murghab. One was the lifeless body of a grey Ford coupé. The others were Vauxhalls, new, dark red, and closed; when it rained, they were covered with tarpaulins. Early in the morning after our arrival, the Governor and his son drove away in the Vauxhall, to Maruchak on the Russian frontier. We looked forlornly at the Ford's engine scattered over the surrounding vegetable-beds and ordered horses.

'I can take you to Maimena in the car if you like,' said a Persian boy named Abbas, plucking the radiator out of a bush. 'We will start in an hour.'

The likelihood of covering more than two or three of the intervening hundred miles in this preposterous vehicle seemed so remote that we took none of the usual precautions before starting, prepared no food, disdained, if only out of courtesy to the driver, to count the car's spare parts, and even went so far as to wear our so-called best suits. The luggage was put into the back, where it reached to the ceiling. When Christopher and I stepped into the front, the chassis subsided a foot, as if we had been the mother-in-law in a slap-stick film. Abbas was winding the crank handle. Suddenly his arm flew over his head, the noise of a blacksmith's shop proceeded from the now collected engine, and we bounded across the Governor's flower-beds, while Abbas, in flying pursuit, just reached the wheel in time to turn us through the gate. Down the main street the population fled; in a minute we were through the town and tearing up a deserted valley.

The luggage fell out of the unglazed window. The radiator, playing fountains to the sky, first declined to the earth in front, then fell backwards on top of the engine, entangling itself in the fan, till we roped it up with our bedding cords. The sound of the machinery became apocalyptic, clanking and fizzing without any sort of rhythm till at last, with a final deafening cannonade, it ceased altogether and Abbas beamed at us with the expression of a conductor laying down his baton after an applauded symphony. A sympathetic report from the near hind tyre, though a beat late, announced that it also needed rest for the moment. We had come ten miles.—Robert Byron, *The Road to Oxiana.*

GEOLOGICAL PROBLEMS

East Falkland Island, March, 1834. I AM quite charmed with Geology, but, like the wise animal between two bundles of hay, I do not know which to like the best; the old crystalline group of rocks, or the softer and fossiliferous beds. When puzzling about stratification, &c., I feel inclined to cry 'a fig for your big oysters, and your bigger megatheriums'. But then when digging out some fine bones, I wonder how any man can tire his arms with hammering granite. By the way I have not one clear idea about cleavage, stratification, lines of upheaval. I have no books which tell me much, and what they do I cannot apply to what I see. In consequence I draw my own conclusions, and most gloriously ridiculous ones they are, I sometimes fancy. . . . Can you throw any light into my mind by telling me what relation cleavage and planes of deposition bear to each other?—Charles Darwin, *Letters.*

THE MISSISSIPPI

1842. BUT WHAT words shall describe the Mississippi, great father of rivers, who (praise be to Heaven) has no young children like him! An enormous ditch, sometimes two or three miles wide, running liquid mud, six miles an hour: its strong and frothy current choked and obstructed everywhere by huge logs and whole forest trees: now twining themselves together in great rafts, from the interstices of which a sedgy lazy foam works up, to float upon the water's top; now rolling past like monstrous bodies, their tangled roots showing like matted hair; now glancing singly by like giant leeches; and now writhing round and round in the vortex of some small whirlpool, like wounded snakes. The banks low, the trees dwarfish, the marshes swarming with frogs, the wretched cabins few and far apart, their inmates hollow-cheeked and pale, the weather very hot, mosquitoes penetrating into every crack and crevice of the boat, mud and slime on everything: nothing pleasant in its aspect, but the harmless lightning which flickers every night upon the dark horizon. . . .

We drank the muddy water of this river while we were upon it. It is considered wholesome by the natives, and is something more opaque than gruel. I have seen water like it at the Filter-shops, but nowhere else.—Charles Dickens, *American Notes*.

A PALACE IN DECAY

Camp, Delhi, Feb. 20, 1838. IN THE afternoon we all . . . went to see the palace. It is a melancholy sight—so magnificent originally, and so poverty-stricken now. The marble hall where the king sits is still very beautiful, all inlaid with garlands and birds of precious stones, and the inscription on the cornice is what Moore would like to see in the original: 'If there be an Elysium on earth, it is this, it is this!'.

The lattices look out on a garden which leads down to the Jumma, and the old king was sitting in the garden with a chowrybadar waving the flies from him; but the garden is all gone to decay too, and 'the Light of the World' had a forlorn and darkened look. All our servants were in a state of profound veneration; the natives all look upon the King of Delhi as their rightful lord, and so he is, I suppose. In some of the pavilions belonging to the princes there were such beautiful inlaid floors, any square of which would have made an enviable table for a palace in London, but the stones are constantly stolen; and in some of the finest baths there were dirty charpoys spread, with dirtier guards sleeping on them. In short, Delhi is a very suggestive and moralising place—such stupendous remains of power and wealth passed and passing away—and somehow I feel that we horrid English have just 'gone and done it', merchandised it, revenued it, and spoiled it all. I am not very fond of Englishmen out of their own country. And Englishwomen did not look pretty at the ball in the evening, and it did not tell well for the beauty of Delhi that the painted ladies of one regiment, who are generally called 'the little corpses' (and very hard it is too upon most corpses) were much the prettiest people there, and were besieged with partners.—Emily Eden, *Up the Country*.

NIGHT IN THE DESERT

THE SUN going down left us drowned in the drooping gloom, which was soon dark night. We held on our march in hope to meet with the Arab, and there fell always a little rain. Serpentine lightning flickered over the ground before us, without thunder; long creasted lightnings shot athwart and seemed suspended, by moments, in the wide horizon; other long cross flashes darted downward in double chains of light. The shape of all those lightnings was as an hair of wool that is fallen in water. Only sometimes we heard a little, not loud, roaring of thunder. In a lull of the weather we beheld the new moon, two days old, at her going down. The first appearing of the virgin moon is always greeted with a religious emotion in the deserts of Arabia, and we saluted her, poor night-wanderers, devoutedly; the day by my reckoning should be the 23rd of April. We held on ever watching for the Beduin fires, and heard about us the night shrieks of I know not what wild birds. At length Hàmed thought he had seen a watch-fire glimmer far in front. As we rode further we saw it sometimes, and otherwhiles it was hidden by the uneven ground of the wilderness. The night darkness was very thick, the *nâga* [1] stumbled, and we could not see the earth. Hàmed, whose wit ever failed a little short of the mark, began to be afraid we might fall from some cragged place: he would adventure no further. We had nothing to eat, and alighting with wet clothes, we lay down in the rain beside our camel; but the wind blew softly, and we soon slept.—Charles Doughty, *Travels in Arabia Deserta*, 1888.

NATIVE LOTUS EATERS

From Papieti, Tahiti, 27th August 1870. BUT I cannot tell you all the wonderful things we've seen—besides, some of them were not quite proper. The natives are happy, contented lotus-eaters. . . . They are far higher, far more beautiful, more graceful than the Maoris, and are bubbling over with life and good-humour and genuine kindliness. As you walk along, the great, strapping brown fellows will greet you with a smile and a cheerful 'Ya rana'='Good morning—God bless you. How I loves to see your 'andsome face'. They wear a loose white shirt, and a sort of kilt of blue or scarlet cotton wrapped round the loins, which is printed with all sorts of fantastic devices of their own imagining. They are as proud of their hair as the women, and wear it in much the same way. The women have long, loose muslin dresses reaching from the neck to the ankles, without any waist, and they arrange them in all sorts of coquettish manners as they walk, or rather trip along. Very pretty green and pink are the favourite colours, though pure white is very popular. Their hair, which is beautiful,

---

[1] A cow camel.

glossy black, is carefully dressed with coco-nut oil, and they have head-dresses of bright yellow plantain or banana leaf, and sometimes a bunch of feathery stuff, which they get from the coco-nut palm, which is really prettier than any ostrich feathers I have ever seen.—George Henry Kingsley, *Notes on Sport and Travel.*

FEVER

On August 18th, I stopped, one day's journey out of Honan Fu, at a pleasant little country inn kept by a Mohammedan—the Mohammedans are much superior to the other Chinese. I had not been feeling at all well of late, and suddenly found that I had a temperature of 104, so stayed in bed all day and tried to perspire it off. I kept a Chinaman fanning me all day—my boy cannot nurse, or feel any more sympathy than a monkey. I asked him if he would mind at all if I died. 'Yes', he replied. 'Master die I should lose face when I get back to Shanghai.' It is always self with the Chinese.—J. W. Brooke, *Through China to Tibet in 1906.*

MONSOON

June 4, 1921. The first shower was smelly and undramatic. Now there is a new India—damp and grey, and but for the unusual animals I might think myself in England. The full Monsoon broke violently, and upon my undefended form. I was under a little shelter in the garden, sowing seeds in boxes with the assistance of two aged men and a little boy. I saw black clouds and felt some spots of rain. This went on for a quarter of an hour, so that I got accustomed to it, and then a wheel of water swept horizontally over the ground. The aged men clung to each other for support. I don't know what happened to the boy. I bowed this way and that as the torrent veered, wet through of course, but anxious not to be blown away like the roof of palm leaves over our head. When the storm decreased or rather became perpendicular, I set out for the Palace, large boats of mud forming on either foot. A rescue expedition, consisting of an umbrella and a servant, set out to meet me, but the umbrella blew inside out and the servant fell down.

Since then there have been some more fine storms, with lightning very ornamental and close. The birds fly about with large pieces of paper in their mouths. They are late, like everyone else, in their preparations against the rough weather, and hope to make a nest straight off, but the wind blows the paper round their heads like a shawl, and they grow alarmed and drop it. The temperature is now variable, becomes very hot between the storms, but on the whole things have improved. I feel much more alert and able to concentrate. The heat made me so stupid and sleepy, though I kept perfectly well. We have had cholera in the city—a very little, still it was a worry, and I went in to Indore and was reinoculated to be perfectly safe. My colleagues rather despised me for doing this—thought me cowardly and impious, for if one is to die of cholera one will die.—E. M. Forster, *The Hill of Devi.*

HORRIBLE DRUNKENNESS

1792. KING NAIMBANNA and several native chiefs paid me a visit this afternoon. The fatigue and unpleasantness of such a visit is not to be described. So many people jabbering together, others speaking to you through an interpreter, and the whole drinking to excess. My continued fear of giving them offence and not being at all satisfied at the appearance of sanctioning such proceedings, made me extremely ill for the night. The officers take good care to retire from such scenes when their inclination leads them, but I have *all these weighty anxieties* to contend with, and am obliged to stay till the last. I make it a rule to be as circumspect as possible in my conduct upon every occasion, that the natives may never see an inconsistency in my deportment; and, although I am fearful of refusing them liquor when they come to see me, yet, whenever I have a suitable opportunity, I never lose it, in pointing out to them the fatal consequences of drinking to excess; but I feel the absolute necessity of bearing for a time with their deep-rooted prejudices and customs as the only way to secure their friendship towards us. . . .—Governor Clarkson's Diary, *Sierra Leone after a Hundred Years.*

FAREWELL

December 16th Sunday, 1792. ALTHOUGH I have been accustomed to read the prayers and a sermon for many months, yet the idea of taking a public leave of the whole colony has excited sensations which I cannot describe, and I felt a dread of ascending the pulpit which I had never felt before; but as I considered it a duty, I could not but embrace the last opportunity in my power of admonishing them and giving them some wholesome advice. . . . I thought it my duty to be very plain with them, I pointed out their faults with mildness, but without disguise. Many of them felt stung by the truth, and there were several who could not stand it and went away. Some of them, I fear, are too far gone to be reclaimed, until they have received a long lesson in the school of adversity. . . . Yet I hope they were all benefited by my discourse, and many, very many, felt greatly affected. . . . In the course of the day I received a letter from one of the Nova Scotians, which I think justice to him requires me to record. I shall therefore transcribe it, particularly as the feeling which dictated it was not confined to himself; for upon my quitting the chapel, numbers crowded to shake hands with me, and to thank me for the good advice I had given them.

Free Town, December 16th, 1792.

HONNEREBEL SIR,—I reproved of your sermon very much. I am very much oblig to your honer for your good advice this day of our Lord, and I hope it will pleas the God of heaven to bliss you safe over the see to your home, and I hope it will pleas God to bring you safe here agin to rule over ous all. Sir, I hope Mr Clarkson won't frown on all for this bad behavyer this day of leaving the church, as for my part I love the and fear the, and am sorry to part from the. I hope from the bottom of my heart that God will blis you for ever, for your goodness to ous all.—I remain your humble servant, Ely Ackim.

—Governor Clarkson's Diary, *Sierra Leone after a Hundred Years.*

THE NEW WORLD

1913. IN THE bush of certain islands of the South Seas you may hear a crashing on windless noons, and, looking up, see a corpse swinging along head downwards at a great speed from tree to tree, holding by its toes, grimacing, dripping with decay. Americans, so active in this life, rest quiet afterwards. And though every stone of Wall Street have its separate Lar, their kind have not gone out beyond city-lots. The maple and the birch conceal no dryads, and Pan has never been heard amongst these reed-beds. Look as long as you like upon a cataract of the New World, you shall not see a white arm in the foam. A godless place. And the dead do not return. That is why there is nothing lurking in the heart of the shadows, and no human mystery in the colours, and neither the same joy nor the kind of peace in dawn and sunset that older lands know. It is, indeed, a new world. How far away seem those grassy, moonlit places in England that have been Roman camps or roads, where there is always serenity, and the spirit of a purpose at rest, and the sunlight flashes upon more than flint! Here one is perpetually a first-comer. The land is virginal, the wind cleaner than elsewhere, and every lake new-born, and each day is the first day. The flowers are less conscious than English flowers, the breezes have nothing to remember, and everything to promise. There walk, as yet, no ghosts of lovers in Canadian lanes. This is the essence of the grey freshness and brisk melancholy of this land. And for all the charm of those qualities, it is also the secret of a European's discontent. For it is possible, at a pinch, to do without gods. But one misses the dead.— Rupert Brooke, *Letters from America.*

FAMILY MANNERS

THE MANNERS of the Americans (in America) are the best I ever saw: and these are seen to the greatest advantage in their homes, and as to the gentlemen, in travelling. But for the drawback of inferior health, I know of no such earthly paradise as some of the homes in which I have had the honour and blessing of spending portions of the two years of my absence. The hospitality of the country is celebrated; but I speak now of more than usually meets the eye of a stranger; of the family manners, which travellers have rarely leisure or opportunity to observe. If I am asked what is the peculiar charm, I reply with some hesitation: there are so many. But I believe it is not so much the outward plenty, or the mutual freedom, or the simplicity of manners, or the incessant play of humour, which characterise the whole people, as the sweet temper which is diffused like sunshine over the land. They have been called the most good-tempered people in the world: and I think they must be so.—Harriet Martineau, *Society in America,* 1837.

MELANCHOLY THOUGHTS

Moradabad, Saturday, Jan. 27, 1838. THERE IS not a day that I do not think of those dear lines of Crabbe's—

> But when returned the youth? The youth no more
> Returned exulting to his native shore;
> But in his stead there came a worn-out man.

They were always good lines, and always had a tendency to bring tears into my eyes; but now, when I look at either the youth or the worn-out men, and think what India does for them all, I really could not venture to say those lines out loud. Please to remember that I shall return a worn-out woman.—Emily Eden, *Up the Country.*

ENCOUNTER WITH THE SUN

THE HEAT grew fierce; there was no valley nor hollow, no hill, no mound, no shadow of hill nor of mound, by which I could mark the way I was making. Hour by hour I advanced, and saw no change—I was still the very centre of a round horizon; hour by hour I advanced, and still there was the same, and the same, and the same—the same circle of flaming sky—the same circle of sand still glaring with light and fire. Over all the heaven above, over all the earth beneath, there was no visible power that could balk the fierce will of the sun; 'he rejoiced as a strong man to run a race; his going forth was from the end of the heaven, and his circuit unto the ends of it: and there was nothing hid from the heat thereof'. From pole to pole, and from the east to the west, he brandished his fiery sceptre as though he had usurped all heaven and earth. As he bid the soft Persian in ancient times, so now, and fiercely too, he bid me bow down and worship him; so now in his pride he seemed to command me, and say, 'Thou shalt have none other gods but me'. I was all alone before him. There were those two pitted together, and face to face; the mighty sun for one—and for the other, this poor, pale, solitary self of mine that I always carry about with me.—A. W. Kinglake, *Eothen*, 1844.

FISHING EXPEDITION

THE OTHER day I went out for a day's fishing on an African river, I and two black men, in a canoe, in company with a round net, three stout fishing-lines, three paddles, Dr. Günther's *Study of Fishes*, some bait in an old Morton's boiled-mutton tin, a little manioc, stinking awfully (as is its wont), a broken calabash baler, a lot of dirty water to sit in, and happy and contented minds. . . . We paddled away, far up a mangrove creek, and then went up against the black mud-bank, with its great network of grey-white roots, surmounted by the closely-interlaced black-green foliage. Absolute silence reigned, as it can only reign in Africa in a mangrove swamp. The water-laden air wrapped round us like a warm, wet blanket. The big mangrove flies came silently to feed on us and leave their progeny behind them in the wounds to do likewise. The stink of the mud, strong enough to break a window, mingled fraternally with that of the sour manioc.

I was reading, the negroes, always quiet enough when fishing, were silently carrying on that great African native industry—scratching themselves—so, with our lines over side, life slid away like a dreamless sleep, until the middle man hooked a cat-fish. It came on board with an awful grunt, right in the middle of us; flop, swish, scurry and yell followed; I tucked the study of fishes in general under my arm and attended to this individual specimen, shouting 'Lef em, lef em; hev em for water one time, you sons of unsanctified house lizards', and such like valuable advice and admonition. The man in the more remote end of the canoe made an awful swipe at the 3 ft.-long, grunting, flopping, yellow-grey, slimy, thing, but never reached it owing to the paddle meeting in mid-air with the flying leg of the man in front of him, drawing blood profusely. I really fancy, about this time, that, barring the cat-fish and myself, the occupants of the canoe were standing on their heads, with a view of removing their lower limbs from the terrible pectoral and dorsal fins, with which our prey made such lively play.

'*Brevi spatio interjecto*', as Caesar says, in the middle of a bad battle, over went the canoe, while the cat-fish went off home with the line and hook. One black man went to the bank, whither, with a blind pre-science of our fate, I had flung, a second before, the most valuable occupant of the canoe, *The Study of Fishes*. I went personally to investigate fluvial desposit *in situ*. When I returned to the surface—accompanied by great swirls of mud and great bubbles of the gases of decomposition I had liberated on my visit to the bottom of the river—I observed the canoe floating bottom upwards, accompanied by Morton's tin, the calabash, and the paddles, while on the bank one black man was engaged in hauling the other one out by the legs. . . . However, all ended happily. We collected all our possessions, except the result of the day's fishing—the cat-fish—but we had had as much of him as we wanted, and so, adding a thankful mind to our contented ones, went home.—Mary Kingsley, *West African Studies*, 1899.

PLEASURES OF THE PIPE

As to diet,—our party are all of opinion that it is the safest way to eat and drink, as nearly as possible, as one does at home. It may be worth mentioning that the syrups and acids which some travellers think they shall like in the Desert are not wholesome, nor so refreshing as might be anticipated. Ale and porter are much better;—as remarkably whole-some and refreshing as they are at sea. Tea and coffee are pleasant every where. Ladies who have courage to do what is good for them, and agreeable to them, in new circumstances, in disregard of former prejudices, will try the virtues of the chibouque while in the East: and if they like it, they will go on with it as long as they feel that they want it. The chibouque would not be in such universal use as it is in the East, if there were not some reason for it: and the reason is that it is usually found eminently good for health. I found it so: and I saw no more reason why I should not take it than why English ladies should not take their daily glass of sherry at home;—an indulgence which I do not need. I continued the use of my chibouque for some weeks after my return; and then left it off only on account of its inconvenience: and in the East, it is not inconvenient. The traveller there finds that his reasonable disgust at the cigar-smoking of our streets does not apply to the Eastern practice. The quality of the tobacco, and the length of the pipe (in which the essential oil is condensed, instead of being imbibed by the smoker) make the whole affair something wholly different from any smoking known in England. I need not say that every traveller is absolutely obliged to appear to smoke, on all occasions of visiting in the East: and if any lady finds refreshment and health in the practice, I hope I need not say that she should continue it, as long as she is subject to the extraordinary fatigues of her new position.—Harriet Martineau, *Eastern Life, Present and Past*, 1846.

DISTURBING MEMORIES

Valparaiso, July 23, 1834. WHEN I return to England, you must take me in hand with respect to the fine arts. I yet recollect there was a man called Raffaelle Sanctus. How delightful it will be once again to see, in the Fitzwilliam, Titian's Venus. How much more than delightful to go to some good concert or fine opera. These recollections will not do. I shall not be able to-morrow to pick out the entrails of some small animal with half my usual gusto.—Charles Darwin, *Letters*.

PURDAH

Camp, Benares, Wednesday, Nov. 22, 1837. THE RAJAH OF BENARES asked us to come to his country-house, called Ramnuggur (how it is spelt, I cannot say; probably with none of those letters). It is on the other side of the Ganges. We drove down to the river-side through a dense cloud of dust. I asked one of our servants to *dust* me gently with my pocket-handkerchief, and without any exaggeration a thick cloud came out of my cape. . . .

The rajah met us at the ghaut, and we were all carried off to the elephants, and got on them to go and see his garden, though it was nearly dusk. But the first sight was very striking.

N

Eighteen elephants and crowds of attendants, and then crowds as far as we could see of natives, going on 'Wah! wah! Hi Lord Sahib.' We rode about till it was quite dark, and then the rajah proposed we should return; and when we came to the turn of the road, the whole of the village and his castle, which is an enormous building, was illuminated. ... It was the *largest* illumination I ever saw. We went on the elephants through the great gateway, in a Timour the Tartar fashion, into the court. Such torches and spearmen and drums and crowds, like a melodrama magnified by a solar microscope; it was the sort of scene where Ellen Tree would have snatched up a doll from under Farley's sword, and said, 'My boy, my boy, my rescued Agib!' or words to that effect, while the curtain fell slowly. We got off at the door of an immense hall, a sort of court, and the rajah's servants spread a path of scarlet and gold kincob from the door to the seat at the farthest end, for us to walk on. ... Then the Ranee sent for us, and F. and I set off in tonjauns for the women's apartments, with the ladies who were with us. They carried us through a great many courts, and then the rajah gave me his cold, flabby little hand, and handed us up some narrow, dirty stairs, and came in with us behind the purdah and introduced us to the Ranee his mother, who was very splendidly dressed, and to some of his sisters, who were ugly. Then they asked us to go and see an old grandmother, and the Ranee laid hold of my hand, and one of the sisters took F., and they led us along an immense court on the roof, to the old lady, who is blind and very ill; but they had dressed her up for us, and we had to kiss her, which was not very nice. There was another immense nautch provided, which we had not time to look at. We gave our rings, and they brought the trays of presents which are usually given, a diamond ring and drops for earrings, two necklaces (very trashy), some beautiful shawls and kincobs, and some muslin; then they put immense skipping-ropes of silver braid, bigger than a common boa, round our necks, and small ones on the other ladies, and then poured attar of roses on our hands, and we left the old lady. When we came back to the Ranee's room, she showed us her little *chapel*, close to her sofa, where there were quantities of horrid-looking idols—Vishnu, and so on. Several native girls were introduced to us, but only one who was pretty, and who has just been betrothed to the father of the rajah. The young Ranees, or whatever they are called, are very shy, and stand with their eyes closed, but the older ones had great fun when we were going away in pouring the attar over our gowns, and utterly spoiled mine, which was silk: next time I shall go in muslin.—Emily Eden, *Up the Country*.

DESERT MEETING

. . . I DELIBERATED for a minute, and then determined that I would abandon all hope of seeing my party again in the Desert, and would push forward as rapidly as possible towards Suez.

It was not without a sensation of awe that I swept with my sight the vacant round of the horizon, and remembered that I was all alone and unprovisioned in the midst of the arid waste; but this very awe gave tone and zest to the exultation with which I felt myself launched. Hitherto in all my wanderings I had been under the care of other people—sailors, Tartars, guides, and dragomen had watched over my welfare; but now, at last, I was here in this African desert, and I *myself, and no other, had charge of my life.* I liked the office well: I had the greatest part of the day before me, a very fair dromedary, a fur pelisse, and a brace of pistols, but no bread, and worst of all, no water; for that I must ride,—and ride I did.

For several hours I urged forward my beast at a rapid though steady pace, but at length the pangs of thirst began to torment me. I did not relax my pace, however; and I had not suffered long, when a moving object appeared in the distance before me. The intervening space was soon traversed, and I found myself approaching a Bedouin Arab, mounted on a camel, attended by another Bedouin on foot. They stopped. I saw that there hung from the pack-saddle of the camel one of the large skin water-flasks commonly carried in the Desert, and it seemed to be well filled. I steered my dromedary close up alongside of the mounted Bedouin, caused my beast to kneel down, then alighted, and keeping the end of the halter in my hand, went up to the mounted Bedouin without speaking, took hold of his water-flask, opened it, and drank long and deep from its leathern lips. Both of the Bedouins stood fast in amazement and mute horror; and really if they had never happened to see a European before, the apparition was enough to startle them. To see for the first time a coat and a waistcoat with the semblance of a white human face at the top, and for this ghastly figure to come swiftly out of the horizon, upon a fleet dromedary—approach them silently, and with a demoniacal smile, and drink a deep draught from their water-flask—this was enough to make the Bedouins stare a little; they, in fact, stared a great deal—not as Europeans stare with a restless and puzzled expression of countenance, but with features all fixed and rigid, and with still glassy eyes. Before they had time to get decomposed from their state of petrification, I had remounted my dromedary, and was darting away towards the east.—A. W. Kinglake, *Eothen*, 1844.

NEW ENGLAND

Cambridge, Mass., February 19, 1874. NEW YORK was a great rattle, dining, and speechifying, and being received, and so has Boston been; and the courtesy, and generosity, and compliments would really turn any one's head who was not as disgusted with himself, as I always (thank God) am. . . . New England is, in winter at least, the saddest country, all brown grass, ice-polished rocks, sticking up through the copses, cedar scrub, low, swampy shores; an iron land which only iron people could have settled in. The people must have been heroes to make what they have of it. Now, under deep snow, it is dreadful. But the summer, they say, is semi-tropic, and that has kept them alive. And, indeed already, though it is hard frost under foot, the sun is bright, and hot, and high, for we are in the latitude of Naples! I cannot tell you a thousandth part of all I've seen, or of all the kindness we have received, but this I can say, that R. is well, and that I feel better than I have felt for years; but Mr. Longfellow and others warn me not to let this over-stimulating climate tempt me to over-work. One feels ready to do anything, and then suddenly very tired. But I am at rest now. . . . —Charles Kingsley, *Letters*.

CRAB COLONIES

Port St. Vincent, New Caledonia, 16th October, 1869. AT LOW tide the mud in the mouths of these rivers presents a most curious appearance. Imagine a bed of early dwarf tulips, without leaves, all in active motion, appearing and disappearing in the most unaccountable manner, and then you will have a dreamy idea of a colony of calling-crabs, each one, apparently, leading off three rousing cheers with his one big claw, and picking something off its mandibles with his little one. On your approach he subsides into his hole, and if you follow him up with a piece of stick, you may or may not drive him out at the other end of his burrow, but, at any rate, out of one or the other hole there is sure to bolt a fish, something like a loach, running on two pairs of tiny compasses fixed under his chin, who will not only scud deftly over the mud, but, in his terror or artfulness, will often run up the aerial roots of the neighbouring mangroves and down the other side into the water with a splash.—George Henry Kingsley, *Notes on Sport and Travel*.

DRESSED AS A MAN

HAMAR ('a very quizzical town upon the Orontes, on the border of the desert'), January 22nd, 1813. YOU HAVE heard, I suppose, that I am dressed as a man; sometimes as Chief of Albanians, sometimes as a

Syrian soldier, sometimes as a Bedouin Arab (the famous robbers in the desert), and at other times like the son of a Pacha. The dress of the great is like something in a play, and in fact much more decent than that of our fine ladies; that of the soldiers as much so, only they wear arms; the Bedouin's quite ridiculous. I will try and describe it, and will begin by the head. A square handkerchief made of coarse cotton and silk, folded from corner to corner, this put over a red nightcap, or skull crown, as if to protect it from a shower of rain, with one corner behind, and one on each side, like an old-fashioned wig; round the head, to bind it on, are several rows of thick cord, as big as two fingers, made of horse or camel's hair, put round three or four times. A shirt, a pair of large drawers, and a thing of the coarsest materials, sometimes cotton (white), or sometimes silk (red), not unlike a *bedgown*, fastened with a leather belt, over that a pelisse of curly white sheepskin, the leather dressed white, or orange colour, or copper colour, and over that a sort of immense cloak with armholes (called *abba*), made of a sort of carpeting, of two different sorts, one with stripes of black and white, six inches wide, or a white sort, with gold on the right shoulder, which is the kind worn by the sons of great chiefs, and that which I wear; then a large pair of yellow boots, and a lance twelve feet long decorated with black feathers. This figure am I, now writing to you.—Lady Hester Stanhope, *Letters*.

PERSIAN GARDEN

Kavar, February 20, 1934. THE GARDENER let me in by a wicket in a thatched wall, and I spent the afternoon wandering about the straight grass paths that divide Persian gardens into squares and oblongs. Each path is an avenue of poplars or planes, and is accompanied by irrigation runnels; inside these, each square contains fruit trees or bare plough. Squares sound formal; but really, Plantation or Wilderness is the proper word to describe a Persian garden. Winter and spring had met on this afternoon. A strong warm wind carried a sound of chopping with it and a rustle of dead plane-leaves; through those leaves perked the green crooks of young ferns. Here and there the rose-leaves had budded too early, and were blackened with frost. The bare apple branches bore tangles of dead mistletoe; another such tangle in the fork of a massive chestnut some hundreds of years old, was the nest of a *palamdar*—according to the gardener; did he mean magpie or squirrel? its dome was of one or the other. The first butterflies were out: a dusty white, of a kind I did not know, newly hatched and flying in a puzzled sort of way as if the world was still too brown for it; and a painted lady, newly awakened, and surveying the garden it knew in September with familiar swoops from point to point. There were some flowers for them. A peach (or plum) was in blossom, and I caught my breath at the dazzle of its red buds, white transparent petals and black stalks defined by the shimmering blue sky. From over the wall peered the endless mountains, mauve and lion-coloured, deathly barren.— Robert Byron, *The Road to Oxiana*.

NEW YORK

1861. SPEAKING OF New York as a traveller I have two faults to find with it. In the first place there is nothing to see; and in the second place there is no mode of getting about to see anything.—Anthony Trollope, *North America*.

PARASITES

1831, St. Paul's Rocks, (Atlantic Ocean). WE FOUND on St. Paul's only two kinds of birds—the booby and the noddy. The former is a species of gannet, and the latter a tern. Both are of a tame and stupid disposition, and are so unaccustomed to visitors, that I could have killed any number of them with my geological hammer. The booby lays her eggs on the bare rock; but the tern makes a very simple nest with seaweed. By the side of many of these nests a small flying-fish was placed; which, I suppose, had been brought by the male bird for its partner. It was amusing to watch how quickly a large and active crab (*Graspus*), which inhabits the crevices of the rock, stole the fish from the side of the nest, as soon as we had disturbed the parent birds. Sir W. Symonds, one of the few persons who have landed here, informs me that he saw the crabs dragging even the young birds out of their nest, and devouring them. Not a single plant, not even a lichen, grows on this islet; yet it is inhabited by several insects and spiders. The following list completes, I believe, the terrestrial fauna: a fly (*Olfersia*) living on the booby, and a tick which must have come here as a parasite on the birds; a small brown moth, belonging to a genus that feeds on feathers; a beetle (*Quedius*) and a woodlouse from beneath the dung; and lastly, numerous spiders, which I suppose prey on these small attendants and scavengers of the waterfowl. The often repeated description of the stately palm and other noble tropical plants, then birds, and lastly man, taking possession of the coral islets as soon as formed, in the Pacific, is probably not quite correct; I fear it destroys the poetry of this story, that feather and dirt-feeding and parasitic insects and spiders should be the first inhabitants of newly-formed oceanic land.—Charles Darwin, *The Voyage of the Beagle*.

RIO 150 YEARS AGO

Dec. 15th (1806). WENT ON shore, and was highly delighted with the town of Rio Janeiro. It is very large but irregularly built, situated on a spacious and commodious bay. You land nearly opposite the Viceroy's palace, which stands on the south side of a large and regular square. You see nothing scarcely but poor slaves carrying immense loads, and friars in their cocked hats going to and from the monasteries. Their carriages resemble in some manner our single-horse chaises, but badly made and drawn by two mules. On the near one rides the charioteer, in a huge cocked hat; the off one is in the shafts. They go astonishingly quick. Saw but few horses, those small and bad. The mules are most beautiful animals, and the inhabitants tell you are much more serviceable then the horses. They are as clean about the legs as our race-horses, and full of spirit. Fowls and ducks plentiful, but rather dear. The oxen and sheep are small and bad. Pigs in abundance. Fruits of all sorts. Pines are larger than ours, but not so fine flavoured; you get them for 6*d* apiece. Oranges, lemons, limes, sweet and sour, bananas, yams, etc., etc. They make no butter or cheese. They get it from England or America. The grandees, when they appear abroad, are carried in a kind of palanquin, which is borne on two negroes' shoulders. Most of these are blue, and adorned with fringes in general of the same colour. They have a velvet pillow, and above the head a kind of tester with curtains. He may either lie down or sit up.—Sir Harry Smith, *Autobiography*.

THE BIRDS OF AMERICA

1818. THERE ARE *two things*, which I have not yet mentioned, and which are almost wholly wanting here, while they are so amply enjoyed in England. The *singing birds* and the *flowers*. Here are many birds in summer, and some of very beautiful plumage. There are some wild flowers, and some English flowers in the best gardens. But, generally speaking, they are birds without song, and flowers without smell. The *linnet* (more than a thousand of which I have heard warbling upon one scrubbed oak on the sand hills in Surrey), the *sky-lark*, the *goldfinch*, the *wood-lark*, the *nightingale*, the *bull-finch*, the *black-bird*, the *thrush*, and all the rest of the singing tribe are wanting in these beautiful woods and orchards of garlands.—When these latter have dropped their bloom, all is gone in the flowery way. No *shepherd's rose*, no *honey-suckle*, none of that endless variety of beauties that decorate the hedges and the meadows in England. No *daisies*, no *primroses*, no *cowslips*, no *blue-bells*, no *daffodils*, which, as if it were not enough for them to charm the sight and the smell, must have names, too, to delight the ear. All these are wanting in America. Here are, indeed, birds, which bear the *name* of robin, blackbird, thrush, and goldfinch; but, alas! the thing that Westminster has, in like manner, the *name* of parliament, and speaks the voice of the people, whom it pretends to represent, in much about the same degree that the black-bird here speaks the voice of its namesake in England.—William Cobbett, *A Year's Residence in America.*

HOTEL LIFE

1861. WE WERE certainly rather melancholy at Newport. . . . I confess that I could not stand the drawing-room—the ladies' drawing-room as such-like rooms are always called at the hotels, and that I basely deserted my wife. I could not stand it either here or elsewhere, and it seemed to me that other husbands,—ay, and even lovers,—were as hard pressed as myself. I protest that there is no spot on the earth's surface so dear to me as my own drawing-room, or rather my wife's drawing-room at home; that I am not a man given hugely to clubs, but one rather rejoicing in the rustle of petticoats. I like to have women in the same room with me. But at these hotels I found myself driven away,—propelled as it were by some unknown force,—to absent myself from the feminine haunts. Anything was more palatable than them; even 'liquoring up' at a nasty bar, or smoking in a comfortless reading-room among a deluge of American newspapers. And I protest also . . . that this comes from no fault of the American women. They are as lovely as our own women. Taken generally, they are better instructed—though perhaps not better educated. They are seldom troubled with *mauvaise honte*,—I do not say it in irony, but begging that the words may be taken at their proper meaning. They can always talk, and very often can talk well. But when assembled together in these vast, cavernous, would-be luxurious, but in truth horribly comfortless hotel drawing-rooms,—they are unapproachable. I have seen lovers, whom I have known to be lovers, unable to remain five minutes in the same cavern with their beloved ones.

And then the music? There is always a piano in an hotel drawing-room, on which, of course, some one of the forlorn ladies is generally employed. I do not suppose that these pianos are in fact, as a rule, louder and harsher, more violent and less musical, than other instruments of the kind. They seem to be so, but that, I take it, arises from the exceptional mental depression of those who have to listen to them. Then the ladies, or probably some one lady, will sing, and as she hears her own voice ring and echo through the lofty corners and round the empty walls, she is surprised at her own force, and with increased efforts sings louder and still louder. She is tempted to fancy that she is suddenly gifted with some power of vocal melody unknown to her before, and filled with the glory of her own performance shouts till the whole house rings. At such moments she at least is happy, if no one else is so. Looking at the general sadness of her position, who can grudge her such happiness?—Anthony Trollope, *North America.*

FOUR IMPORTANT PEOPLE

April 1, 1921. THE PALACE is inhabited by four chief people—me, H.H., Malarao Sahib, and Deolekr Sahib—and if there ever was a normal meal we should find ourselves at it. Malarao is of lofty lineage —a sallow young man with a headache on which I have been trying aspirin. I think he is nice, and he's as pleasant as his lack of English permits. He is Mayor of the Palace, and I apply to him when a door won't shut or a drawer closes with the jaws of death on its contents, or I want my bed carried out on to the roof, or if dead flowers are put on the table for a dinner party, or sparrows build in the ceiling. Deolekr Sahib is my assistant in the office, likewise nobly born. It was in the midst of his broken English (here a squirrel runs down the stairs) that I discovered the £1,000 motor batteries. The works of Science are his —all the garages, which I inspected yesterday—imagine me inspecting garages! A monkey nearly bit me and rightly—all wells and cisterns, including the Krishna waterworks—and the 'electric men' (here the squirrel runs back: it has gone to the state drawing room to sit inside a piano). I really must stop now. I will finish this evening and post at Indore. For I am going in about my clothes to Mhow—over 30 miles drive each way.—'Yes, of course, dear Morgan—any day any car.'— E. M. Forster, *The Hill of Devi.*

A NATURALIST IN BRAZIL

1848, Pará, Brazil. THE IMPRESSIONS received during this first walk can never wholly fade from my mind. After traversing the few streets of tall, gloomy, convent-looking buildings near the port, inhabited chiefly by merchants and shopkeepers, along which idle soldiers, dressed in shabby uniforms, carrying their muskets carelessly over their arms, priests, negresses with red water-jars on their heads, sad-looking Indian women carrying their naked children astride on their hips. . . .

Beyond this, our road lay across a grassy common into a picturesque lane leading to the virgin forest. The long street was inhabited by the poorer class of the population. The houses were of one storey only, and had an irregular and mean appearance. The windows were without glass, having, instead, projecting lattice casements. The street was unpaved and inches deep in loose sand. Groups of people were cooling themselves outside their doors: people of all shades in colour of skin, European, Negro and Indian, but chiefly an uncertain mixture of the three. Amongst them were several handsome women, dressed in a slovenly manner, barefoot or shod in loose slippers; but wearing richly-decorated ear-rings, and around their necks strings of very large gold beads. They had dark expressive eyes, and remarkably rich heads of hair. It was a mere fancy, but I thought the mingled squalor, luxuriance and beauty of these women were pointedly in harmony with the rest of the scene; so striking, in the view, was the mixture of natural riches and human poverty.... But amidst all, and compensating every defect, rose the overpowering beauty of the vegetation. The massive dark crowns of shady mangos were seen everywhere amongst the dwellings, amidst fragrant blossoming orange, lemon, and many other tropical fruit trees; some in flower, others in fruit, at varying stages of ripeness. ... On the boughs of the taller and more ordinary-looking trees sat tufts of curiously-leaved parasites. Slender woody lianas hung in festoons from the branches, or were suspended in the form of cords and ribbons; whilst luxuriant creeping plants overran alike tree-trunks, roofs and walls, or toppled over palings in copious profusion of foliage. The superb banana (Musa paradisiaca), of which I had always read as forming one of the charms of tropical vegetation, here grew with great luxuriance: its glossy velvety-green leaves, twelve feet in length, curving over the roofs of verandahs in the rear of every house. The shape of the leaves, the varying shades of green which they present when lightly moved by the wind, and especially the contrast they afford in colour and form to the more sombre hues and more rounded outline of the other trees, are quite sufficient to account for the charm of this glorious tree. Strange forms of vegetation drew our attention at almost every step. ... There was the bread-fruit tree—an importation, it is true; but remarkable from its large, glossy, dark green, strongly digitated foliage, and its interesting history. Many other trees and plants, curious in leaf, stem, or manner of growth, grew on the borders of the thickets along which lay our road; they were all attractive to new comers, whose last country ramble of quite recent date was over the bleak moors of Derbyshire on a sleety morning in April.—Henry Walter Bates, *The Naturalist on the River Amazons.*

A CRAVING FOR OPIUM

1887. 'AFTER ALL', I said to myself, 'a great deal of exaggeration is current about these things; for how few of those in England who talk so glibly about the evils of opium-smoking, and waste their time and other people's money in trying to put a stop to it, have any practical acquaintance at all with it; and, on the other hand, how many of my friends here, when they feel depressed and worried, or want to pass a quiet evening with a few congenial friends in discussing metaphysics and ontology, indulge in an occasional pipe. However, this resolution I make, that on the day when I shall be well enough to go out of this garden again I lay aside my pretty opium-pipe (*váfúr*), with its *síkh* (cleaning rod) and its *anbur* (charcoal tongs), which shall be to me thenceforth but as curiosities to hang up in my college-rooms when I get back to Cambridge.'

Well, to-night, as I reluctantly admitted to myself, the time had come to put my resolution into practice. And how did I do it? I kept it, after a fashion, just for that one night—and what a night it was! In vain I longed for sleep, in vain I tossed to and fro on my couch . . ., for an indefinable craving, to which was presently superadded a general sense of uneasiness pervading all the facial nerves, warred with the weariness which possessed me. I was ashamed to wake my servant and bid him kindle a fire, else had my resolution not held even for one night; indeed, as it was, it can hardly be said to have held, since at last in desperation I drenched some tobacco in laudanum, taken from the medicine-chest I had with me, rolled it into a cigarette, and tried, though with but little satisfaction, to smoke it.

And this is the way of opium. You may smoke it occasionally at long intervals, and feel no after-craving. You may smoke it for two or three days consecutively, and abandon it without difficulty; then you may, after an interval of one or two days, do the like once more, and again forsake it; and then, having smoked it once or twice again, you will try to put it from you as before, and you will find you cannot. . . . So next day I relapsed . . ., and, when a few days later I told my plight to a friend of mine (the prince's secretary and an Ezelí Bábí), who was a confirmed 'váfúrí' (opium-smoker), he clapped his hand on his thigh and exclaimed, '*Hálá dígar guẓasht! Váfúrí shudé-id!*' ('Now at any rate, it is all over! You have become an opium-smoker!'). Neither did he say this without a certain air of contentment, if not of exultation; for it is a curious fact that, although the opium-smoker will, as a rule, never tire of abusing his tyrant, he will almost always rejoice to see another led into the same bondage, and will take the new captive by the hand as a brother.—Edward G. Browne, *A Year Among the Persians*, 1893.

A LAND OF MUD

Baghdad, September 27, 1933. IT IS little solace to recall that Mesopotamia was *once* so rich, so fertile of art and invention, so hospitable to the Sumerians, the Seleucids, and the Sasanids. The prime fact of Mesopotamian history is that in the thirteenth century Hulagu destroyed the irrigation system; and that from that day to this Mesopotamia has remained a land of mud deprived of mud's only possible advantage, vegetable fertility. It is a mud plain, so flat that a single heron, reposing on one leg beside some rare trickle of water in a ditch, looks as tall as a wireless aerial. From this plain rise villages of mud and cities of mud. The rivers flow with liquid mud. The air is composed of mud refined into a gas. The people are mud-coloured; they wear mud-coloured clothes, and their national hat is nothing more than a formalised mud-pie. Baghdad is the capital one would expect of this divinely favoured land. It lurks in a mud fog; when the temperature drops below 110, the residents complain of the chill and get out their furs. For only one thing is it now justly famous: a kind of boil which takes nine months to heal, and leaves a scar.—Robert Byron, *The Road to Oxiana*.

THE CHILLY WIND OF CHANGE

THE LAND of the Pharaohs is becoming civilised, and unpleasantly so: nothing can be more uncomfortable than its present middle-state, between barbarism and the reverse. The prohibition against carrying arms is rigid as in Italy; all 'violence' is violently denounced, and beheading being deemed cruel, the most atrocious crimes, as well as those small political offences, which in the days of the Mamelukes would have led to a beyship or a bow-string, receive fourfold punishment by deportation to Faizoghli, the local Cayenne. If you order your peasant to be flogged, his friends gather in threatening hundreds at your gate; when you curse your boatman, he complains to your consul; the dragomans afflict you with strange wild notions about honesty; a government order prevents you from using vituperative language to the 'natives' in general; and the very donkey boys are becoming cognisant of the right of man to remain unbastinadoed.—Sir Richard Burton, *Pilgrimage to El-Medinah and Meccah*, 1855.

APPROACH TO JERUSALEM

1833. IT WAS curious to observe the different effect which our approach to Jerusalem had upon the various persons who composed our party. A Christian pilgrim, who had joined us on the road, fell down upon his knees and kissed the holy ground; two others embraced each other, and congratulated themselves that they had lived to see Jerusalem. As for us Franks, we sat bolt upright upon our horses, and stared and said nothing; whilst around us the more natural children of the East wept for joy, and, as in the army of the Crusaders, the word Jerusalem! Jerusalem! was repeated from mouth to mouth; but we, who consider ourselves civilized and superior beings, repressed our emotions; we were above showing that we participated in the feelings of our barbarous companions. As for myself, I would have got off my horse and walked barefooted towards the gate, as some did, if I had dared: but I was in fear of being laughed at for my absurdity, and therefore sat fast in my saddle. At last I blew my nose, and, pressing the sharp edges of my Arab stirrups on the lank sides of my poor weary jade, I rode on slowly towards the Bethlehem gate.—Hon. Robert Curzon, *Monasteries of the Levant.*

JAPANESE DANCING

FACTORIES, SMOKE, innumerable Woolworths, mud—were these Japan? We were assured they were not. The 'real' Japan (all countries have a 'real' self, which no stranger can ever hope to see) was something different, was somewhere else. Looking at the celebrated Cherry Dances in Kyoto, we were almost ready to believe it. The costumes, it is true, were extraordinarily vulgar and garish. The scenery in Western style—the Western style of the pre-war provincial pantomime—was deplorable. Any self-respecting producer of revues in London or New York could have staged a far more adequate Old Japan. But he could not have got the dancing. That was an enchantment. A chorus of thirty or forty geishas, drilled to a pitch of almost Prussian efficiency, their farded faces impassive as white masks, performed a ballet that was the formalization of the gestures of courtesy, that was polite conversation made more gracefully polite, that was the apotheosis of good manners at the tea-table. And hardly less lovely were the movements of the orchestra. In Europe one pays to listen to music; in Japan one pays to see it played. When European performers make their appearance upon the platform one generally wants to shut one's eyes; in a Japanese concert-room, on the other hand, one desires to keep one's eyes wide open and to close one's ears. Not that the music is unpleasant. What I heard at Kyoto might have been the remote and geological ancestor of Russian music. It stood in relation to Rimsky Korsakoff as pithecanthropus stands to man; it was a kind of *ur*-Stravinsky, a fossil and primitive form of the genus of Moussorgsky. Not unpleasing, I repeat, but after a while a little boring. The guitars, on which twenty geishas played with plectrums that looked like ivory combs, were singularly poor in tone. And the tambourines, the cymbals, and the drums, which were being played by twenty of their sisters on the opposite side of the hall, beat out only the simplest and most obvious rhythms. No, the orchestra was not much to listen to. But what a ravishment to behold! They were as well drilled as the ballerinas. The twenty guitar players sat in identically the same position, and when they combed the strings of their instruments their hands performed the same movements simultaneously, as though they were synchronously moving parts of one machine. Similar machines actuated the eight hour-glass-shaped tambourines, the eight small kettle-drums, the two sets of cymbals, the two little gongs. Most exquisite of all were the drummers. They knelt in front of their instruments as though before a row of little gods. Each held a pair of enormous white drumsticks, so thick that the tiny hands could hardly grasp them. With these, in unison, they tapped the little gods before whom they knelt; and the little drum gods answered them, boom boom—a response, it must be admitted, rather more clear and comprehensible than that which deities are accustomed to vouchsafe to their worshippers. But then the ritual of these Japanese adorers was so beautiful that it could hardly fail to be magically compelling. Their arms, prolonged by the enormous white drumsticks, were held out before them almost at full stretch. And when they beat, they beat from the shoulder, lifting and letting fall the whole arm. But 'letting fall' is not the right expression; it connotes a loose and undeliberate movement, and the drummers did nothing undeliberately. On the contrary, each stroke was applied with a perfectly controlled precision. Tap, tap, tap-a-tap, tap; they touched the drum face as though they were fitting into position, one by one, the tesserae, now large, now small, of an elaborate mosaic.—Aldous Huxley, *Jesting Pilate*, 1926.

INDEPENDENCE

Richmond, Virginia, March 4th, 1853. A GREAT GOOD w.h an Englishman who has seen men and cities gets by coming hither, is that he rubs a deal of Cockney arrogance off, and finds men and women above all as good as our own. You learn to sympathise with a great hearty nation of 26 millions of English-speakers, not quite ourselves but so like, the difference is not worth our scorn certainly; nay I'm not sure I don't think the people are our superiors. There's a rush and activity of life quite astounding, a splendid recklessness about money w^h has in it something admirable too. Dam the money says every man. He's as good as the richest for that day. If he wants champagne he has champagne, Mr Astor can't do more. You get an equality w^h may shock ever so little at first, but has something hearty and generous in it. I like the citizenship and general freedom. And in the struggles w^h every man with whom you talk is pretty sure to have had, the ups and downs of his life, the trades or professions he has been in—he gets a rough and tumble education w^h gives a certain piquancy to his talk and company.—W. M. Thackeray, *Letters*.

CAIRO FUNERALS

WHEN FIRST I arrived in Cairo the funerals that daily passed under my windows were many, but still there were frequent and long intervals without a single howl. Every day, however (except one, when I fancied that I observed a diminution of funerals), these intervals became less frequent and shorter, and at last, the passing of the howlers from morn to noon was almost incessant. I believe that about one half of the whole people was carried off by this visitation. The orientals, however, have more quiet fortitude than Europeans under afflictions of this sort, and they never allowed the plague to interfere with their religious usages. I rode one day round the great burial-ground. The tombs are strewed over a great expanse among the vast mountains of rubbish (the accumulations of many centuries) which surround the city. The ground, unlike the Turkish 'cities of the dead', which are made so beautiful by their dark cypresses, has nothing to sweeten melancholy—nothing to mitigate the hatefulness of death. Carnivorous beasts and birds possess the place by night, and now in the fair morning it was all alive with fresh comers—alive with dead. Yet at this very time when the plague was raging so furiously, and on this very ground which resounded so mournfully with the howls of arriving funerals, preparations were going on for the religious festival called the Kourban Bairam. Tents were pitched, and *swings hung for the amusement of children*—a ghastly holiday! but the Mahometans take a pride, and a just pride, in following their ancient customs undisturbed by the shadow of death.—A. W. Kinglake, *Eothen*, 1844.

SALT LAKE CITY

Salt Lake City, Utah, May 17, (1874). HERE WE are after such a journey of luxury—through a thousand miles of desert, plain, and mountain, treeless, waterless almost, sage brush and alkali. Then cañons and gorges, the last just like Llanberris Pass, into this enormous green plain, with its great salt lake; and such a mountain ring, 300 to 400 miles in circumference! The loveliest scene I ever saw. . . . Yesterday we were running through great snowdrifts, at from 5,000 to 7,000 feet above the sea (we are at 5,000 here), and all along by our side the old trail, where every mile is fat with Mormon bones. Sadness and astonishment overpower me at it all. The 'city' is thriving enough, putting one in mind, with its swift streams in all streets, and mountain background, of Tarbes, or some other Pyrenean town. But, ah! what horrors this place has seen. Thank God it is all breaking up fast. The tyrant is 70, and must soon go to his account, and what an awful one.—Charles Kingsley, *Letters*.

COCO-NUTS

GROVES OF coco palms are no favourites of mine. I don't like them. The trees are nice enough to look on, and nice enough to use in the divers ways you can use a coco-nut palm; but the noise of the breeze in their crowns keeps up a perpetual rattle with their hard leaves that sounds like heavy rain day and night, so that you feel you ought to live under an umbrella, and your mind gets worried about it when you are not looking after it with your common sense.

Then the natives are such a nuisance with coco-nuts. For a truly terrific kniff give me even in West Africa a sand beach with coco-nut palms and natives. You never get coco-nut palms without natives, because they won't grow out of sight of human habitation. I am told also that one coco will not grow alone; it must have another coco as well as human neighbours, so these things, of course, end in a grove. It's like keeping cats with no one to drown the kittens.

Well, the way the smell comes about in this affair is thus. The natives bury the coco-nuts in the sand, so as to get the fibre off them. They have buried nuts in that sand for ages before you arrive, and the nuts have rotted, and crabs have come to see what was going on, a thing crabs will do, and they have settled down here and died in their generations, and rotted too. The sandflies and all manner of creeping things have found that sort of district suits them, and have joined in, and the natives, who are great hands at fishing, have flung all the fish offal there, and there is usually a lagoon behind this sort of thing which contributes its particular aroma, and so between them the smell is a good one, even for West Africa.—Mary Kingsley, *West African Studies*, 1899.

PRIMEVAL FOREST

Pará, Brazil, 1848. WE USED to rise soon after dawn, when Isidoro would go down to the city, after supplying us with a cup of coffee, to purchase the fresh provisions for the day. The two hours before breakfast were devoted to ornithology. At that early period of the day the sky was invariably cloudless (the thermometer marking 72° or 73° Fahr.); the heavy dew or the previous night's rain, which lay on the moist foliage, becoming quickly dissipated by the glowing sun, which rising straight out of the east, mounted rapidly towards the zenith. All nature was fresh, new leaf and flower-buds expanding rapidly. Some mornings a single tree would appear in flower amidst what was the preceding evening a uniform green mass of forest—a dome of blossom suddenly created as if by magic. The birds were all active; from the wild-fruit trees, not far off, we often heard the shrill yelping of the Toucans (*Rhamphastos vitellinus*). Small flocks of parrots flew over on most mornings, at a great height, appearing in distinct relief against the blue sky, always two by two chattering to each other, the pairs being separated by regular intervals; their bright colours, however, were not apparent at that height. After breakfast we devoted the hours from 10 a.m. to 2 or 3 p.m. to entomology; the best time for insects in the forest being a little before the greatest heat of the day. We did not find them at all numerous, although of great variety as to species. The only kinds that appeared in great numbers of individuals were ants, termites, and certain species of social wasps; in the open grounds dragon-flies were also amongst the most abundant kinds of insects. Beetles were certainly much lower in the proportion of individuals to species than they are in England, and this led us to the conclusion that the ants and termites here must perform many of the functions in nature which in temperate climates are the office of Coleoptera. . . .

The heat increased rapidly towards two o'clock (92° and 93° Fahr.), by which time every voice of bird or mammal was hushed; only in the trees was heard at intervals the harsh whirr of a cicada. The leaves, which were so moist and fresh in early morning, now became lax and drooping; the flowers shed their petals. Our neighbours the Indian and Mulatto inhabitants of the open palm-thatched huts, as we returned home fatigued with our ramble, were either asleep in their hammocks

o

or seated on mats in the shade, too languid even to talk. On most days in June and July a heavy shower would fall some time in the afternoon, producing a most welcome coolness. . . . Meantime all nature is refreshed; but heaps of flower-petals and fallen leaves are seen under the trees. Towards evening life revives again, and the ringing uproar is resumed from bush and tree. The following morning the sun again rises in a cloudless sky, and so the circle is completed; spring, summer, and autumn, as it were, in one tropical day. The days are more or less like this throughout the year in this country. A little difference exists between the dry and wet seasons; but generally, the dry season, which lasts from July to December, is varied with showers, and the wet, from January to June, with sunny days. It results from this, that the periodical phenomena of plants and animals do not take place at about the same time in all species, or in the individuals of any given species, as they do in temperate countries. Of course there is no hybernation; nor, as the dry season is not excessive, is there any aestivation as in some tropical countries. Plants do not flower or shed their leaves, nor do birds moult, pair, or breed, simultaneously. In Europe, a woodland scene has its spring, its summer, its autumnal, and its winter aspects. In the equatorial forests the aspect is the same or nearly so every day in the year: budding, flowering, fruiting, and leaf shedding are always going on in one species or other. The activity of birds and insects proceeds without interruption, each species having its own separate times; the colonies of wasps, for instance, do not die off annually, leaving only the queens, as in cold climates; but the succession of generations and colonies goes on incessantly. It is never either spring, summer, or autumn, but each day is a combination of all three.— Henry Walter Bates, *The Naturalist on the River Amazons*.

FREE MEN

1817–1819. THE AMERICAN labourers, like the tavern-keepers, are never *servile*, but always *civil*. Neither *boobishness* nor *meanness* mark their character. They never *creep* and *fawn*, and are never *rude*. Employed about your house as day-labourers, they never come to interlope for victuals or drink. They have no idea of such a thing: Their pride would restrain them if their plenty did not; and, thus would it be with all labourers, in all countries, were they left to enjoy the fair produce of their labour. Full pocket or empty pocket, these American labourers are always the *same men*; no saucy cunning in the one case, and no base crawling in the other. This, too, arises from the free institutions of government. A man has a voice *because he is a man*, and not because he is the *possessor of money*. And, shall I *never* see our English labourers in this happy state?—William Cobbett, *A Year's Residence in America*.

WASHINGTON

1842. TAKE THE worst parts of the City Road and Pentonville, or the straggling outskirts of Paris, where the houses are smallest, preserving all their oddities, but especially the small shops and dwellings, occupied in Pentonville (but not in Washington) by furniture-brokers, keepers of poor eating-houses, and fanciers of birds. Burn the whole down; build it up again in wood and plaster; widen it a little: throw in part of St. John's Wood; put green blinds outside all the private houses, with a red curtain and a white one in every window; plough up all the roads; plant a great deal of coarse turf in every place where it ought *not* to be; erect three handsome buildings in stone and marble, any-where, but the more entirely out of everybody's way the better; call one the Post Office, one the Patent Office, and one the Treasury; make it scorching hot in the morning, and freezing cold in the after-noon, with an occasional tornado of wind and dust; leave a brick-field without the bricks, in all central places where a street may naturally be expected: and that's Washington.—Charles Dickens, *American Notes*.

A SERIOUS LABOUR

EGYPT IS not the country to go to for the recreation of travel. It is too suggestive and too confounding to be met but in the spirit of study. One's powers of observation sink under the perpetual exercise of thought: and the lightest-hearted voyager, who sets forth from Cairo eager for new scenes and days of frolic, comes back an antique, a citizen of the world of six thousand years ago, kindred with the mummy. Nothing but large knowledge and sound habits of thought can save him from returning perplexed and borne down;—unless indeed it be ignorance and levity. A man who goes to shoot crocodiles and flog Arabs, and eat ostrich's eggs, looks upon the monuments as so many strange old stone-heaps, and comes back 'bored to death with the Nile'; as we were told we should be. . . . But for all between these two extremes of levity and wisdom, a Nile voyage is as serious a labour as the mind and spirits can be involved in; a trial even to health and temper such as is little dreamed of on leaving home. The labour and care are well bestowed, however, for the thoughtful traveller can hardly fail of returning from Egypt a wiser, and therefore a better man.—Harriet Martineau, *Eastern Life, Present and Past*, 1846.

LADY HESTER STANHOPE

FOR THE last fifteen years of her life, Lady Hester Stanhope seldom quitted her bed till between two and five o'clock in the afternoon, nor returned to it before the same hours the next morning. The day's business never could be said to have well begun until sunset. But it must not be supposed that the servants were suffered to remain idle during daylight. On the contrary, they generally had their work assigned them over-night, and the hours after sunset were employed by her ladyship in issuing instructions as to what was to be done next day; in giving orders, scoldings, writing letters, and holding those interminable conversations which filled so large a portion of her time, and seemed so necessary to her life. When these were over, she would prepare herself to go to bed, but always with an air of unwillingness, as if she regretted that there were no more commands to issue. . . .

Her bedstead was nothing but planks nailed together on low tressels. A mattress, seven feet long and about four and a half broad, was spread on these planks, which were slightly inclined from head to foot. Instead of sheets, she had Barbary blankets, which are like the finest English ones, two over her, and one under. There was no counterpane, but, as occasion required, a wollen *abah*, or cloak, or a fur pelisse would be used for that purpose. Her pillow-case was of Turkish silk, and under it was another covered in coloured cotton. Behind this were two more of silk, ready at hand, if wanted.

Her night-dress was a chemise of silk and cotton, a white quilted jacket, a short pelisse, a turban on her head, and a kefféyah tied under her chin in the same manner as when she was up, and a shawl over the back of her head and shoulders. Thus she slept nearly dressed.

As it had become a habit with her to find nothing well done, when she entered her bedroom, it was rare that the bed was made to her liking; and, generally, she ordered it to be made over again in her presence. Whilst this was doing, she would smoke her pipe, then called for the sugar-basin to eat two or three lumps of sugar, then for a clove to take away the mawkish taste of the sugar. The girls, in the mean time, would go on making the bed, and be saluted every now and then, for some mark of stupidity, with all sorts of appellations. The night-lamp was then lighted, a couple of yellow wax lights were placed ready for use in the recess of the window; and, all things being apparently done for the night, she would get into bed, and the maid, whose turn it was to sleep in the room, (for, latterly, she always had one) having placed herself, dressed as she was, on her mattress behind the curtain which ran across the room, the other servant was dismissed.

But hardly had she shut the door and reached her own sleeping-room, flattering herself that her day's work was over, when the bell would ring, and she was told to get broth, or lemonade, or orgeat directly.... Lady Hester Stanhope took it on a tray placed on her lap as she sat up in bed, and it was necessary for one of the two servants to hold the candle in one hand and shade the light from her mistress's eyes with the other. The contents of the basin were sipped once or twice and sent away; or, if she ate a small bit of dried toast, it was considered badly made, and a fresh piece was ordered, perhaps not to be touched.

This being removed, the maid would again go away, and throw herself on her bed; and, as she wanted no rocking, in ten minutes would be sound asleep. But, in the mean time, her mistress has felt a twitch in some part of her body, and ding dong goes the bell again.—*Memoirs of the Lady Hester Stanhope*, 1845.

THE PLEASURES OF HARD LABOUR

In the Mountain, Apia, Samoa, Monday, November 2nd, 1890. THIS IS a hard and interesting and beautiful life that we lead now. Our place is in a deep cleft of Vaea Mountain, some six hundred feet above the sea, embowered in forest, which is our strangling enemy, and which we combat with axes and dollars. I went crazy over outdoor work, and had at last to confine myself to the house, or literature must have gone by the board. *Nothing* is so interesting as weeding, clearing, and path-making; the oversight of labourers becomes a disease; it is quite an effort not to drop into the farmer; and it does make you feel so well. To come down covered with mud and drenched with sweat and rain after some hours in the bush, change, rub down, and take a chair in the verandah, is to taste a quiet conscience. And the strange thing that I mark is this: If I go out and make sixpence, bossing my labourers and plying the cutlass or the spade, idiot conscience applauds me; if I sit in the house and make twenty pounds, idiot conscience wails over my neglect and the day wasted.—R. L. Stevenson, *Letters*.

QUEEN OF THE ARABS

January 25th, 1813. I WENT with the great chief, Mohanna El-Fadel, into the desert for a week, and marched three days with their encampment. I was treated with the greatest respect and hospitality, and it was, perhaps, altogether the most curious sight I ever saw—horses and mares fed upon camel's milk, Arabs living upon little else, except a little rice, and sometimes a sort of bread, the space around me covered with living creatures, twelve thousand camels coming to water from one tribe only. The old poets from the banks of the Euphrates, singing the praises and the feats of ancient heroes; children quite naked; women with lips dyed light blue and their nails red, and hands all over flowers and designs of different kinds; a chief who is obeyed like a great king; starvation and pride so mixed, that I really could not have had an idea of it; even the cloths I presented to the sons of Mohanna they could not carry, indeed hold, but called a black slave to take them. However, I have every reason to be perfectly contented with their conduct towards me, and I am the *Queen* with them all.—Lady Hester Stanhope, *Letters*.

SOPHISTICATED CHILDREN

1861. AND THEN the children. . . . The actual age of these perfectly civilized and highly educated beings may be from three to four. One will often see five or six such seated at the long dinner-table of the hotel, breakfasting and dining with their elders, and going through the ceremony with all the gravity, and more than all the decorum of their grandfathers. When I was three years old I had not yet, as I imagine, been promoted beyond a silver spoon of my own wherewith to eat my bread and milk in the nursery. . . . But at hotel life in the States the adult infant lisps to the waiter for everything at table, handles his fish with epicurean delicacy, is choice in his selection of pickles, very particular that his beef-steak at breakfast shall be hot, and is instant in his demand for fresh ice in his water. But perhaps his, or in this case her, retreat from the room when the meal is over, is the *chef d'œuvre* of the whole performance. The little precocious, full-blown beauty of four signifies that she has completed her meal,—or is 'through' her dinner, as she would express it,—by carefully extricating herself from the napkin which has been tucked around her. Then the waiter, ever attentive to her movements, draws back the chair on which she is seated, and the young lady glides to the floor. . . . Her father and mother, who are no more than her chief ministers, walk before her out of the saloon, and then she,—swims after them. . . . The peculiar step to which I allude is to be seen often on the Boulevards in Paris. It is to be seen more often in second rate French towns, and among fourth rate French women. Of all signs in women betokening vulgarity, bad taste, and aptitude to bad morals, it is the surest. . . .—Anthony Trollope, *North America*.

TEA DURING AN AIR-RAID

China. WE WERE to stay at Paak Hok Tung, a village half a mile down the river. American and English missionaries have made a settlement there. Walking up the tidy path between playing-fields, college buildings, and villa gardens, you might fancy yourself at home in one of the pleasanter London suburbs. And it was in a pleasant, cultured suburban drawing-room that our missionary host and hostess gave us tea. Had we had a nice journey? Yes, thank you, very nice. Any trouble at the customs? Well, unfortunately, yes: Auden had had to pay thirty dollars duty on his camera. Oh, how tiresome; but you'll get it back. Was it usually so hot in Canton at this time of year? No, it wasn't. Five days ago, it had been quite chilly.

Somewhere, from far away across the river, came a succession of dull, heavy thuds; felt rather than heard. And then, thin and distinct, the whine which a mosquito makes, when it dives for your face in the dark. Only this wasn't a mosquito. More thuds. I looked round at the others. Was it possible that they hadn't noticed? Clearing my throat, I said as conversationally as I could manage: 'Isn't that an air-raid?'

Our hostess glanced up, smiling, from the tea-tray: 'Yes, I expect it is. They come over about this time, most afternoons. . . . Do you take sugar and milk?'

Yes, I took both; and a piece of home-made sultana cake as well, to cover my ill-bred emotions. It was all very well for Auden to sit there so calmly, arguing about the Group Movement. He had been in Spain. My eyes moved over this charming room, taking in the tea-cups, the dish of scones, the book-case with Chesterton's essays and Kipling's poems, the framed photograph of an Oxford college. My brain tried to relate these images to the sounds outside; the whine of the power-diving bomber, the distant thump of the explosions. Understand, I told myself, that these noises, these objects are part of a single, integrated scene. Wake up. It's all quite real. And, at that moment, I really did wake up. At that moment, suddenly, I arrived in China.

'They're moving off now', our hostess told me. She had the kindly air of one who wishes to reassure a slightly nervous child about a thunderstorm. 'They never stay very long.'—W. H. Auden and Christopher Isherwood, *Journey to a War*, 1939.

SLIME PITS OF GENESIS

Circa 1906. THE JERICHO road is bare enough, but the valley of Jordan has an aspect of inhumanity that is almost evil. If the prophets of the Old Testament had fulminated their anathemas against it as they did against Babylon or Tyre, no better proof of their prescience would exist; but they were silent, and the imagination must travel back to flaming visions of Gomorrah and of Sodom, dim legends of iniquity that haunted our own childhood as they haunted the childhood of the Semitic races. A heavy stifling atmosphere weighed upon this lowest level of the earth's surface; the wind was racing across the hill tops above us in the regions where men breathed the natural air, but the valley was stagnant and lifeless like a deep sea bottom. We brushed through low thickets of prickly sidr trees, the Spina Christi of which the branches are said to have been twisted into the Crown of Thorns. . . . The sidrs dwindled and vanished, and before us lay a sheet of hard mud on which no green thing grows. It is of a yellow colour, blotched with a venomous grey-white salt: almost unconsciously the eye appreciates its enmity to life. As we rode here a swirl of heavy rain swooped down upon us from the upper world. The muleteers looked grave, and even Mikhail's face began to lengthen, for in front of us were the Slime Pits of Genesis, and no horse or mule can pass over them except they be dry. The rain lasted a very few minutes, but it was enough. The hard mud of the plain had assumed the consistency of butter, the horses' feet were shod in it up to the fetlocks, and my dog Kurt whined as he dragged his paws out of the yellow glue. So we came to the Slime Pits, the strangest feature of all that uncanny land. A quarter of a mile to the west of Jordan—the belt is much narrower to the east of the stream—the smooth plain resolves itself suddenly into a series of steep mud banks intersected by narrow gullies. The banks are not high, thirty or forty feet at the most, but the crests of them are so sharp and the sides so precipitous that the traveller must find his way across and round them with the utmost care. The shower had made these slopes as slippery as glass, even on foot it was almost impossible to keep upright. My horse fell as I was leading him; fortunately it was on a little ridge between mound and mound, and by the most astonishing gymnastics he managed to recover himself. I breathed a short thanks-giving when I saw my caravan emerge from the Slime Pits; we might, if the rain had lasted, have been imprisoned there for several hours, since if a horseman falls to the bottom of one of the sticky hollows he must wait there till it dries.—Gertrude Bell, *The Desert and the Sown.*

THE NEGRO CHARACTER

Maldonado, Rio Plata, May 22, 1833. I ALWAYS much enjoy political gossip and what you at home think will, &c., &c., take place. I steadily read up the weekly paper, but it is not sufficient to guide one's opinion; and I find it a very painful state not to be as obstinate as a pig in politics. I have watched how steadily the general feeling, as shown at elections, has been rising against Slavery. What a proud thing for England if she is the first European nation which utterly abolishes it! I was told before leaving England that after living in slave countries all my opinions would be altered; the only alteration I am aware of is forming a much higher estimate of the negro character. It is impossible to see a negro and not feel kindly towards him; such cheerful, open, honest expressions and such fine muscular bodies. I never saw any of the diminutive Portuguese, with their murderous countenances, without almost wishing for Brazil to follow the example of Hayti; and, considering the enormously healthy-looking black population, it will be wonderful if, at some future day, it does not take place.—Charles Darwin, *Letters*.

BEAUTIES OF THE TROPICS

1836, Bahia, Brazil. LEARNED NATURALISTS describe these scenes of the tropics by naming a multitude of objects, and mentioning some characteristic feature of each. To a learned traveller this possibly may communicate some definite ideas: but who else from seeing a plant in an herbarium can imagine its appearance when growing in its native soil? Who from seeing choice plants in a hothouse, can magnify some into the dimensions of forest trees, and crowd others into an entangled jungle? Who when examining in the cabinet of the entomologist the gay exotic butterflies, and singular cicadas, will associate with these lifeless objects, the ceaseless harsh music of the latter, and the lazy flight of the former,—the sure accompaniments of the still, glowing noonday of the tropics? . . .

When quietly walking along the shady pathways, and admiring each successive view, I wished to find language to express my ideas. Epithet after epithet was found too weak to convey to those who have not visited the inter-tropical regions, the sensation of delight which the mind experiences. I have said that the plants in a hothouse fail to communicate a just idea of the vegetation, yet I must recur to it. The land is one great wild, untidy, luxuriant hothouse, made by Nature for herself, but taken possession of by man, who has studded it with gay houses and formal gardens. How great would be the desire in every admirer of nature to behold, if such were possible, the scenery of another planet! yet to every person in Europe, it may be truly said, that at the distance of only a few degrees from his native soil, the glories of another world are opened to him. In my last walk I stopped again and again to gaze on these beauties, and endeavoured to fix in my mind for ever, an impression which at the time I knew sooner or later must fail. The form of the orange-tree, the cocoa-nut, the palm, the mango, the tree-fern, the banana, will remain clear and separate; but the thousand beauties which unite these into one perfect scene must fade away; yet they will leave, like a tale heard in childhood, a picture full of indistinct, but most beautiful figures.—Charles Darwin, *The Voyage of the Beagle.*

TOBACCO CHEWING

Washington, 1842. I WAS surprised to observe that even steady old chewers of great experience, are not always good marksmen, which has rather inclined me to doubt that general proficiency with the rifle, of which we have heard so much in England. Several gentlemen called upon me who, in the course of conversation, frequently missed the spittoon at five paces; and one (but he was certainly short-sighted) mistook the closed sash for the open window, at three. On another occasion when I dined out, and was sitting with two ladies and some gentlemen round a fire before dinner, one of the company fell short of the fireplace, six distinct times. I am disposed to think, however, that this was occasioned by his not aiming at that object; as there was a white marble hearth before the fender which was more convenient, and may have suited his purpose better.—Charles Dickens, *American Notes.*

SCENE BY THE GANGES

Patna, Sunday, Nov. 5, 1837. I MUST do the Hindus the justice to say that they make as many holidays out of one year as most people do out of ten; and I am not at all sure whether a small importation of Hindus would not be acceptable to you, to accompany your boys to school as regulators to their school-days. It would be a safeguard against their being overworked. The whole bank was lined with natives bringing immense baskets of fruit for 'the Ganges to look at', as the Nazir [1] expressed it; and they were dipping their baskets into the river with their graceful salaams and then bowing their heads down to the water. They are much more clothed here than in Bengal, and the women wear bright crimson veils, or yellow with crimson borders, and sometimes purple dresses with crimson borders, and have generally a little brown baby, with a scarlet cap on, perched on their hips. I wish you would have one little brown baby for a change; they are so much prettier than white children. Behind these crowds of people, there were old mosques and temples and natives' houses, and the boats of rich natives in front

[1] The Governor-General's head native servant.

with gilded sterns, and painted peacocks at the prow. In short, just what people say of India; you know it all, but it is pretty to see; and I mean the 'moral' of my Indian experience to be, that it is the most picturesque population, with the ugliest scenery, that ever was put together.—Emily Eden, *Up the Country.*

FIRST GLIMPSES OF WESTERN AUSTRALIA

May 26th, 1829. WALKED TO the Side of the River & killed a Wild duck & some parroquets; heard the natives holloaing to us. Walked to meet them, their number consisted of ten & they accompanied us to our Tents in perfect good humour, imitating our walking & repeating everything we told them. I gave them all the little birds I had shot & made them understand that it was with the gun that they were killed; they each had a parroquet which they placed in the gingle on the lower part of the body, which had a most ludicrous appearance, as the wings of some of the birds were extended & answered all the purpose of a fig leaf; they are perfectly unconscious of any kind of indecency & were amused with our laughing. On their arrival at the Tents, I shewed them a looking glass at which they shouted and were perfectly delighted, all except the Old men; but I was determined that they should see their old worn out Countenances, but one look satisfied them, whilst the Younger ones of the party were continually pushing forward to look at themselves & did not appear to be displeased with their appearances. I made some of our men strip and shew their Arms, the Size of which astonished them very much & they could not refrain from feeling them & in fact were not satisfied without seeing all the parties', then our legs which excited more surprise than our Arms; & well they might as I think the limbs of some of our people would make three of some of theirs. I have a couple of good looking young lads in my Gig, whose chins happened to be particularly smooth, & they evidently believed them to be women, also the Youngsters with me, & I do not think that they would be brought to believe the contrary. They wanted the men to take off their trowsers after the shirts, but Jack had too much decency to think of satisfying their curiosity in that particular.—Admiral Sir C. H. Fremantle, *Diary and Letters.*

E. M. FORSTER IN INDIA

Guest House, August 28th, 1921. FOR FOUR hours yesterday evening I walked barefoot in petticoats through the streets with black and red powders smeared over my forehead, cheeks and nose.

Things began to warm up at 11.30 p.m. on the 26th when, dressed in our best, we sat cross-legged in the temple aisles, awaiting the Birth. The altar was as usual smothered in mess and the gold and silver and rich silks that make up its equipment were so disposed as to produce no effect. . . . My memory is so bad and the muddle so great, that I forget the details of the Birth already, but the Maharajah announced it from his end of the carpet and then went to the altar and buried his face in the rose leaves, much moved. Next, a miniature cradle was set up in the aisle, and a piece of crimson silk, folded so that it looked like an old woman over whom a traction engine has passed, was laid in it and rocked by him, Bhau Sahib, the Dewan, the Finance Member, and other leading officials of the state. Noise, I need hardly add, never stopped— the great horn brayed, the cymbals clashed, the harmonium and drums did their best, while in the outer courtyard the three elephants were set to bellow and the band played 'Nights of Gladness' as loudly as possible. Under these circumstances the child was named 'Krishna' by H.H. I was now nearly dead with the heat. What I thought were little animals running down my legs proved to be streams of sweat. But I sat while the chief personages revisited the altar and were concealed by a pink and green curtain from our gaze, behind which they ate.—I forgot to say that we were each given a paper tray of red powder and that when the Birth was announced we threw it in the air so that the whole aisle was filled with crimson smoke. Or that H.H. carried the folded silk (which did *not* contain the image, who mustn't be moved) in his arms among the people who squatted row behind row far into the distance. And I must not waste time telling of my troubles with the decorations, of the mottoes from English Poetry that wouldn't stick up, or of the glass battery-cases that I filled with water and live fish and into which some humanitarian idiot dropped handfuls of flour so that the fish should not starve. You couldn't have seen a whale. Oh such an emptying and slopping to get it right, and two of the fish died, through over-eating, and had to be buried in a flower pot in case H.H. should see them.—E. M. Forster, *The Hill of Devi*.

ISLAND HUNT

April 28th, 1829. AFTER DINNER went on shore and tried to walk over the Island,[1] but from the thickness of the trees and underwood it was impossible to move; tried to find fresh water; not succeeding, commenced digging a well, & after about seven feet succeeded in finding a Spring. Found nothing on the Island but Seals; killed three or four;

[1] Buacke Island.

they took to the shore from the water & the boats Crew with Toma-
hawks had a capital hunt after one, which they succeeded in killing
with the assistance of two or three shot through him. An immense
monster, so large that the four men could not carry him to the boat;
most likely a Sea Elephant. Saw one or two kangeroos but could not
get a shot at one. . . . Dined late on board after our seal hunt, great fun.
I had no idea they could travel so fast, they started on the hind legs or
fins & went erect faster than we could run; one when tired put his back
against a tree & gave battle, but we soon tamed him with a shot.—
Admiral Sir C. H. Fremantle, *Diary and Letters.*

ARROGANCE

Canton, 1769. BOB POTT passed most of his time in our rooms,
generally coming before I was up of a morning. He breakfasted with
us, and if he took it into his head that McClintock was too long at the
meal, or drank too much tea, he without the least ceremony overset
the table. The first time he practised this, I was very angry at such a
quantity of handsome China being thus mischievously demolished, and
expressed my displeasure thereat, which only excited the mirth of
young pickle. 'Why, zounds!' said he, 'you surely forget where you
are. I never suffer the servants to have the trouble of removing a tea
equipage, always throwing the whole apparatus out of window or
down stairs. They easily procure another batch from the steward's
warehouse.'—William Hickey.

THACKERAY AND THE OYSTERS

THACKERAY ANNOUNCED to me by letter in the early autumn of 1852
that he had determined to visit America. . . . He arrived on a frosty
November evening, and went directly to the Tremont House, where
rooms had been engaged for him. I remember his delight in getting
off the sea, and the enthusiasm with which he hailed the announcement
that dinner would be ready shortly. A few friends were ready to sit
down with him, and he seemed greatly to enjoy the novelty of an
American repast. In London he had been very curious in his enquiries
about American oysters, as marvellous stories, which he did not
believe, had been told him of their great size. We apologized—
although we had taken care that the largest specimens to be procured
should startle his unwonted vision when he came to the table—for
what we called the extreme *smallness* of the oysters, promising that we
would do better next time. Six bloated Falstaffian bivalves lay before
him in their shells. I noticed that he gazed at them anxiously with fork

upraised; then he whispered to me, with a look of anguish, 'How shall I do it?' I described to him the simple process by which the free-born citizens of America were accustomed to accomplish such a task. He seemed satisfied that the thing was feasible, selected the smallest one in the half-dozen . . . and then bowed his head as if he were saying grace. All eyes were upon him to watch the effect of a new sensation in the person of a great British author. Opening his mouth very wide, he struggled for a moment, and then all was over. I shall never forget the comic look of despair he cast upon the other five over-occupied shells. I broke the perfect stillness by asking him how he felt. 'Profoundly grateful', he gasped, 'and as if I had swallowed a little baby.'—James T. Fields, *Yesterdays with Authors*, 1872.

MEETING WITH GERTRUDE BELL

1926. . . . a door in the blank wall, a jerky stop, a creaking of hinges, a broadly smiling servant, a rush of dogs, a vista of garden-path edged with carnations in pots, a little verandah and a little low house at the end of the path, an English voice—Gertrude Bell.

I had known her first in Constantinople, where she had arrived straight out of the desert, with all the evening dresses and cutlery and napery that she insisted on taking with her on her wanderings; and then in England; but here she was in her right place, in Iraq, in her own house, with her office in the city, and her white pony in a corner of the garden, and her Arab servants, and her English books, and her Babylonian shards on the mantelpiece, and her long thin nose, and her irrepressible vitality. I felt all my loneliness and despair lifted from me in a second. Had it been very hot in the Gulf? got fever, had I? but quinine would put that right; and a sprained ankle—too bad!—and would I like breakfast first, or a bath? and I would like to see her museum, wouldn't I? did I know she was Director of Antiquities in Iraq? wasn't that a joke? and would I like to come to tea with the king? and yes, there were lots of letters for me. I limped after her as she led me down the path, talking all the time, now in English to me, now in Arabic to the eager servants. She had the gift of making everyone feel suddenly eager; of making you feel that life was full and rich and exciting. I found myself laughing for the first time in ten days. The garden was small, but cool and friendly; her spaniel wagged not only his tail but his whole little body; the pony looked over the loose-box door and whinnied gently; a tame partridge hopped about the verandah; some native babies who were playing in a corner stopped playing to stare and grin. A tall, grey sloughi came out of the house, beating his tail against the posts of the verandah; 'I want one like that', I said, 'to take up into Persia.' I did want one but I had reckoned without Gertrude's promptness. She rushed to the telephone, and as I poured cream over my porridge I heard her explaining—a friend of hers had arrived—must have a sloughi at once—was leaving for Persia next day—a selection of sloughis must be sent round that morning. Then she was back in her chair, pouring out information: the state of Iraq, the excavations at Ur, the need for a decent museum, what new books had come out? what was happening in England? The doctors had told her she ought not to go through another summer in Bagdad, but what should she do in England, eating out her heart for Iraq? next year, perhaps . . . but I couldn't say she looked ill, could I? I could, and did. She laughed and brushed that aside. Then, jumping up—for all her movements were quick and impatient—if I had finished my breakfast wouldn't I like my bath? and she must go to her office, but would be back for luncheon. Oh yes, and there were people to luncheon; and so, still talking, still laughing, she pinned on a hat without looking in the glass, and took her departure.—V. Sackville-West, *The Letters of Gertrude Bell.*

TRAVELLING IN AMERICA

America, Sunday, 14.12.84. THE PEOPLE who are not pleased with America must be those whose sympathies are fossilized or whose eyes have no power of observation. Such delightful and entertaining schemes for hoodwinking nature you never saw, such ingenuities for beating the terrible forces of the seasons, such daring inventions and heroic tricks of luxury. The people are bluff and good-natured, civil if you are civil to them, as sharp as needles to detect and defy pretension. Come with a simple civility and an obvious desire to be pleased, and you will be surprised at the good time you will have.— *The Life and Letters of Sir Edmund Gosse.*

BEDOUIN WOMEN

THE BEDOUIN women are not treasured up like the wives and daughters of other orientals, and indeed they seemed almost entirely free from the restraints imposed by jealousy. The feint which they made of concealing their faces from me was always slight: when they first saw me, they used to hold up a part of their drapery with one hand across their faces, but they seldom persevered very steadily in subjecting me to this privation. They were sadly plain. The awful haggardness that gave something of character to the faces of the men was sheer ugliness in the poor women. It is a great shame, but the truth is, that except when we refer to the beautiful devotion of the mother to her child, all the fine things we say and think about women apply only to those who are tolerably good-looking or graceful. These Arab women were not within the scope of the privilege, and indeed were altogether much too plain and clumsy for this vain and lovesome world. They may have been good women enough, so far as relates to the exercise of the minor virtues, but they had so grossly neglected the prime duty of looking pretty in this transitory life that I could not at all forgive them; they seemed to feel the weight of their guilt, and to be truly and humbly penitent. I had the complete command of their affections, for at any moment I could make their young hearts bound and their old hearts jump by offering a handful of tobacco; yet, believe me, it was not in the first *soirée* that my store of Latakiah was exhausted.—A. W. Kinglake, *Eothen*, 1844.

PALM TREES

Port of Spain, Trinidad, Christmas Eve, 1869. ACTUALLY SETTLED in a West Indian country house, amid a multitude of sights and sounds so utterly new and strange, that the mind is stupefied by the continual effort to take in, or, to confess the truth, to gorge, without hope of digestion, food of every conceivable variety. The whole day long new objects, and their new names, have jostled each other in the brain, in dreams as well as in waking thoughts. Amid such a confusion, to describe this place as a whole, is as yet impossible. . . .

To begin with the weeds on the path, like, and yet unlike, all at home—then the rattle of the bamboo, the clashing of the huge leaves of the young fan-palms, the flower-fence, the guinea-grass, the sand-box, the hibiscus, with its scarlet flowers—a long list; but for the climax, the groo groo palms, a sight never to be forgotten—to have once seen palms breaking through, and as it were defying the soft rounded forms of the broad-leaved vegetation by the stern force of their simple lines; the immovable pillar-stem, looking the more immovable beneath the toss, the lash, and flicker of the long leaves, as they awake out of their sunlit sleep, and rage impotently for a while before the mountain gusts, to fall to sleep again. Like a Greek statue in a luxurious drawing-room, sharpcut, cold, virginal, showing, by the mere grandeur of form, the voluptuousness of mere colour, however rich and harmonious; so stands the palm tree, to be worshipped rather than to be loved.—Charles Kingsley, *Letters*.

AFRICAN INSECTS

But it's against the insects ashore that you have to be specially warned. During my first few weeks of Africa I took a general natural historical interest in them with enthusiasm as of natural history; it soon became a mere sporting one, though equally enthusiastic at first. Afterwards a nearly complete indifference set in, unless some wretch aroused a vengeful spirit in me by stinging or biting. I should say, looking back calmly upon the matter, that 75 per cent. of West African insects sting, 5 per cent. bite, and the rest are either permanently or temporarily parasitic on the human race. And undoubtedly one of the many worst things you can do in West Africa is to take any notice of an insect. If you see a thing that looks like a cross between a flying lobster and a figure of Abraxas on a Gnostic gem, do not pay it the least attention, never mind where it is; just keep quiet and hope it will go away—for that's your best chance; you have none in a stand-up fight with a good thorough-going African insect.—Mary Kingsley, *West African Studies*, 1899.

CEYLON

'Ardnaree', Kandy, Ceylon, 11 April, 1922. I've been in Ceylon a month and nearly sweated myself into a shadow. Still it's a wonderful place to see and experience. There seems to be a flaw in the atmosphere, and one sees a darkness, and through the darkness the days before the Flood, marshy, with elephants mud-grey and buffaloes rising from the mud, and soft-boned voluptuous sort of people, like plants under water, stirring in myriads.—D. H. Lawrence, *Letters*.

GLORIOUS LANDSCAPE

India, 1834–38. The plain of Mysore lay before us—a vast ocean of foliage on which the sun was shining gloriously. I am very little given to cant about the beauties of nature, but I was moved almost to tears. I jumped off the palanquin, and walked in front of it down the immense declivity. In two hours we descended about three thousand feet. Every turning in the road showed the boundless forest below in some new point of view. I was greatly struck with the resemblance which this prodigious jungle, as old as the world and planted by nature, bears to the fine works of the great English landscape gardeners. It was exactly a Wentworth Park as large as Devonshire. After reaching the foot of the hills, we travelled through a succession of scenes which might have

P

been part of the garden of Eden. Such gigantic trees I never saw. In a quarter of an hour I passed hundreds the smallest of which would bear a comparison with any of those oaks which are shown as prodigious in England. The grass, the weeds, and the wild flowers grew as high as my head. The sun, almost a stranger to me, was now shining brightly; and, when late in the afternoon I again got out of my palanquin and looked back, I saw the large mountain ridge from which I had descended twenty miles behind me, still buried in the same mass of fog and rain in which I had been living for weeks.—Lord Macaulay, *Letters.*

A NEW LINE IN SOUVENIRS

OUR OWN part of the ship was not invaded by anybody, except one solitary figure. He was a man in European dress, with wistful eyes and a fine Hellenic face. He spoke English well, and, advancing to us with dignity, he asked us if we would buy what he called 'special photographs'. 'Be off', said one of my friends. 'Take the beastly things away with you.' 'Not beastly', he said gently, 'academic.' Then opening a leather case which he carried, he produced from its depths some polished cubes of olive-wood, and with no change of manner except an increased gravity, 'Perhaps', he went on, 'you would like a piece of the true Cross.'—W. H. Mallock, *In An Enchanted Island*, 1889.

SUPERSTITION

1837. LADY HESTER STANHOPE once built a new room; and, just before she was going to inhabit it, from some cause, imagined, or pretended to imagine, it was charmed. We may judge of the builder's surprise, when she sent for him, and said, 'Tomorrow you must assemble your workmen, and pull down the new room.' The man, fancying some defect had been discovered in his workmanship, humbly begged her to say what it was that moved her displeasure, as, perhaps, he might be able to find a remedy for it, without destroying the whole. 'Your business, sir', answered Lady Hester, in that tone of voice which she made so terrible when she chose, 'is to pull down if I like it, I suppose, as well as to build; so be so good as to obey my orders without farther question.' 'When they were removing the arch of the door, doctor', said Lady Hester, who related the story to me, 'I saw a paper fall out. I took it up, and sent it to a man versed in charms. He told me it was a charm, written by one of my deadly enemies: and, if I had dwelt in the room, I should have died. Only think, how lucky it was I did what I did!'—*Memoirs of the Lady Hester Stanhope.*

WHITE MAN'S BURDEN

ONE OF the most intricate *cruces* that is at present taxing the ingenuity
of the transport officers of the Mission is how to convey the flag-staff
to the frontier. It is a solid and weighty structure in three pieces, each
about 16 feet long, so that the whole, when erected, will be about 45
feet high. It is to be hoped we shall experience no revival of the 'flag
question' which proved such an annoyance to Sir Fred. Goldsmid on
the Seistan Boundary Commission. I must not omit to mention another
important member of the Mission—viz., the Bull-dog that will keep
watch at the foot of the British flag-staff. Such a guardian may be
necessary, if it be true, as some suggest, that the British Lion will not
be sent to support the British Mission.—Lt. A. C. Yate, *Travels with
the Afghan Boundary Commission,* 1885.

THE SILENCE OF THE EAST

THE MOSLEM quarter of a city is lonely and desolate; you go up and
down, and on, over shelving and hillocky paths through the narrow
lanes walled in by blank, windowless dwellings; you come out upon an
open space strewed with the black ruins that some late fire has left; you
pass by a mountain of castaway things, the rubbish of centuries, and
on it you see numbers of big, wolf-like dogs lying torpid under the sun,
with limbs outstretched to the full, as if they were dead; storks or
cranes, sitting fearless upon the low roofs, look gravely down upon
you; the still air that you breathe is loaded with the scent of citron and
pomegranate rinds scorched by the sun, or (as you approach the
bazaar) with the dry, dead perfume of strange spices. You long for
some signs of life, and tread the ground more heavily, as though you
would wake the sleepers with the heel of your boot; but the foot falls
noiseless upon the crumbling soil of an Eastern city, and silence follows
you still. Again and again you meet turbans, and faces of men, but they
have nothing for you,—no welcome—no wonder—no wrath—no
scorn; they look upon you as we do upon a December's fall of snow—
as a 'seasonable', unaccountable, uncomfortable work of God that may
have been sent for some good purpose, to be revealed hereafter.—
A. W. Kinglake, *Eothen,* 1844.

A BITTER MOMENT

Djoun, Mount Lebanon, March 8, 1838. SHE COMPLAINED bitterly, as
usual, of her servants—of neglect—ignorance—heartlessness: she said
she would rather be surrounded by robbers; for there is some principle

amongst thieves. 'Oh', she exclaimed, 'that I could find one human being who knew his Creator!'

She went on:—'I have had a very bad night, and whether I shall live or die, I don't know: but this I can tell you beforehand, that if I do die, I wish to be buried like a dog, in a bit of earth just big enough to hold this miserable skin, or else to be burnt, or thrown into the sea. And, as I am no longer an English subject, no consuls, nor any English of any sort, shall approach me in my last moments; for, if they do, I will have them shot. Therefore, the day before I die, if I know it, I shall order you away, and not only you, but everything English; and if you don't go, I warn you beforehand, you must take the consequences. Let me be scorched by the burning sun—frozen by the cold blast—and let my ashes fly in the air—let the wolves and jackals devour my carcase; but'—here the agitation she was in, and which had kept increasing, brought on a severe fit of coughing, and it was a quarter of an hour before she could recover strength enough to speak again.—Lady Hester Stanhope, *Memoirs of the Lady Hester Stanhope.*

DYLAN THOMAS IN PERSIA

1951. No, PERSIA wasn't all depressing. Beautiful Ispahn and Shiraz. Wicked, pompous, oily British. Nervous, cunning, corrupt, and delightful Persian bloody bastards. Opium no good. Persian vodka, made of beetroot, like stimulating sockjuice, very enjoyable. Beer full of glycerine and pips. Women veiled, or unveiled ugly, or beautiful and entirely inaccessible, or hungry. The lovely camels who sit on their necks and smile. I shan't go there again.—Dylan Thomas, *Dylan Thomas in America.*

A CIVILIZED PEOPLE

1817–1819. THERE ARE very few really *ignorant* men in America of native growth. Every farmer is more or less of a *reader*. There is no *brogue*, no *provincial dialect*. No class like that which the French call *peasantry*, and which degrading appellation the miscreant spawn of the Funds have, of late years, applied to the whole mass of the most useful of the people in England, those who do the work and fight the battles. And, as to the men, who would naturally form *your* acquaintances, they, I know from experience, are as kind, frank, and sensible men as are, on the general run, to be found in England, even with the power of selection. They are all well-informed; modest without shyness; always free to communicate what they know, and never ashamed to acknowledge that they have yet to learn. You never hear them *boast* of their possessions, and you never hear them *complaining* of their wants. They have all been *readers* from their youth up; and there are few subjects upon which they cannot converse with you, whether of a political or scientific nature. At any rate, they always *hear* with patience. I do not know that I ever heard a native American interrupt another man while he was speaking. Their *sedateness* and *coolness,* the *deliberate* manner in which they say and do every thing, and the *slowness* and *reserve* with which they express their assent; these are very wrongly estimated, when they are taken for marks of *a want of feeling.* It must be a tale of woe indeed, that will bring a tear from an American's eye; but any trumped up story will send his hand to his pocket, as the ambassadors from the beggars of France, Italy and Germany can fully testify.— William Cobbett, *A Year's Residence in America.*

CHINESE MEAL

ONE'S FIRST sight of a table prepared for a Chinese meal hardly suggests the idea of eating, at all. It looks rather as if you were sitting down to a competition in water-colour painting. The chopsticks, lying side by side, resemble paint-brushes. The paints are represented by little dishes of sauces, red, green, and brown. The tea-bowls, with their lids, might well contain paint-water. There is even a kind of tiny paint-rag, on which the chopsticks can be wiped.

You begin the meal by wiping hands and face with hot moistened towels. (These towels are, perhaps, China's most brilliant contribution to the technique of material comfort; they should certainly be introduced into the West.) Then comes the food. It is served in no recognizable order of progression—fish does not necessarily follow soup, nor meat fish. Nor can the length of the meal be foreseen by the guest. His favourite dish may well appear at the very end, when he is too bloated even to taste it. *Hors-d'oeuvre* delicacies remain in presence throughout —and this, too, is like painting; for the diners are perpetually mixing them in with their food, to obtain varying combinations of taste.

To-day we had shark's fin soup (one of the great soups of the world; quite equal to minestrone or borsch), lobster, chicken, rice, and fish. The drink, which was served in small metal teapots, resembled Korn or Bols. It was made from rose-petals and maize. The Governor had considerately provided us with knives and forks, but these we declined to use. We had eaten already with chopsticks in Hongkong, and were anxious for more practice. In China, it is no social crime to drop your food on the table. When a new dish comes in, the host makes a gesture towards it with his chopsticks, like a cavalry-commander pointing with his sabre to an enemy position, and the attack begins. This scramble, so informal yet so scrupulously polite, is the greatest charm of a Chinese meal; and even the most expert eater can hardly avoid making a certain amount of mess. One of the English guests was showing me how to pick up a shrimp patty, when he let it fall on to the carpet. His face was promptly saved by Mr Tong, who exclaimed: 'Ah, that shrimp must be alive!'—W. H. Auden and Christopher Isherwood, *Journey to a War*, 1939.

HUMBLING EXPERIENCE

Philadelphia. Jan. 17, 1853. THERE ARE 500000 people in this city about w? we know so little—there's one street with shops on each side 6 miles long—there's New York with 700000—Boston, Cincinnati, scores more vast places—only beginning too and evidently in their very early youth whereas we are past our prime most likely. Empires more immense than any the old world has known are waiting their time here. In 10 years we shall cross to Europe in a week and for 5£; in 50 the population will treble that of Britain—Everybody prospers. There are scarce any poor. For hundreds of years more there is room and food and work for whoever comes. In travelling in Europe our confounded English pride only fortifies itself, and we feel that we are better than 'those foreigners' but it's worth while coming here that we may think small beer of ourselves afterwards.—W. M. Thackeray, *Letters.*

ACKNOWLEDGMENTS

THE publishers are grateful to the following for permission to include copyright material:

Messrs Allen & Unwin Ltd for an extract from *The Path to Rome* by Hilaire Belloc; Messrs Edward Arnold Ltd and Mr E. M. Forster for extracts from *The Hill of Devi* and the photograph facing page 188; Messrs Ernest Benn Ltd for extracts from *The Letters of Gertrude Bell* and *The Letters of Disraeli to Lady Bradford*; Sir Geoffrey Keynes, Mr Brian Hill, and Messrs Jonathan Cape Ltd for extracts from *The Note-books of Samuel Butler*; Messrs Jonathan Cape Ltd for extracts from *Letters between Samuel Butler and Miss E. M. A. Savage*, and *Arabia Deserta* by C. M. Doughty; Messrs Cassell & Co. Ltd for extracts from Corvo's *The Desire and Pursuit of the Whole*, and *The Quest for Corvo* by A. J. A. Symons; Messrs Chatto & Windus Ltd for extracts from *Jesting Pilate* and *Along the Road* by Aldous Huxley; Constable & Co. Ltd for extracts from *The Letters of George Meredith*; Messrs Curtis Brown Ltd and Faber & Faber Ltd for extracts from *Letters From Iceland* by W. H. Auden and Louis MacNeice; Messrs J. M. Dent & Sons Ltd for an extract from *Dylan Thomas in America* by John Brinnin; Messrs André Deutsch Ltd for extracts from *Portrait of a Whig Peer* by John Connell; Messrs Faber & Faber Ltd for extracts from *Journey to a War* by W. H. Auden and Christopher Isherwood, and from *Bitter Lemons* by Lawrence Durrell; Messrs Hamish Hamilton Ltd for extracts from *The Unquiet Grave* by Palinurus; Messrs William Heinemann Ltd for extracts from *Amurath To Amurath* and *The Desert and the Sown* by Gertrude Bell, and from *The Life and Letters of Sir Edmund Gosse* by the Hon. Evan Charteris, and from *Boswell on the Grand Tour* and *Boswell in Holland*; Messrs David Higham Associates Ltd for extracts from *The Scarlet Tree* by Osbert Sitwell, published by Macmillan & Co. Ltd; the Estate of the late Mrs Frieda Lawrence and Messrs William Heinemann Ltd for extracts from *Sea and Sardinia* and *The Letters of D. H. Lawrence*; Messrs Macmillan & Co. Ltd for extracts from *The Journals of Dorothy Wordsworth*, edited by Professor E. de Selincourt; Messrs John Murray Ltd for an extract from *The Order of Release*; the Hon. Sir Harold Nicolson for an extract from *Some People*; Oxford University Press for extracts from *The Journals and Papers of Gerard Manley Hopkins*, edited by Humphry House and Graham Storey; A. D. Peters for extracts from *Black Lamb and Grey Falcon* by Rebecca West, and for extracts from *The Road to Oxiana* by Robert Byron; Messrs Max Reinhardt Ltd for extracts from *Portugal* by Roy Campbell; Messrs Martin Secker & Warburg Ltd for extracts from *Down and Out in Paris and London* by George Orwell and an extract from *Old Calabria* by Norman Douglas; Messrs Sidgwick & Jackson Ltd for extracts from *Letters from America* by Rupert Brooke; Messrs Chapman & Hall Ltd and Richard Steele & Son for extracts from *By the Ionian Sea* by George Gissing; The Hogarth Press for extracts from *Blue Skies, Brown Studies* by William Sansom.

INDEX OF TITLES

INDEX OF AUTHORS